DEDICATION

To the *Newman Reader* website: which has brought virtually all of the great man's works to the public for many years now. It's an example of the very best use of the powerful resources of the Internet.

INTRODUCTION

Blessed John Henry Cardinal Newman wrote in a letter dated 10 February 1869:

> I am *not* a theologian. A theologian is one who has mastered theology – who can say how many opinions there are on every point, what authors have taken which, and which is the best – who can discriminate exactly between proposition and proposition, argument and argument, who can pronounce which are safe, which allowable, which dangerous – who can trace the history of doctrines in successive centuries, and apply the principles of former times to the conditions of the present. This it is to be a theologian – this and a hundred things besides – which I am not, and never shall be.

He stated "I am not a theologian" many times in his letters. He often qualified any theological instruction he gave, making sure to note that it was not cast in stone, and subject to correction by the Church or credentialed theologians. In the above, strict "academic" or "scholarly" sense, indeed he was not a theologian. Yet in another broader (and in my opinion, far more important) sense, he certainly *was* one.

Whether Newman was a *theologian* or not, he wrote exquisitely on theology. The very fact that he was seeking to write (especially in his personal letters) on a popular, non-technical level, makes his work in this regard so important. In effect, he becomes a catechist, and in part, an apologist, in these informal remarks in his voluminous correspondence.

Scholars – for the most part – write to and for *other scholars*, whereas the goal of Catholic catechists, apologists, and evangelists is to reach the masses (and Catholics) with the joyous good news of the glorious fullness of the Catholic Christian faith.

Furthermore, in Cardinal Newman's writing we find (always and everywhere) extraordinary prose almost unequaled in its eloquence: a feast of 19th century English style. Lastly – of supreme relevance and importance – we encounter a *saintly* (as of this writing, beatified) man, who will most likely one day be canonized as a saint. I personally firmly believe that he will also be honored as a Doctor of the Church in due course.

This is the third book of Newman quotations that I have compiled. I do so partly out of obligation for the central role that he played in my own spiritual and theological odyssey, but primarily to widen the availability of his lesser-known writings, and to share his profound thought and insights with as wide an audience as possible.

My present goal (and what makes this book different from the previous two) is to create almost a "systematic theology" from Cardinal Newman. By use of categories, I have sought to arrange his thoughts in such a way that they can be accessed all the more quickly.

Cardinal Newman (as one can see in the Table of Contents) covered a very wide range of topics in his correspondence. I have sought to collect the "cream" of his theological thoughts therein. As such, this volume might be regarded as Newman's "catch-all" book, in which he deals with many theological subjects; very unlike most of his books, which are devoted to a single topic.

May you enjoy this treasure-trove of wonderful theology, as well as Newman's ruminations on Church history and the complexities of the conversion process. In conversion, often theology, Church history, personal experience, and apologetics are all merged together. No one exemplified this mixture and the process of conversion more than Blessed Cardinal Newman.

Thus, this volume may be of particular usefulness for possible converts, as well as Catholics seeking to revive an uncertain or tentative personal Catholic faith. In these fabulous quotations, in any event, there is much precious treasure for *anyone* who loves theology and God, Who is at the center of it.

CONTENTS

I. Apologetics

II. Philosophy of Religion

III. Church History

IV. Development of Doctrine

V. Anglicanism

VI. Conversion (to Catholicism)

VII. Lay Participation

VIII. Bible, Tradition, and Authority

IX. Doctrine of the Church (Ecclesiology)

X. The Papacy / Papal Supremacy and Infallibility

XI. Theology of Salvation (Soteriology)

XII. Jesus Christ (Christology)

XIII. God the Father (Theology Proper)

XIV. The Holy Spirit (Pneumatology) and Trinitarianism

XV. The Blessed Virgin Mary (Mariology)

XVI. Angels and the Communion of Saints

XVII. Purgatory

XVIII. Penance and Asceticism

XIX. The Holy Eucharist and Sacrifice of the Mass

XX. Devotions, Liturgy, and Worship

XXI. The Sacrament of Baptism

XXII. Sacraments and Sacramentals

XXIII. Heaven and Hell / Satan and Demons

XXIV. Education

XXV. Atheism, Agnosticism, Liberalism, and Secularism

XXVI. Ecumenism

XXVII. Science

XXVIII. Miscellaneous

BIBLIOGRAPHICAL SOURCES

Drawn from *The Letters and Diaries of John Henry Newman*
[excluding volumes 11-12, 27-30, 32]

Vol. 1 Edited by Ian Ker and Thomas Gornall, S.J.; *Ealing, Trinity, Oriel: February 1801 to December 1826* (Oxford: Clarendon Press, 1978).

Vol. 2 Edited by Ian Ker and Thomas Gornall, S.J.; *Tutor of Oriel: January 1827 to December 1831* (Oxford: Clarendon Press, 1979).

Vol. 3 Edited by Ian Ker and Thomas Gornall, S.J.; *New Bearings: January 1832 to June 1833* (Oxford: Clarendon Press, 1979).

Vol. 4 Edited by Ian Ker and Thomas Gornall, S.J.; *The Oxford Movement: July 1833 to December 1834* (Oxford: Clarendon Press, 1980).

Vol. 5 Edited by Thomas Gornall, S.J.; *Liberalism in Oxford: January 1835 to December 1836* (Oxford: Clarendon Press, 1981).

Vol. 6 Edited by Gerard Tracey; *The Via Media and Froude's Remains: January 1837 to December 1838* (Oxford: Clarendon Press, 1984).

Vol. 7 Edited by Gerard Tracey; *Editing the* British Critic: *January 1839 – December 1840* (Oxford: Clarendon Press, 1995).

Vol. 8 Edited by Gerard Tracey; Tract 90 *and the Jerusalem Bishopric: January 1841 – April 1842* (Oxford: Clarendon Press, 1999).

Vol. 9 Edited by Francis J. McGrath, F.M.S. and Gerard Tracey; *Littlemore and the Parting of Friends: May 1842-October 1843* (Oxford University Press, 2006).

Vol. 10 Edited by Francis J. McGrath, F.M.S.; *The Final Step: 1 November 1843 – 6 October 1845* (Oxford University Press, 2006).

Vol. 13 Edited by Charles Stephen Dessain; *Birmingham and London: January 1849 to June 1850* (London: Thomas Nelson and Sons Ltd, 1963).

Vol. 14 Edited by Charles Stephen Dessain and Vincent Ferrer Blehl, S.J.; *Papal Aggression: July 1850 to December 1851* (London: Thomas Nelson and Sons Ltd, 1963).

Vol. 15 Edited by Charles Stephen Dessain and Vincent Ferrer Blehl, S.J.; The Achilli Trial: January 1852 to December 1853 (London: Thomas Nelson and Sons Ltd, 1964).

Vol. 16 Edited by Charles Stephen Dessain; *Founding a University: January 1854 to September 1855* (London: Thomas Nelson and Sons Ltd, 1965).

Vol. 17 Edited by Charles Stephen Dessain; *Opposition in Dublin and London: October 1855 to March 1857* (London: Thomas Nelson and Sons Ltd, 1967).

Vol. 18 Edited by Charles Stephen Dessain; *New Beginnings in England: April 1857 to December 1858* (London: Thomas Nelson and Sons Ltd, 1968).

Vol. 19 Edited by Charles Stephen Dessain; *Consulting the Laity: January 1859 to June 1861* (London: Thomas Nelson and Sons Ltd, 1969).

Vol. 20 Edited by Charles Stephen Dessain; *Standing Firm Amid Trials: July 1861 to December 1863* (London: Thomas Nelson and Sons Ltd, 1970).

Vol. 21 Edited by Charles Stephen Dessain and Edward E. Kelly, S.J.; *The Apologia: January 1864 to June 1865* (London: Thomas Nelson and Sons Ltd, 1971).

Vol. 22 Edited by Charles Stephen Dessain; *Between Pusey and the Extremists: July 1865 to December 1866* (London: Thomas Nelson and Sons Ltd, 1972).

Vol. 23 Edited by Charles Stephen Dessain and Thomas Gornall, S.J.; *Defeat at Oxford. Defence at Rome: January to December 1867* (Oxford: Clarendon Press, 1973).

Vol. 24 Edited by Charles Stephen Dessain and Thomas Gornall, S.J.; *A Grammar of Assent: January 1868 to December 1869* (Oxford: Clarendon Press, 1973).

Vol. 25 Edited by Charles Stephen Dessain and Thomas Gornall, S.J.; *The Vatican Council: January 1870 to December 1871* (Oxford: Clarendon Press, 1973).

Vol. 26 Edited by Charles Stephen Dessain and Thomas Gornall, S.J.; *Aftermaths: January 1872 to December 1873* (Oxford: Clarendon Press, 1974).

Vol. 31 Edited by Charles Stephen Dessain and Thomas Gornall, S.J.; *The Last Years: January 1885 to August 1890; With a Supplement of Addenda to Volumes XI – XXX* (Oxford: Clarendon Press, 1977).

Chapter One

Apologetics

What Are Some Basic Guidelines in Defending Our Faith?

I think theology, even when introduced, should always be *in undress*, and should address itself to common sense, reason, received maxims, etc ere not to authority or technical dicta. Of course the hidden basis of a discussion must be the voice of tradition, the consent of the schools, the definitions of the Church; but, as I do believe that the whole of revelation may be made more or less palatable to English common sense, (for e.g. tho' so sacred a doctrine as the Holy Trinity is necessarily above reason, yet it is *common sense* to say that from the nature Of the case it *must* be) so think that to go beyond the line of English common sense, (e.g. to continue my instance to prove the doctrine of the Holy Trinity as St Augustine does by the memory, intellect, and will) would be a great mistake in a Magazine. (v. 21; To Henry James Coleridge, 16 June 1865)

The first duty of charity is to try to enter into the mind and feelings of others..This is what I love so much in you, my dear Keble; but I much desiderate it in this new book of Pusey's – and I deplore the absence of it there . . . (v. 22; To John Keble, 8 Oct. 1865)

Objections are for the most part like blots or disfigurements on a picture; we understand that the picture represents a definite scene, and what that scene is, in spite of such drawbacks. (v. 25; To an Unknown Correspondent, 19 June 1870)

Every one has his own difficulties and his own way of solving them. Others can but give him suggestions from time to time, and on particular points. (v. 25; To William Dunn Gainsford, 10 Nov. 1870)

It is simply impossible I can to any good purpose answer your difficulties, unless we agree in principles . . . (v. 26; To Henry Tenlon, 23 March 1873)

My view has ever been to answer, not to suppress, what is erroneous – merely as a matter of expedience for the cause of truth, at least at this day. It seems to me a bad policy to suppress. Truth has a power of its own, which makes its way – it is stronger than error – according to the Proverb. (v. 26; To W. J. Copeland, 20 April 1873)

Is Apologetics Only for Non-Catholics or Non-Christians?

[T]here are two reasons for writing quite distinct from conversion, and, considering all things, I prefer them to any other reason – the one is to edify Catholics. Catholics are so often *raw.* Many do not know their religion – many do not know the reasons for it. And there is in a day like this, a vast deal of semi-doubting. There are those who only wish to convert, and then leave the poor converts to shift for themselves, as far as knowledge *of their religion* goes. The other end which is so important, is what I call levelling up. If we are to convert souls savingly they must have the due preparation of heart, and if England is to be converted, there must be a great move of the national mind to a better sort of religious sentiment. (v. 25; To Sister Mary Gabriel du Boulay, 2 Jan. 1870)

Should Laymen Have a Working Knowledge of Apologetics?

It is to be considered, that our students are to go out into the world, and a world not of professed Catholics, but of inveterate, often bitter, commonly contemptuous Protestants; nay, of Protestants who, so far as they come from Protestant Universities and public schools, do know their own system, do know, in proportion to their general attainments, the doctrines and arguments of Protestantism. I should desire, then, to encourage in our students an intelligent apprehension of the relations, as I may call them, between the Church and society at large; for instance, the difference between the Church and a religious sect; between the Church and civil power; what the Church claims of necessity, what it cannot dispense with, what it can; what it can grant, what it cannot. A Catholic hears the celibacy of the clergy discussed; is that usage of faith, or is it not of faith? He hears the Pope accused of interfering with the prerogatives of her Majesty, because he appoints an hierarchy. What is he to answer? What principle is to guide him in the remarks which he cannot escape from the necessity of making? He fills a station of importance, and he is addressed by some friend who has political reasons for wishing to know what is the difference between Canon and Civil Law, whether the Council of Trent has been received in France, whether a priest cannot in certain cases absolve prospectively, what is meant by his *intention*, what by the *opus operatum*; whether, and in what sense, we consider Protestants to be heretics; whether any one can be saved without sacramental confession; whether we deny the reality of natural virtue, and what worth we assign to it. Questions may be multiplied without limit, which occur in conversation between friends in social intercourse, or in the business of life, where no argument is needed, no subtle and delicate disquisition, but a few direct words stating the fact. Half the controversies which go on in the world arise from ignorance of the facts of the case; half the prejudices against Catholicity lie in the misinformation of the prejudiced parties. Candid persons are set right, and enemies silenced, by the mere statement of what it is that we believe. It will not answer the purpose for a Catholic to say, "I leave it to theologians," "I will ask my priest;" but it will commonly give him a triumph, as easy as it is complete, if he can then and there lay down the law. I say, "lay down the law;" for remarkable it is, that even those who speak against Catholicism like to hear about it, and will excuse its advocate from alleging arguments, if he can gratify their curiosity by giving them information. Generally speaking, however, as I have said, such mere information will really be an argument also. I recollect some twenty-five years ago three friends of my own, as they then were, clergymen of the Establishment, making a tour through Ireland. In the West or South they had occasion to become pedestrians for the day; and they took a boy of thirteen to be their guide. They amused themselves with putting questions to him on the subject of his religion; and one of them confessed to me on his return that that poor child put them all to silence. How? Not of course by any train of argument or refined theological disquisition, but merely by knowing and understanding the answers in his catechism. Nor will argument itself be out of place in the hands of laymen mixing with the world. As secular power, honour, and resources are never more suitably placed than when they are in the hands of Catholics; so secular knowledge and secular gifts are then best employed when they minister to Divine Revelation. Theologians inculcate the matter and determine the details of that revelation; they view it from within; philosophers view it from without; and this external view may be called the Philosophy of Religion, and the office of delineating it externally is most gracefully performed by laymen. In the first age laymen were most commonly the apologists. Such were Justin, Tatian, Athenagoras, Aristides, Hermias [sic], Minucius Felix, Arnobius, and Lactantius. In like manner, in this age some of the most prominent defences of the Church are from laymen; as De Maistre, Chateaubriand, Nicolas, Montalembert, and others. If laymen may write, lay-students may read; they surely may read what their fathers may have written. They might surely study other works too, ancient and modern, whether by ecclesiastics or laymen, . . . (v. 19; "Lay Students in Theology," *The Rambler*, May 1859)

How is Faith Related to Apologetic Inquiry?

The advantage of subscription (to my mind) is its witnessing to the principle that religion is to be approached with a submission of the understanding. Nothing is so common, as you must know, as for young men to approach serious subjects, as judges – to study them, as mere sciences. Aristotle and Butler are treated as teachers of *a* system, not as if there was more truth in them than in Jeremy Bentham. The study of the Evidences now popular (such as Paley's) encourages this evil frame of mind – the learner is supposed *external* to the system – our Lord is 'a young Galilean peasant' – His Apostles, 'honest men, trustworthy witnesses' and the like. . . . In all these cases the student is supposed to look upon the system from without, and to have to choose it by an act of reason before he submits to it – whereas the great lesson of the Gospel is faith, an obeying prior to reason, and *proving* its reasonableness by making experiment of it – a casting of heart and mind into the system, and investigating the truth by practice. (v. 5; To Arthur Philip Perceval, 11 Jan. 1836)

No truth, no conclusion about what is true, is without its difficulties. You must give up faith, if you will not believe till all objections are first solved. (v. 10; To an Unknown Correspondent, August [?] 1845)

As to the divine foundation of the certitude of faith being not historical but from the grace of God, this is quite true, but irrelevant. It only means you cannot make an act of faith by your own strength, and that, when you make a saving act of faith, you believe in *God*, not in man, though you *come* to believe in Him *through* history, *through* argument. Private judgment *must* be your guide, *till* you are in the Church. You do not begin with faith, but with reason, and you *end* with faith. How are you to get into the way of faith, but by history or some other equivalent method of inquiry? You *must* have some *ground* of becoming a Catholic, . . . (v. 24; To Mrs. Helbert, 10 Sep. 1869)

If there is any definite question that I can answer you, I will do so – but I can't give the gift of faith. (v. 25; To Mrs. Wilson, 8 Jan. 1870)

How is Grace Related to Apologetics and Rational Argument?

Grace alone surely can guide our argumentative power into truth, and grace is not attained in such anxious and difficult enquiries as those which are in question between us without fasting and prayer. (v. 7; To W. C. A. MacLaurin, 8 and 16 Oct. 1840)

I would gladly help you in your difficulties of faith, if I could – but, as you know well, you must wait upon God, and He will hear you and not forsake you. If you ask Him to teach you the truth, He will do so, slowly perhaps, but surely. (v. 25; To S. S. Shiel, 25 Jan. 1870)

Is Logical Demonstration All There is to Apologetics?

You say that 'the dry external argument is inadequate as a demonstration of Christianity' etc I most entirely agree with you, . . . I have been for some years preaching University Sermons, as I have had opportunity, on this one subject, that men judge in religion, and are meant to judge by antecedent probability much more than by external evidences, and that their view of antecedent probability depends upon their particular state of mind) I consider with you that 'the alleged historical proof of miracles is unsatisfactory', separate from the knowledge of the moral character of the doctrine. (v. 7; To [brother] Francis W. Newman, 10 Nov. 1840)

How Are Faith and Reason Related?

The Catholic doctrine concerning Faith and Reason is this – that Reason proves that Catholicism *ought* to be believed, and that in that form it comes before the Will, which accepts it or rejects it, as moved by grace or not. Reason does not prove that Catholicism' is *true*, as it proves mathematical propositions are true; but it proves that there is a *case* for it so strong that we see we ought to accept it. There may be many difficulties, which we cannot answer, but still we see on the whole that the grounds are sufficient for conviction. This is not the same thing as conviction. If conviction were unavoidable, we might be said to be *forced* to believe, as we are forced to confess that two sides of a triangle are greater than the third; but, while there is enough evidence for conviction, whether we *will* be convinced or not, rests with ourselves. (v. 31; To Catherine Ward, 12 Oct. 1848)

Surely, enough has been written – all the writing in the world would not destroy the necessity of faith – if all were made clear to reason, where would be the exercise of faith? The simple question is whether *enough* has been done to *reduce* the difficulties so far as to hinder them absolutely blocking up the way, or excluding those direct and large arguments on which the reasonableness of faith is built. (v. 14; To James Hope, 20 Nov. 1850)

Theology tells us that faith is *more certain* than demonstration – this is a theological truth – it *must* be true- but it is not deduced from experiment, from testimony, from feeling. *A man's consciousness does not attest it.* (v. 14; To J. Spencer Northcote, 25 March 1851)

[C]an a more fatal suicidal act be committed on the part of our controversialists, than to imply an opposition between reason and faith, or at least to encourage the notion that the intellect of the world is naturally and properly on the side of infidelity [?]. (v. 15; To Edward Healy Thompson, 7 Oct. 1853)

God will be sure to prosper, guide, and reward so strong and pure a resolve. The self command you go on to speak about, by which the mind rules itself to believe, I consider in the highest degree meritorious, and sure of a reward – but I don't *word* it as you do. It is not, that faith is an act of the *will* – but the will obliges the *reason* to believe. Nor is there a want of faith and of acts of faith in the *reason*, in the case you put- but a languor of the *imagination*. For I consider the 'realization' you speak of is to be as distinct from faith, as emotion is. It is a state of the imagination. (v. 18; To Catherine Anne Bathurst, 22 March 1858)

[T]here is scarce a subject in Theology which can be fully demonstrated to the conviction of the world, by reason, or by antiquity, or by Scripture – that most doctrines admit of proof up to a certain point – but that, whereas to receive them savingly, we must receive them on the authority of the Church, so for receiving them with *certainty* we are thrown upon her enunciation, not on our own individual investigations and conclusions. After all our reasonings, something must be ever left to faith. (v. 20; To William Robert Brownlow, 16 Oct. 1863)

[Y]ou argue as follows: That which is a conclusion in reason cannot also be an object of faith; since then the being of a God is an object of faith, it is not a conclusion of the reason. Now here a great deal might be said, did my paper admit of it, on the difference between a conclusion and an object; but I will only say this, that the same truth may at once be proved by reason and held by faith. For instance, the truth of the Newtonian system is a conclusion in reason; yet by the mass of the community it is held, not as a conclusion which they have proved, but as a truth received on faith in scientific men, . . . Or, (what is more simple,) the fact that, contrary to the evidence of sight, the earth turns on its axis, some conclude on grounds of reason, most men only believe 'because every one says so, because men of science say so.' Nay, the very same person may hold the same fact at once upon faith and upon reason. 1. I may have satisfactorily proved to myself by pure reason that the nebular theory is true; and then, on turning to Scripture, may find that light was created before the sun. Here faith confirms reason, or I hold a fact first by reason, and then in addition by faith. 2. I may receive on faith that the whole human race descends from Adam, and at some future time may be able to prove it from philology, ethnology, geology, and archeology. Here reason confirms faith, or I hold a fact, first by faith, and then in addition by reason. 1. I do not cease to conclude because I believe. 2. I do not cease to believe because I conclude. (v. 21; To an Unknown Correspondent, 23 Sep. 1864)

It is an odd sort of faith, which only believes what the reason understands, what the reason approves of. (v. 26; To Lady Chatterton, 13 June 1873)

What I have written about Rationalism requires to be expanded. If you will let me be short and abrupt, I would contrast it with *faith*. Faith cometh by hearing, by the *Word of God*. Rationalists are those who are content with conclusions to which they have been brought by reason, but 'we are saved by faith,' and even in cases and persons where true conclusions can be arrived at those conclusions must be believed on the ground that 'God has spoken.' A man may be a true and exact theist and yet not have faith. What he lacks in order to faith is the grace of God, which is given in answer to prayer. (v. 31; To Richard A. Armstrong, 23 March 1887)

Is Apologetics the Same as Proselytyzing?

I willingly talk to young men on Church subjects . . . they are most elevating and striking and therefore from their novelty most exciting subjects . . . and they will excite when preached just in proportion to the degree in which they have beforehand been neglected. . . . I never have tried to proselyte – but when persons are perplexed and come to me for information, then I am induced to write Lectures to meet that existing perplexity. (v. 6; To Thomas Henderson, 2 August 1838)

I did not make his state of mind: I found it. *I* could not change it, even if I had been called to do so. *I* did not intrude my advice upon him; he asked it. . . . It has never been my way . . . 'to make a proselyte to my communion.' But when a man comes to me and asks me plain questions, how can I answer it to God, if I conceal from him what I believe God has taught me? (v. 24; To James Skinner, 13 May 1868)

I can quite understand a man being in good faith a member of the Anglican Church – and I feel the greatest difficulty of attempting in that case to stir him from his position – for I might merely unsettle him, and lead him to give up the truth which he already has instead of embracing what is fuller truth. (v. 24; To H. A. Woodgate, 30 Dec. 1868)

Is "Controversy" in Apologetics a Good Thing?

You caught at that Lutheran's saying that Dr. W. [Nicholas Wiseman] was an unscrupulous controversialist. I dare say he is. But who is not? Is Jeremy Taylor, or Laud, or Stillingfleet? I declare I think it is as rare a thing, candour in controversy, as to be a Saint. (v. 8; To Frederic Rogers, 10 Jan. 1841)

The one thing I feared and deprecated years ago, when we began the Tracts for the Times, was utter neglect of us on the part of the Church. I was not afraid of being misrepresented, censured or illtreated – and certainly hitherto it has done no harm. Every attack hitherto has turned to good, or at least is dying a natural death. But *Controversy* does but delay the sure victory of truth by making people angry. When they find out they are wrong of *themselves*, a generous feeling rises in their minds towards the persons and things they have abused and resisted. Much of this reaction has already taken place. Controversy too is a waste of time – one has other things to do. Truth can fight its own battle. It has a reality in it, which shivers to pieces swords of earth. As far as we are not on the side of truth, *we* shall shiver to bits, and I am willing it should be so. (v. 8; To Robert Delaney, 25 Jan. 1841)

Everyone knows how commonly it happens in life, that you *cannot* defend yourself without attacking your opponent, little as you wish to do so. *One or other* must be *bad.* Now this is emphatically the case in the controversy with Rome – *either* the Holy See is tyrannical, *or* Protestants are rebels. (v. 13; To Frederick A. Faber, 22 Nov. 1849)

I don't think I have written anything controversial for the last 14 years. Nor have I ever, as I think, replied to any controversial notice of what I have written. Certainly, I let pass without a word the various volumes which were written in answer to my Essay on Doctrinal Development, and that on the principle that truth defends itself, and falsehood refutes itself – and that, having said my say, time would decide for me, without any trouble, how far it was true, and how far not true. And I have quoted Crabbe's line as to my purpose, (though I can't quote correctly):-

> Leaving the case to Time, who solves all doubt,
> By bringing Truth, his glorious daughter, out.

(v. 22; To Edward B. Pusey, 5 Sep. 1865)

Should a Person Exercise Faith if Still Plagued by Difficulties?

What Mrs H. [Houldsworth] requires is for one to write a book. Any one can ask questions and in no time, but it requires many words to answer any one of them. Some of her present questions she has asked me, and I have answered, already. You doubtless have answered others. She *must* take *something* on faith. The question is whether she has not enough evidence in order to make it her duty to put away questions she cannot answer to her satisfaction, as mere difficulties. If she inquired into the New Testament in the same minute way, she would not believe in the Bible – if into the proofs of a God, the bare existence of evil would hinder her from believing in Him. . . . Adverse arguments, must, when we have once made up our minds, be ignored entirely. If a jury find a man guilty, because ten credible witnesses have sworn against him, and one or two for him, they consider that the testimony of the ten annihilates that of the two.' This is a law of the human mind – that is, the will of God. I am sure that it is for her good that I thus insist. Till she understands that she cannot have a proof devoid of difficulties, she will believe nothing. . . . She has written to me herself within the last month – and told me that, at the end of the time which I appointed her, she found herself so confused by contrary arguments that she did not know where she stood. On this I said to her – 'Well then – put aside all arguments on both sides – don't read or think about them – don't talk with anyone – But for two months give yourself simply to prayer and communing with God – and then see *where you are* at the end of the time –' . . . (v. 25; To Catherine Froude, 24 July 1871)

Should we Avoid Ad Hominem *Attacks in Argument?*

I detested a certain peculiarity which he was apt to let his language run into, and that is, *abuse* – and on this certainly I ever have had a very strong opinion. By 'abuse' I mean strong and violent expressions of *opinion* on persons and things as distinct from the expression of *facts*. I see nothing of this in his speeches in Parliament – they are *measured* in *language*, and *profuse* in *facts*; – the truest virtues in controversy and debate. (v. 15; To Mrs. William G. Ward, 17 March 1853)

Abuse is as great a mistake in controversy, as panegyric in biography. Of course a man must state strongly his opinion, but that is not personal vituperation. (v. 22; To Henry James Coleridge, 13 April 1866)

What is the Reward of Apologetics?

[O]f course it is a most welcome thing to be told that anything oneself has written has been made at all instrumental in impressing religious convictions on the mind of another . . . (v. 7; To Miss Mary Holmes, 29 May 1840)

Should we Know People Before Trying to Persuade Them?

I have a great dislike of controverting or the like with people I do not know. I do not think it answers. Very seldom have I been persuaded into the attempt – and never, I think, with success. I have hitherto succeeded in keeping people in our Church whose turn of mind, opinions etc I know – but I have failed whenever I have been asked to write to strangers. (v. 9; To Miss Mary Holmes, 24 March 1843)

Does Proclaiming Theological Truth Offend Some People?

It is a very difficult thing to speak the truth without giving offence. . . . I think my greatest friendliness will be shown in speaking out what I think to be christian truth; with God's help I will ever do so, and I doubt not that, tho' I may be misunderstood and thought harsh for a while, yet in the end I shall get honor for my honesty even from those who differ from me. (v. 4; To Mr. Jubber, 19 July 1834)

Are There Times When Trying to Argue with People is Futile?

As to Mr Askew's Letter, it is at once angry and pompous, and it would be very easy to demolish his whole structure – but I do not think it is worthwhile. There is no call on you to answer everyone who chooses to make free with you – and I do not suppose it would do any kind of good for anyone else to get into controversy with persons who have prejudged the matter, and who think every refutation of their opinions only serves to make those opinions more irrefragable and more engaging. (v. 14; To Viscount Feilding, 15 Nov. 1850)

[I]t is hopeless for two men to talk when they more or less have different principles, or see the true [first principles] variously. (v. 15; To Robert Isaac Wilberforce, 27 Dec. 1853; Greek word used for the bracketed translation)

Does the "Argument from Longing" Suggest that Heaven Exists?

I am very regular in my riding, . . . It is so great a gain to throw off Oxford for a few hours so completely as one does in dining out, that it is almost sure to do me good. The country too is beautiful – the fresh leaves, the scents, the varied landscape. Yet I never felt so intensely the transitory nature of this world as when most delighted with these country scenes – and in riding out today I have been impressed, more powerfully than I had before an idea was possible, with the two lines – 'Chanting with a *solemn* voice, mind us of our better choice.' I could hardly believe the lines were not my own and Keble had not taken them from me. I wish it were possible for words to put down those indefinite vague and withal subtle feelings which quite pierce the soul and make it sick. . . . What a veil and curtain this world of sense is! beautiful but still a veil . . . (v. 2; To [sister] Jemima Newman, 10 May 1828)

How Can we Communicate Catholic Truths to Protestants?

You have shown that a *case* may be made out for Catholics. You can't expect to prove the truth of their religion, much less to convert the Protestants of Stafford by a letter, or twenty letters, in a Newspaper; but you can show them, and this you have done, that it is not so easy to show Catholicism is false, or that it is not as good as Protestantism, as some people think. (v. 21; To Michael O'Sullivan, 1 February 1864)

Of course your weak point is the cultus of our Lady – but so it will be, if you are bound to take St Alfonso's words as de fide. I think they would, (taken in the lump,) startle, not to say shock, most Catholics of our latitude . . . They may be very well for the South. . . . What is beautiful as devotion, is harsh as dogma – St Alfonso is devotional – but if people do not spontaneously *run with* that devotionalness, then it looks to them like dogma and startles them. Subjectively received, it is pleasant – objectively contemplated, it is perplexing[.] (v. 21; To Michael O'Sullivan, 1 February 1864)

Chapter Two

Philosophy of Religion

How Important is Philosophy of Religion?

To show that there is a true philosophy of religion is the first step in the development and reception on a large scale of Christian and Catholic truth. (v. 25; To John Campbell Shairp, 18 Dec. 1870)

What is "Philosophical Theology"?

I consider it but as a *defence of* the Truth. Faith submits and receives – the intellect, suborned by the rebellious principle, interferes – therefore faith takes it as its instrument to combat its own difficulties. To use a common proverb, it is like setting a thief to catch a thief. (v. 5; To James Stephen, 16 March 1835)

What is "Certitude" or Faith Held in "Certainty"?

I consider there is no such thing [[(in the province of facts)]] as a perfect logical demonstration; there is always a margin of objection – even in mathematics, except in the case of short proofs, as the propositions of Euclid. Yet on the other hand it is a paradox to say there is not such a state of mind as certitude. It is as well ascertained a state of mind, as doubt – to say that such a phenomenon in the human mind is a mere extravagance or weakness is a monstrous assertion which I cannot swallow. Of course there may be abuses and mistakes in particular cases of certitude, but that is another matter. It is *a law of our nature* then, that we are certain on premises which do not touch <reach> demonstration. This seems to me undeniable. Then what is the faculty, since it is not the logical Dictum de omni et hullo, which *enables* us to be certain, to have the *state of mind* called certitude, though the syllogism before us is not according to the strict rules of Barbara and Celarent? . . . No syllogism can prove to me that nature is uniform – but the argument is so strong, though not demonstrative, that I should . . . be . . . a fool, to doubt. . . . So again in History etc. a cumulative argument, though not demonstrative, may claim of us, i.e. by the law of our nature, by our duty to our nature, i.e. by our duty to God, *an act of certitude.* . . . Now I know that to say all this and no more, is to open the door to endless disputes. The only thing to be done is to rest the whole on Certain first principles, and to say if you can't take my first principles, I can't help it. But to find the first principles is the difficulty. . . . Should not I be an ass if I did not believe in the existence of India? Yet are there not scores of persons who have evidence of a quality and quantity indefinitely higher than mine? for I have not been there, and they have. I should think myself a fool if I said 'I have some doubt about the existence of India,' or 'I am not certain about it,' . . . (v. 24; To Henry Wilberforce, 27 July 1868)

[T]here *is* an evidence, which leads to (more than an opinion) viz to an assent or certitude, as to the fact. . . . My main proposition, in my Essay [*in Aid of a Grammar of Assent*] is, that by the nature of the human mind we assent absolutely on reasons which taken separately are but probabilities[.] (v. 25; To Henry Bleckly, 10? Jan. 1871)

Does Certainty Derive from Demonstration or Probabilities?

Certainty in the business of life means a *conviction sufficient for practice.* You seem to think that no evidence for an alledged fact is certain, which admits of the chance of the fact being otherwise – i.e. you would hold that demonstration alone is certain proof. I differ – and again demand your reasons, and no reasons can I find. Here again the world is against you – and you besides are the assailant – yet you coolly take it for granted that no evidence from probabilities amounts to a certainty sufficient for action, and leave me to refute your assumption. The world is against you – for every thing we do, is done on probabilities. Even when we trust our senses and memory, we rely on evidence, which, in your own words, 'is not certain and *may* be false.' No facts are known, no practical matters conducted, on demonstrative proof, which is found in pure mathematics alone and subjects of a similar nature: – there is always *a* chance of error. (v. 2; To [brother] Charles Robert Newman, 19 Aug. 1830)

Time alone can turn a view into a conviction – It is most unsatisfactory to be acting on a syllogism, or a solitary, naked, external, logical process. But surely it is possible in process of time to have a proposition so wrought into the mind, both ethically and by numberless fine conspiring and ever-recurring considerations as to become part of our mind, to be inseparable from us, and to command our obedience. And then the greater the sacrifice, the more cogent the testimony shall we have to its authority, for to overcome impediments is a token of power. (v. 10; To Mrs. William Froude, 9 Dec. 1843)

As to the question of certainty, to which you refer, it is both a very interesting one, and, as I think, a difficult one. As far as I can make out, our conclusion in reason (about the truth etc) is not demonstrative, but goes so far towards absolute proof, that it is our duty by an act of the will to believe it *as* firmly as if it were; – somewhat in the same way, that (as *I* should say) we (personally) have no *demonstration* that *we* (personally) shall *die* – but a man would be a fool who did not hold it certain. (v. 18; To J. M. Capes, 27 Sep. 1858)

I have no demonstration that I shall die – but . . . the evidence is such and so much, as to make it clear to me that I should be a fool not absolutely and implicitly to believe it. It has a claim on my speculative belief that England is an island, even though I have no demonstration of it. Reason goes just so far, not as to prove it, but to tell me it is but common sense in me to order my mind to believe, or to direct my mind to believe it. I do not merely say to myself, 'It is *safe* to act as if I believed it.' . . . I cannot see that induction is ever a demonstration – but it makes the conclusion 'credibile' – viz 'claiming belief.' . . . I daily control and direct my mind into a firm belief, or speculative certainty, of truths which I cannot prove, on the ground that I should be a fool not to believe them, or, that reason bids my will to bid my mind to believe. *How* it is that we are so constituted as to be bound by our reason to believe what we cannot prove, is a question which I do not pretend to solve. (v. 18; To J. M. Capes, 1 Oct. 1858)

I should say that I never supposed that such. reasons as I assigned were *demonstrations*, but I considered them arguments, as far as they went, for they all went one way, and therefore were satisfactory. *No arguments from Scripture are demonstrations.* They are as good arguments surely, i.e. they tend towards proving the doctrine, as much as any texts go to *demonstrate* the Athanasian doctrine of the Trinity. What is true of Scripture is true of the writings of the, Fathers. It is always possible to pick a hole in the proof gathered from them. (v. 19; To Arthur Osborne Alleyne, 8 June 1860)

No one on earth can have evidence strictly *sufficient* for an *absolute* conclusion, but I may have evidence so strong that I may see it is my duty to give my absolute assent to it. I have not absolute demonstration that my father was not a murderer, or my intimate friend a sharper, but it would not only be heartless, but irrational not to disbelieve these hypotheses or possibilities *utterly* – and, anyhow, in matter of fact men generally *do* disbelieve them absolutely- and therefore the Church, as the Minister of God, asks us for nothing more in things supernatural than common sense, as nature asks of us in matters of this world. I believe absolutely that there is a North America – and that the

United States is a Republic with a President – why then do I not absolutely believe, though I see it not, that there is a Heaven and that God is there? If you say that there is *more* evidence for the United States than for Heaven, that is intelligible – but it is not a question of more or less; since the *utmost* evidence only leads to probability and yet you believe absolutely in the United States, it is no reason against believing in heaven absolutely, though you have not 'experience' of it. But you have said all this to her. She says there are persons who are *certain* of the Christian religion *because* they have strictly proved it – no one is certain for this reason. Every one believes by an act of will, more or less ruling his intellect (as a matter of duty) to believe absolutely *beyond* the evidence. She says 'acts of certitude are always made about things of which our senses or our reason do, or can take cognizance' – our senses do not tell us that there is a 'United States' and our reason does not *demonstrate* it, only makes it probable. Try to analyze the reasons *why* one believes in the United States. We not only *do* not, but we *could* not make a demonstration; yet we assent absolutely. (v. 25; To William Robert Brownlow, 29 April 1871)

How Compelling is Cumulative Evidence?

[G]ranting and maintaining that there are various independent arguments separately conclusive for the credibility of Revelation, need *any one such* be present in the individual, and may not his conclusion be sufficiently logical, if it be the result of converging probabilities, and a cumulative proof? May not 12 probable arguments, make by their aggregate force a conclusive one? This is the circumstantial evidence you have spoken of; certainly, it seems to be most clear, and in the experience of every day, that we are positively and absolutely . . . certain of a thing by a combination of arguments, each of which is only probable; and if so, why not in the case of Faith? Provided that I am *logically certain* that faith is rational and right, who has a right to say the logic takes this shape rather than that? and I certainly do think a *logical* demonstration is possible from cumulating probabilities. (v. 15; To Edward Healy Thompson, 7 Oct. 1853)

Now, is not the proof of Religion of *this* kind? I liken it to the mechanism of some triumph of skill, tower or spire, geometrical staircase, or vaulted roof, . . . where all display of strength is carefully avoided, and the weight is ingeniously thrown in a variety of directions, upon supports which are distinct from, or independent of each other. It would be most difficult to analyze, and put on paper briefly and intelligibly, the rationale of such a happy construction. And so in the case of the religious fabric – not indeed that it is so contrived for the sake of the contrivance, but from the nature of the case, man being what he is and facts being external to him – and so far it may be said to have an end in its very delicacy and subtlety, that it subserves the purposes of moral probation, as is often said. (v. 19; To Sir John Simeon, 12 Feb. 1861)

The best illustration of what I hold is that of a *cable* which is made up of a number of separate threads, each feeble, yet together as sufficient as an iron rod. An iron rod represents mathematical or strict demonstration; a cable represents moral demonstration, which is an assemblage of probabilities, separately insufficient for certainty, but, when put together, irrefragable. A man who said 'I cannot trust a cable, I must have an iron bar,' *would, in certain given cases*, be irrational and unreasonable: – so too is a man who says I must have a rigid demonstration, not moral demonstration, of religious truth. You have illustrated the point yourself most appositively. Thus I thought as a Protestant; and I observe there are Catholic theologians of authority who go *further* in their estimate of the legitimate force of probability in creating certitude than I went, – maintaining that the *greater* probability is a sufficient, or rather the intended and ordinary, ground of certainty with men in general; or that that Religion, which is evidently more credible than the rest, is that very religion which is revealed by God, and therefore most certainly true, or demonstrated, for there is a way, by which the highest certainty of religion may be arrived at by fundamental articles which are only *more* probable. For myself, I never, that I recollect, took this ground of 'the more probable,' but of a certitude which lay in an assemblage and accumulation of probabilities, which *rationally demanded* to be considered sufficient for certitude[.] (v. 21; To J. Walker of Scarborough, 6 July 1864)

As to the question of 'certainty,' I conceive that the certainty, (human) arising from the cumulus of probabilities, is rewarded by the certainty of faith,which is firmer and more satisfying. The aggregate of probabilities does not create the faith, or its certainty, which is a gift direct from God – but they create the same sort of certainty, which an infidel may have that our Lord suffered under Pontius Pilate. If then Manning meant (as I do not suppose) that the probabilities did not create legitimately a human certainty, he differed from me – but if he meant that the human certainty was swallowed up by the faith from God's grace, which is its reward, (and I think he meant this) I agree with him. However, in my book I have nothing to do with supernatural faith – but with the human process. Children may have divine faith without any logical process whatever – but Butler is speaking of the logical value of probabilities, and so was I. Butler *tends* to reduce the certainty to a *practical* certainty, viz that it is *safer to act, as if* the conclusion were true; I maintain that probabilities lead to a speculative certainty legitimately; so that it is quite *rational* to come to that conviction, that human faith, which is rewarded by divine faith. In thus speaking, of course I do not mean to say, that, in matter of fact, that human conclusion is reached, or the reward of divine certainty given, *without* the influence of *actual* grace, both being present and being obeyed. (v. 21; To J. Walker of Scarborough, 24 Oct. 1864)

Does Conscience Surpass Intellect as a Way to God?

Another thought which I wish to put before you is, whether our nature does not tell us that there is something which has more intimate relations with the question of religion than intellectual exercises have, and that is our conscience. We have the idea of duty – duty suggest something or some one to which it is to be referred, to which we are responsible. That something that has dues upon us is to us God. I will not assume it is a personal God, or that it is more than a law (though of course I hold that it is the Living Seeing God) but still the idea of duty, and the terrible anguish of conscience, and the irrepressible distress and confusion of face which the transgression of what we believe to be our duty, cause us, all this is an intimation, a clear evidence, that there is something nearer to religion than intellect; and that, if there is a way of finding religious truth, it lies, not in exercises of the intellect, but close on the side of duty, of conscience, in the observance of the moral law. (v. 24; To Louisa Simeon, 25 June 1869)

[T]he dictate of conscience, which is natural and the voice of God, is a moral *instinct*, and its own evidence – as the *belief* in an external world is an *instinct* on the apprehension of sensible phenomena. . . . to *deny* those instincts is an absurdity, *because* they are the voice of nature. . . . it is a duty to trust, or rather to use our nature – and not to do so is absurdity. (v. 24; To Charles Meynell, 25 July 1869)

Is Reasoning Key in Arriving at First Premises and Axioms?

You must not suppose that I am denying the intellect its real place in the discovery of truth; but it must ever be borne in mind that its exercise mainly consists in reasoning, – that is, in comparing things, classifying them, and inferring. It ever needs points to start from, first principles, and these it does not provide – but it can no more move one step without these starting points, than a stick, which supports a man, can move without the man's action. In physical matters, it is the senses which gives us the first start – and what the senses give is physical fact – and physical facts do not lie on the surface of things, but are gained with pains and by genius, through experiment. Thus Newton, or Davy, or Franklin ascertained those physical facts which have made their names famous. After these primary facts are gained, intellect can act; it acts too of course in gaining them; but they *must* be gained; it is the senses which *enable* the intellect to act, by giving it something to act upon. In like manner we have to ascertain the starting points for arriving at religious truth. The intellect will be useful in gaining them and after gaining them – but to attempt to *see* them by means of the intellect is like attempting by the intellect to see the physical facts which are the basis of physical exercises of the intellect, a method of proceeding which was the very mistake of the Aristotelians of the middle age, who, instead of what Bacon calls 'interrogating nature' for facts, reasoned out every thing by syllogisms. To gain religious starting points, we must in a parallel way, interrogate our hearts, and (since it is a personal, individual matter,) our *own* hearts, – interrogate our own consciences, interrogate, I will say, the God who dwells there. (v. 24; To Louisa Simeon, 25 June 1869)

Is the Epistemology of Religion Primarily Subjective?

I agree with you too in feeling the incommensurability (so to speak) of the human mind – we cannot gauge and measure by any common rule the varieties of thought and opinion. We all look at things with our own eyes m and invest the whole face of nature with colors of our own. – Each mind pursues its own course and is actuated in that course by ten thousand in-describable incommunicable feelings and imaginings. It would be comparatively easy to enumerate the various external impulses which determine the capricious motions of a floating feather or web, and to express in an algebraical formula the line it describes – so mysterious are the paths of thought. Nay I might even be tempted to say that on no single point do any two individuals agree – no single object do their minds view from the same spot and in the same light. And this will of course hold good in religious matters – Necessary as it is, that we should all hold the same truths (as we would be saved) still each of us holds them in his own way; and differs from his nearest and most loved friends either in the relative importance he gives to them, or in the connected view he takes of them, or in his perception of the particular consequences resulting from them. – Accordingly I trust I shall always be very slow to *quarrel* with persons differing from me in matters of *opinion*. For *words* are not *feelings* . . . Intellect seems to be but the attendant and servant of right moral feeling in this . . . weak and dark state of being – defending it when attacked, accounting tor it, and explaining it in a poor way to others. – It supplies a medium of communication between mind and mind – yet only to a certain extent . . . I have Froude's authority for lowering the intellectual powers into handmaids of our moral nature. (v. 2; To Joseph Blanco White, 1 March 1828)

Must Christianity Necessarily be Proven, to be Rationally Held?

That indeed I have all along assumed (*when not arguing*) that Christianity is true, this I allow – and so I certainly ever shall, till I am convinced otherwise. – In my last letter to you, which you call 'unjustifiable,' doubtless I assumed it – but, *not on the ground that I had proved its truth*, but because you had not *dis*proved it. (v. 2; To [brother] Charles Robert Newman, 19 Aug. 1830)

How Do Most Intellectuals Regard Natural Law?

In medieval times you might appeal to supernatural principles as axioms, and start from them. At a later date you might speak of the moral sense, and take truths for granted on the ground that every one held them. You might speak of the idea of a Supreme Being as common to the whole human family – but now nothing is received as true without and before *proof*, except what the senses or our consciousness conveys to us, for nothing else is universally held. (v. 19; To Richard Simpson, 6 July 1859)

What is the Moral Law?

[T]he Moral law is in the Nature of God Himself. . . . to recognize our nature is really to *recognize God.* Hence those *instincts* come from *God* – and as the moral law is an inference or generalization from those instincts, the moral law is ultimately taught us from God, *whose* nature it is. (v. 24; To Charles Meynell, 25 July 1869)

This is what I meant to say by consensus – *why* do men *agree* to say this deed is right, that man is good, that maxim is praiseworthy? *Why* is there a 'consensus'? how comes it about? The *reason why* they agree is the *proper* definition of right, goodness, truth and beautifulness, not the mere fact of their agreeing. They agree, because there is an objective right, goodness etc which they mentally see – that objective right etc is the *moral* law – and if I am asked where the moral law is, I answer, that it is realized in God. What all men dimly see, one and all, and therefore they agree in, is the shadow of the divine attributes. These moral truths are eternal . . . and very different from the facts of Revelation, (even though some of them are eternal too.) . . . That there is a right and a wrong, that certain things in the concrete are right, that it is a sin to murder, this is clear to the individual mind by nature, and if I wish to persuade another, I need no test external to him, but I appeal to his intuition. (v. 26; To H. A. Woodgate, 23 Feb. 1872)

What is Rationalism and its Fundamental Deficiency?

Rationalism is the attempt to know *how* things are, about which you can know nothing. . . . (v. 5; To [sister] Harriet Newman, 10 Oct. 1835)

How Are People Usually Convinced of Christian Truths?

The heart is commonly reached, not through the reason, but through the imagination, by means of direct impressions, by the testimony of facts and events, by history, by description. Persons influence us, voices melt us, looks subdue us, deeds inflame us. Many a man will live and die upon a dogma: no man will be a martyr for a conclusion. A conclusion is but an opinion; it is not a thing which *is*, but which *we are* "*certain about*;" and it has often been observed, that we never say we are certain without implying that we doubt. To say that a thing *must* be, is to admit that *it may not* be. No one, I say, will die for his own calculations; he dies for realities. . . . Logic makes but a sorry rhetoric with the multitude; first shoot round corners, and you may not despair of converting by a syllogism. . . . To most men argument makes the point in hand only more doubtful, and considerably less impressive. After all, man is *not* a reasoning animal; he is a seeing, feeling, contemplating, acting animal. He is influenced by what is direct and precise. . . . Now I wish to state all this as matter of fact, to be judged by the candid testimony of any persons whatever. Why we are so constituted that Faith, not Knowledge or Argument, is our principle of action, is a question with which I have nothing to do; but I think it is a fact, and if it be such, we must resign ourselves to it as best we may, . . . no Religion has yet been a Religion of physics or of philosophy. It has ever been synonymous with Revelation. It never has been a deduction from what we know: it has ever been an assertion of what we are to believe. It has never lived in a conclusion; it has ever been a message, or a history, or a vision. (v. 8: Letter to the *Times* by "Catholicus" in Response to Robert Peel ["Tamworth"], Feb. 1841)

Religious truth is reached, not by reasoning, but by an inward perception. Anyone can reason; only disciplined, educated, formed minds can perceive. (v. 9; To Miss Mary Holmes, 8 March 1843)

I feel more and more, and have for years, how little one's mind is in one's own power. Difficulties of years are sometimes overcome in a moment – yet one cannot foresee the time. It is very mysterious, and brings before one the great Christian truth, that man in purls naturalibus is a most imperfect being and depends on principles and powers external to him for the power of thinking and acting. What I *want* to do and can't, and it falls into your subject, is to construct a *positive* argument for Catholicism. The negative is most powerful – 'Since there must be one true religion, it can *be none other* than this –' but the fault of this is that it involves what many people call scepticism – a cutting away everything else but Catholicism – showing the difficulties of such portions of truth as Protestantism contains etc. Hence what I have written (e.g. difficulties of the Canon) has been much objected to. Now as to *positive* proof, I can only rest the argument on antecedent probabilities or verisimilia – which are to my mind most powerful, . . . but they seem argumentatively imperfect; and I would give much to be able to strike out something – but I feel myself quite helpless. (v. 13; To J. M. Capes, 2 Dec. 1849)

If I wrote a new work, it would be on 'the popular, practical, and personal evidence of Christianity –' i.e. as contrasted to the scientific, and its object would be to show that a given individual, high or low, has as much right (has as real rational grounds) to be certain, as a learned theologian who knows the scientific evidence. (v. 19; To Charles Meynell, 23 Jan. 1860)

What is the Essence of Religion?

The essence of Religion is the idea of a Moral Governor and a particular Providence; . . . are not virtue and vice, and responsibility, and reward and punishment, anything else than moral matters, and are *they* not of the essence of Religion? (v. 8: Letter to the *Times* by "Catholicus" in Response to Robert Peel ["Tamworth"], Feb. 1841)

What is the Relation of Faith to Culture?

I consider, then, that intrinsically excellent and noble as are scientific pursuits, and worthy of a place in a liberal education, and fruitful in temporal benefits to the community, still they are not, and cannot be, *the instrument* of an ethical training; that physics do not supply a basis, but only materials for religious sentiment; that knowledge does but occupy, does not form the mind; that apprehension of the unseen is the only known principle capable of subduing moral evil, educating the multitude, and organizing society; and that, whereas man is born for action, action flows not from inferences, but from impressions,—not from reasonings, but from Faith. (v. 8: Letter to the *Times* by "Catholicus" in Response to Robert Peel ["Tamworth"], Feb. 1841)

Do Catholics Love the Philosophy of Plato and Socrates?

It has been a great pleasure to receive your volumes, and I thank you very much for them. The Plato reads as easily as if he wrote in English, and must be the means of introducing to many who otherwise could know nothing of him, the great phenomenon which his picture of Socrates presents to us – a phenomenon so important to those who hold the principles of what may be called Catholic philosophy. (v. 20; To Lady Chatterton, 16 June 1863)

How Strong is the Teleological (Design) Argument for God?

I have not insisted on the argument from *design*, because I am writing for the 19th century, by which, as represented by its philosophers, design is not admitted as proved. And to tell the truth, though I should not wish to preach on the subject, for 40 years I have been unable to see the logical force of the argument myself. I believe in design because I believe in God; not in a God because I see design. . . . Half the world know nothing of the argument from design – and, when you have got it, you do not prove by it the moral attributes of God – except very faintly. Design teaches me power, skill and goodness – not sanctity, not mercy, not a future judgment, which three are of the essence of religion. (v. 25; To William Robert Brownlow, 13 April 1870)

I should maintain that the very fact of the world's existence implies an Almighty, intelligent, personal Creator. And again, the same great truth is proved from what I should call the argument from *design*, that is, from the wonderful order, harmony, unity, and beautifulness of the Universe . . . (v. 31; To William Barry, 4 Nov. 1885)

Does the Argument from Final Causes Prove God's Existence?

In an Oxford Sermon, preached in 1839, . . . I have expressed a doubt whether the argument from *final causes* is, as facts stand, sufficient to prove the being of God . . . but that is not all one with denying that the *physical universe* was sufficient to prove it. (v. 31; To William Barry, 4 Nov. 1885)

Chapter Three

Church History

Are the Church Fathers Closer to Catholicism or Protestantism?

I cannot deny that from the first the Fathers do teach doctrines and a temper of mind which we commonly identify with Romanism. (v. 7; To [sister] Jemima Mozley, 17 Nov. 1839)

For myself, this only I see for certain that there is indefinitely more in the Fathers against our own state of alienation from Christendom than against the Tridentine Decrees. (v. 8; To R. W. Church, 24 Dec. 1841)

I am led to speak of the Canons *at all* merely in a *search whether* there be any Protestantism, as the word is popularly understood, in the Primitive church, and I say that the result of my search is, that *whatever* turns up, is so far as it goes the *other way* . . . (v. 8; To William James, 28 March 1842)

As to the Fathers, . . . I *do* now think, far more than I did, that their study leads to Rome. It has thus wrought in me. But of course I *ever* have thought it required a safeguard to keep it from Rome, because in the history of the Church their theology *has* led to Rome on a very large scale. (v. 10; To Edward B. Pusey, 18 Dec. 1843)

I have honestly trusted our Church and wished to defend her as she wishes to be defended. I was not surely wrong in defending her on that basis which our Divines have ever built and on which alone they can pretend to build. And how could I foresee that when I examined that basis I should feel it to require a system different from hers and that the Fathers to which she led me would lead me from her? (v. 10; To Henry Edward Manning, 24 Dec. 1843)

[W]ere St Athanasius and St Ambrose in London now, they would go to worship, not to St Paul's Cathedral, but to Warwick Street or Moor Fields. This my own reading of history has made to me an axiom, and it converted me, though I cannot of course communicate the force of it to another. As an illustration of what I mean, I would direct you to an article in the Dublin [Review], part of which Mr [William G.] Ward reprinted in his Ideal [of a Christian Church, 1844], in which the prima facie appearance of the Church in the 4th and 5th centuries is drawn out: its altars, tombs, pilgrimages, processions, rites, relics, medals etc; whereas I hardly see a trace of the Church of the Fathers, as a *living*, *acting* being, in the Anglican communion. . . . The Church was to be one and the same from Christ's first coming to His second. The modern Roman communion is unmistakeably like the Church of the Fathers; and this great argument is confirmed by finding that the Church of England is unmistakeably unlike it. (v. 13; To A. J. Hanmer, 18 Nov. 1849)

I maintain that the Catholic system, as we now have it, is that to which the *mass* of historical phenomena point – and what remains of fact not taken up by it, consists of odds and ends, and is amorphous, pointing to nothing at all; – that when you confront Catholicism before the facts of history, they are seen almost all tending, converging, absorbed in it – but that place *Protestantism, Anglicanism* etc before the same facts, and there is a simple discord, no sort of relation and sympathy at all existing between the doctrinal system and the phenomena. It is as entertaining this view of the case, that I am so much pained at the general mode of arguing, which Anglicans adopt. *They have nothing to say positive*; they only carp at those historical facts which *we* are unable (if so) to take up and locate in our system Theirs is an 'argument from odds and ends –' i.e. an *objection* –

nothing more. I could enlarge on this at great length. (v. 14; To Francis Richard Wegg-Prosser, 7 Sep. 1851)

Does Christian Truth or Dogma Change Over Time?

I believe it to be a plain external truth, that . . . the Church's religion has been one and the same from first to last. . . . I wish to go by no private judgment. I think that the way I view the fact is the broad practical impression which historical records make on the mind.

    . . . Here then we have one religion in all ages; I profess it. I sacrifice my private judgment to it whenever it speaks; I use my private judgment only in accidental details, where it does not speak, to determine what it speaks.(v. 7; To [brother] Francis W. Newman, 10 Nov. 1840)

How Should Catholics View John Wycliffe?

I can but state the general and superficial view of Wycliffe, which the ordinary histories give us[.] That there were very great social and moral corruptions in the English Church at that time, and in the Church elsewhere, I see no reason to doubt. I see no ground for doubting that there was a great deal to rouse the indignation of men who had a keen sense of what was right and becoming, a love of justice, and the proud, censorious, violent temper which is often found united to these good qualities. Such might be Wycliffe. Then, as all would-be-reformers, he takes upon him duties which are not his – and gets into a false position. From attacking ecclesiastical abuses, he goes on to attack received doctrine – If he took more upon himself, than he had a right to do in his mode of attacking abuses, and therefore was wrong, what reason is there to suppose him right in attacking doctrine? how could he expect to have a blessing, and to have the light of divine guidance? His career is that of many others – Scripture says that 'rebellion is like witch-craft and idolatry;' in other words, that men begin with disobedience and end with spiritual blindness. I suppose Milton is an example – who began with extreme political, or rather revolutionary opinions, and ended with renouncing our Lord's Divinity and the cardinal doctrines connected with it. I am disposed to consider that Wycliffe had many great qualities, but that they were ruined by pride and self will. (v. 19; To Viscount Feilding, 23 Dec. 1859)

Was the Protestant "Reformation" a Praiseworthy Thing?

I fear I must express a persuasion that it requires no deep reading to dislike the Reformation. 'A good tree cannot bring forth evil fruit-' [Mt 7:18] . . . Whence all this schism and heresy, humanly speaking, but for it? – And I fear I must say that the *historical* characteristics of its agents are such, that one need not go into their doctrines or their motives. (v. 8; To Edward B. Pusey, 13 Aug. 1841)

Lutheranism and Calvinism are heresies, repugnant to Scripture, springing up three centuries since, and anathematized by East as well as West . . . (v. 8: Protest Against the Jerusalem Bishopric, 11 Nov. 1841)

Lutheranism and Calvinism . . . *are* heresies just in the sense in which Pelagianism is. (v. 8; To J. R. Hope, 14 Nov. 1841)

I have no sympathy at all with the Reformation, its agents, and leading defenders. (v. 9; Memorandum to Edward B. Pusey, 16 Oct. 1842)

How Has Lutheranism Evolved?

But there is this great difference between German Protestantism 2 centuries ago and now – Then it was Lutheran, now it is a new variety called Evangelical Religion, the produce and compound of Calvinism and Rationalized Lutheranism. (v. 9; To Miss Mary Holmes, 20 Sep. 1842)

Is Church History Fatal to Protestantism?

I would as soon say that Christianity is not true, as say that 'the Church has nothing to do with history.' It is a piece of fanaticism – and no theologian would put his hand to it. I say that 'history read with open eyes is fatal to' Anglicanism, Wesleyanism, Congregationalism, Unitarianism, to every thing but Roman Catholicism. That we have our difficulties I fully admit, and that there are historical points, which if left to oneself one should interpret differently. Of course; – there *are* points in which I must go by faith, not by my private judgment – But to say that history is fatal to Roman Catholicism is the saying of one who should recollect that those who live in glass houses should not throw stones at one which has only glass windows, and those of plate glass. (v. 24; To Mrs. Helbert, 10 Sep. 1869)

Chapter Four

Development of Doctrine

What is the Development of Doctrine?

1. From the first, running up into the obscurity of the Apostolic century, there has been a large body called the Church, claiming the exclusive dispensation of the gospel; and there has been but one such, – large, continuous and commanding.

2. This body, in centuries iv and v, is known to have been of a certain temper, cast of principle, system of doctrine, and character of conduct; in a word of a certain *religion*

3. On tracing backwards, the evidences of the existence of this religion are fainter, but still they exist in their degree.

4. Evidence of any other system of religion, (i.e. in temper, principle, doctrine, conduct) calling itself Christianity, is altogether unproducible. Either this is Christianity, or we do not know (historically) *what* Christianity is. Everything else is the history of mere sects with known authors. The Christian religion, when traced back from the fourth century, vanishes in this form from the pages of history. In proportion as it is known, it is this.

5. There is no reason why this should not be Apostolic Christianity; as it does not differ from Scripture, more than the parts of Scripture differ from each other, and does not resemble foreign systems, which came in contact with it between the first and fourth centuries, more than systems resemble each other which are .acknowledged by all to be independent and distinct.

6. This temper, cast of principle, doctrine, conduct, are singularly consistent with each other, or *one*; so that the existence of e.g. the temper, makes the co-existence of the doctrine at least not improbable.

7. The *temper and principles* of the Church have been precisely

the same from first to last, from the Apostolic age to this; viz what her enemies call dogmatic, mystical, credulous, superstitious, bigotted, legal. I consider no persons doubt this great fact.

8. Its doctrines and course of conduct have developed from external and internal causes; where by development I mean the more accurate statement and the varied application of ideas from the action of the reason upon them according to new circumstances.

9. All systems which have life, have a development, yet do not cease to have an identity though they develop. E.g. Locke or Luther have done far more than they themselves saw.

. . . no one, even at present, denies or disbelieves that Ignatius or Clement Alex. or Irenaeus had the same (what the world calls) narrow, severe, bitter temper and system, and as far as doctrine was developed, the same doctrine as is charged upon the Church now; no one seems to deny that from the first the mass of Christianity tended straight to what is afterwards known as Catholicism, . . . (v. 7; To [brother] Francis W. Newman, 10 Nov. 1840)

If we do not allow of developments, especially in a matter which from the nature of the case *requires* time for its due exhibition, hardly any doctrine can be proved by antiquity. (v. 10; To Mrs. William Froude, 19 May 1844)

The second point was my conviction that certain definite doctrines of Rome were not to be found in Antiquity – and this objection has been removed from my mind by a consideration of the principle of *development*, . . . it is quite plain that the early Christians had no images in worship – there is very little trace of invocation among them, no special honors to St Mary, purgatory in its Roman form was not acknowledged except in places – transubstantiation was not professed or taught, the Holy Communion was commonly administered in two kinds, and the like. In this they differ from Rome, as it is at present – Is not this a *corruption* of Christianity, as originally given? No, I answer, I think it a development of it. . . . I have always held a development of doctrine, at least in some great points in theology. E.g. I have thought that the doctrine of the Holy Trinity and Incarnation are intellectual developments of the inspired declarations of Scripture – but I used to think either that this development was made in the Apostles' life time and given by them traditionally to the Church, or at least that it was made by the Church in the *first* ages. . . . My present view of development is contained in my last University Sermon ['The Theory of Developments in Religious Doctrine']; and differs from this, not in principle, but in two respects. 1. In considering that developments may be made at any time, for the Church is always under the guidance of Divine Grace. 2. that developments are not only *explanations* of the sense of the Creed, but further doctrines involved in and arising from its articles. (v. 10; To Mrs. William Froude, 9 June 1844)

I meant to have drawn out the mode in which I have got reconciled to the (apparently) modem portions of the Roman system. It has been by applying to them that *principle* which, as my last letter showed, had long been in my mind, the principle of developments. From the time I wrote the Arians, or at least from 1836, I have had in my thoughts, though I could not bring it out, that argument or theory, which at last appeared in my closing University Sermon. . . . Yet I must confess that the Sermon does not, . . . go the whole length of theory which is necessary for the Roman system, and that something is still necessary to the discussion of the *theory*, though I have no difficulties about receiving the system in matter of fact. The kind of considerations, which do weigh with me, are such as the following: –

    1. I am far more certain (according to the Fathers) that we *are* in a state of culpable separation *than* that developments do *not* exist under the gospel, and that the Roman developments are *not* true ones.

    2. I am far more certain that *our* (modern) doctrines are

wrong, *than* that the *Roman* (modem) doctrines are wrong.

3. Granting that the Roman (special) doctrines are not found drawn out in the early Church, yet I think there is sufficient trace of them in it, to recommend and prove them, *on the hypothesis* of the Church having a divine guidance, though not sufficient to prove them by itself. So that the question simply turns on the nature of the promise of the Spirit made to the Church.

4. The proof of the *Roman* (modern) <special> doctrines is as strong <(or stronger)> in Antiquity, as that of certain doctrines which *both we and the Romans hold*. E.g. There is more evidence in Antiquity for the necessity of Unity than for that of the Apostolical Succession – for the supremacy of the See of Rome than for the Presence in the Eucharist – for the practice of Invocation than for certain books in the present Canon of Scripture etc etc

5. The Analogy of the Old Testament and the New leads to acknowledgment of doctrinal developments. E.g. the prophetical notices concerning our Lord before His coming. Again the gradual revelation of the calling of the Gentiles through St Peter and St Paul. Again, the distinct theological announcements of St John's gospel compared with those which preceded it. Again it is undeniable that the doctrine of the Holy Trinity, as we now hold it, is historically the result of a great deal of discussion and controversy, of much heresy and much antagonist development. Again the rule for baptizing heretics, or of infant baptism etc., etc. was unsettled and contested in early times, but at last universally obtained as it is at present. (v. 10; To Mrs. William Froude, 14 July 1844)

One age corrects the expressions and statements of even the Saints of the foregoing. Infant Baptism and Confession, Monachism and Roman Supremacy, Original Sin and Purgatory, seem to me equally developments – and the sooner or later does not affect the question. (v. 10; To Edward B. Pusey, 14 March 1845)

As to my Essay [[on doctrinal development]], . . . it is not the argument from unity or Catholicity which immediately weighs with me (in it) but from Apostolicity. If that book is asked, why does its author join the Catholic Church? The answer is, because it is the Church of St Athanasius and St Ambrose. (v. 13; To Henry Wilberforce, 7 March 1849)

My point of issue with the Anti-developmentists seems to be this – whether or not the whole revealed truth, as revealed per modum unius to the Apostles, has been explicitly present to the Church in all its parts from the first – or, whether or not a given *age* may not be inadvertent of a certain portion of the revelation or deposit – or whether or not revealed truth does not grow in its parts to *the Church* as well as to the individual . . . – or, whether or not all knowledge is not like that kind of knowledge which we call memory . . . (or that points de fide, which have been deductions of revelation, are not known by the Church before they are deduced) so that as we know a thing in memory, though memory sleeps, or have latent knowledge, so we may have latent knowledge of doctrine – and as, were a matter which is past sifted, our memory at first might err, but when wide awake would tell truly, so, divines may speak of doctrines carelessly and erroneously till controversy arises, and then be forced by its influence into correctness and completeness. (v. 13; To William G. Ward, 11 March 1849)

The theory of development of doctrine is but a method of *answering objections*. At least this is the primary view I have taken of it in my Essay. Then, in the next place, it becomes an *evidence*, when you see it proceeds on a *law*, which obtains, as now, so in the earliest period. Further, in drawing out the state of. the case in the way of *defence*, the *unity* of the Church *throughout* its apparent changes, is an additional (and to me) most strong evidence. (v. 14; To Francis Richard Wegg-Prosser, 3 Oct. 1851)

The differences and additions in doctrinal teaching observable in the history of the Church are but apparent, being the necessary phenomena incident to deep intellectual ideas . . . (v. 15; To Edmund S. Ffoulkes, 1 June 1853)

[N]o one can religiously speak of development, without giving the *rules* which keep it from extravagating endlessly. And I give seven tests of a true development, founded on the nature of the case. These tests secure the substantial immutability of Christian doctrine – and I think my comparison is, that modern R. Catholicism looks different from primitive Catholicism in no other sense, than a friend, whom we see after a lapse of years, seems at first sight strange to us, till after a few minutes the old features revive in spite of the changes. (v. 20; To John Cowley Fisher, 14 Oct. 1861)

The critical question is, whether there is development in the Christian Apostolic dogma. . . . what is *meant* by *development*? . . . Is it a more intimate apprehension, and a more lucid enunciation of the original dogma? For myself I think it is, and nothing more. . . . I think it is what an Apostle *would* have said, when on earth, what any of his disciples would have said, according as occasion called for it. If St Clement, or St Polycarp, had been asked whether our Lady was immaculately conceived, I think he might have taken some time to understand the meaning of the question, and perhaps (as St Bernard) he might have to the end misunderstood the question; but if he did once understand it, I think he would have said 'Of course she was.' Whether the minute facts of history will bear me out in this view, I leave to others to determine. Accordingly, to me the words 'development in dogma' are substantially nothing but the process by which, under the magisterium of the Church, implicit faith becomes explicit. . . . the differences between the creed then and the creed now, was only . . . of apprehension. I should like to say that the Church apprehends it more clearly . . . (v. 20; To Sir John Acton, 8 July 1862)

You will ask why this doctrine [papal infallibility] (in case it shall be so determined by the Church) was not known as certain before – well, but why was not the whole gospel known from the time of Adam, or of Moses, or of David? Why is it not known to all the world? It has been the will of God to give knowledge gradually; and, as the Angels desired to look into what they knew only in part about the mysteries of redemption, so is it with us who are the redeemed. Prophets too and righteous men desired in vain to see the things which we see} At the same time the plan of redemption, which was determined from eternity, was revealed to chosen men from the beginning, as to Abraham – and so the full truths of Christianity were made known to the Apostles and afterwards to the Church, but have become clearer and clearer, as time has gone on. (v. 24; To Mrs. Helbert, 30 Aug. 1869)

Not till the end of the fourth century did the Church declare the divinity of the Holy Ghost, viz in the 2nd Council A.D. 381 etc. *Of course* it was ever held by implication, since the Holy Trinity was believed from the first – but I mean the bare absolute proposition 'The Holy Ghost is God –' and, as an illustration of what I mean, St Basil in the middle of the fourth century kept from calling Him God when his Arian enemies were on the watch; I say, kept silence on the point, and, when some Catholics found fault with him, St Athanasius took his part. . . . There has been a gradual evolution of the Apostolic doctrine or dogma, as delivered from our Lord to the Church. (v. 24; To Mrs. Helbert, 10 Sep. 1869)

What is the Rule of Secrecy, or "Disciplina Arcani"?

I have used the name *disciplina arcani* in speaking of the reserve of the Primitive Church in inculcating the more sacred doctrines of our faith because the rule of secrecy was professed in the 4th century and the principle of it is at all times binding; but, as far as I can make out, it existed rather as a feeling and a principle than as a rule in the early Church. This is the case with the greater part of the theological and ecclesiastical system, which is implicitly contained in the writings and acts of the Apostles, but was developed at various times according to circumstances. I should in a certain sense say this was true of the doctrine of the Trinity – and of the Incarnation as opposed to Nestorianism. – . . . as time went on what was at first spontaneous . . . what the individual was in the Apostolic age, that the body became in (say) the 4th century. Our Creeds, our Liturgies, our canons are for the most part developed and determined by a definite period after the time of the Apostles; – as would be natural on the above hypothesis. Accordingly I view the existence of the *rule* of secrecy in cent. 4 [as] evidence of the existence of the *principle* in the first (i.e. it being not unscriptural – rather, in matter of fact Scriptural.) . . . it would be a rule renewed again and again after being destroyed. . . . Again I think it consists, whether as a principle or (even) as a rule, rather in not insisting on, than concealing the truth. I suppose a primitive Christian would not have refused to answer questions when directly asked by a heathen. And this being considered, it might exist even where the sacred doctrines were public property – i.e. a catechist would *teach* the simpler doctrine – viz the Messiahship, the Divine Sonship the Mediatorship of Christ etc – not caring to remind the learner of subjects which were above him. If this be so, the *disciplina arcani* i.e. the *rule* would in fact exist, wherever there was the catechetical system – and in this way we seem to have a means of determining the *history* of the rule in early times, as far as it had a history. Further, as to the doctrines which were the *subjects* of the rule of secrecy, at first these were the great Catholic verities – These being at length avowed in the public confessions of faith, there was perhaps some refinement adopted – e.g. the Eucharist etc. though the explanations of the Catholic doctrine, of which the Arian heresy was the cause, doubtless would be of the nature of a secret doctrine. (v. 4; To Thomas Falconer, 26 Jan. 1834)

Does Development of Doctrine Tend to Lead One to Rome?

Also you may purchase the golden Treatise of Vincentius [Lerinensis] for a few shillings, who has more enlightened me (as I fancy) in the Catholic theory and made me more dissatisfied with our 'pure and apostolical' 'established' etc etc [[Church]] than any other thing. (v. 5; To Henry Wilberforce, 10 Sep. 1835; brackets in original)

I have always thought that in my Essay on Development of doctrine I accounted in another way for the facts which in my former work I thought told against the Church . . . (v. 19; To J. Spencer Northcote, 29 june 1861)

How Did Newman Regard His 1845 Essay on Development?

Of course it gave me great comfort to hear what you said about my Development argument. That I should have written it very differently, had I been a Catholic, I know well, and have always said – and the reason, when at Rome, I declined to enter into controversy with old B. [Brownson] was, as I expressed it, that I had come there to learn my religion, not to hold a theological polemic. I always said that my book was a philosophical, not a theological one; and it was on that very distinction that the Cardinal passed it without correction. Nothing has happened from that time to this to make me think the *principle* of the book false – but I had rather, by waiting, let better hands than mine set right the details, than attempt a censureship myself which might need censuring. (v. 16; To Richard Stanton, 15 Aug. 1855)

Chapter Five

Anglicanism

Do Anglicans Regard Themselves as a Species of Protestantism?

Now I should frighten good people if I were to say I disown the word Protestant . . . I 'protest' as much against Calvin as against the Council of Trent . . . The word Protestant does not (as far as I know) occur in our formularies – It is an uncomfortable perplexing word, intended to connect us, and actually connecting us, with the Protestants abroad. We are a 'Reformed' Church, not a 'Protestant'. I care not a whit for the Diet of Augsburg. Calvin is no guide to me, not even an authority – and as for Bucer I wish he had never crossed the seas. That the Puritanic spirit spread in England in Elizabeth and James's time, and did sad havoc, tainting even good and wise men, is certain. . . . The spirit of Puritanism has been succeeded by the Methodistic. (Of course I do not use the word reproachfully, but historically.) We, the while, children of the Holy Church, whencesoever brought into it, whether by early training, or after thought, have had one voice, that one voice which the Church has had from the beginning. . . . Meanwhile the Church of Rome apostatized at Trent. (v. 4; To Samuel Rickards, 30 July 1834)

Are the 39 Articles "Protestant" in Nature?

As to the 39 articles, tho' I believe them to be entirely Scriptural, they are not such favourites of mine, that *if I consulted my own wishes*, I should make an effort to retain them. I think they accidentally countenance a vile Protestantism. (v. 5; To R. F. Wilson, 13 May 1835)

I think it was Mr. Oakeley's view, that he might 'profess all Roman doctrine' in the Church of England, or at least 'hold it' – and consequently that the 39 Articles allowed of it. I never took this view. I knew that they bound me in various ways to oppose the Roman doctrines, . . . [*Tracts for the Times*] Number 90 then was not a resolution of the 39 Articles into the Council of Trent, but an experimental inquiry *how far* they would approximate to it, under the notion that the Church of Rome would have in her turn to approximate to Protestants. The Tract had no wish to force a sense upon the 39 Articles, which they would not admit, but it considered them '*patient* of a Catholic interpretation,' and that on two grounds – (I) historically, because in fact they were drawn up so as to admit the assent of (professed) Catholics, . . . next, logically, that is, on the assumption that the Anglican Church was a branch of the Catholic – for, if so, its formularies *must* necessarily admit of an interpretation consistent with the *Quod semper, quod ubique, quod ab omnibus*, of the Catholic Church, with which also, in spite of its *practical* and *popular* errors, as I called them, the Roman teaching was allowed by me to be consistent. I never to this day have felt necessary to be dissatisfied with the drift or the substance of Number 90, though in detail there are strained interpretations. (v. 18; To Thomas Flanagan, 28 July 1857)

What is the Status of Anglican "Apostolic Succession"?

I said there were two considerations which kept me from having any fear of Rome – the one that we had the Apostolical succession. I have hitherto been employed in showing how I have been forced from this ground, considered as an argument – viz by the question of Schism, which suspends the grace of that succession, even where the succession is found. (v. 10; To Mrs. William Froude, 9 June 1844)

[T]he Bishops, except one, were all expelled when Elizabeth came, as well as the superior clergy, so that a new succession or

Church began, which, never having been recognized, could not be rejected. Again, it was not the case of a Church dissenting on one point of doctrine, which had just turned up in controversy, as the Monophysite; but England (as it avowed) threw off the whole Catholic faith, so accounted for centuries, maintaining that the whole Church had been immersed in Anti christian error for centuries. England then excommunicated itself, since it fell under the anathema of centuries. (v. 13; To Mrs. Martha Lockhart, 5 Nov. 1849)

What Was the State of Anglicanism in 1835?

Indeed in all matters the state of the Church is most deplorable – scarce one man in ten thousand knowing any one reason for any one part of our doctrine or discipline, and relinquishing the most sacred things carelessly from not knowing their value. (v. 5; To Samuel Rickards, 14 Sep. 1835)

Was Anglicanism Flourishing in 1839-40?

Our Church is not at one with itself – there is no denying it. We have an heretical spirit in us. Whether it *can* be cast out, without 'tearing' and destroying the Church itself, is quite beyond me. (v. 7; To [sister] Jemima Mozley, 17 Nov. 1839)

We . . . have never been tried and come out of trial without practical concessions. I cannot see that we *can* receive [[sustain]] the assault of the foe. We are divided among ourselves, like the Jews in their siege] So that it seems to me as if there were coming on a great encounter between infidelity and Rome, and that we should be smashed between them. (v. 7; To [sister] Jemima Mozley, 25 Feb. 1840)

Has Anglicanism Unnecessarily Discarded Catholic Elements?

Surely it is matter of fact, the 'Church of England' has never been one reality, except *as* an Establishment. Viewed *internally*, it is the battle field of two opposite principles; Socinianism and Catholicism – Socinianism fighting for the most part by Puritanism its unconscious ally. . . . why may I not in my own heart deplore the hard heartedness and coarsemindedness of those, whoever they were, who gave up (practically) to the Church of Rome *what we might have kept* – so much that was high, elevating, majestic, affecting, captivating – so depriving us of our birthright that the Latins now claim it as if theirs solely. My heart *is* with Rome, *but not* as Rome, but as, and so far as, she is the faithful retainer of what we have practically thrown aside. (v. 5; To Hugh James Rose, 23 May 1836)

Whatever be the influence of the Tracts, great or small, they may become just as powerful for Rome, if our Church refuses them, as they would be for our Church if she accepted them. If our rulers speak either against the Tracts, or not at all, if any number of them, not only do not favour, but even do not suffer the principles contained in them, it is plain that our members may easily be persuaded either to give up those principles, or to give up the Church. If this state of things goes on, I mournfully prophesy, not one or two, but many secessions to the Church of Rome. (v. 8; To Unknown, 23? Oct. 1841)

For myself, I am too anxious for others, nay for myself, to say anything light about going to Rome. Our Church seems fast protestantizing itself, . . . (v. 8; To John Keble, 24 Oct. 1841)

Did Newman Agonize Over Anglican Difficulties in 1840-1845?

Do you think *I* do not feel difficulties as well as you? – yet I remain as I am – being convinced on the whole that I ought to do so. (v. 7; To Robert Williams, 19 July 1840)

I seem to myself almost to have shot my last arrow in the article on English Catholicity; and I am troubled by doubts, whether, as it is, I have not in what I have published spoken too strongly against Rome; though I think I did it in a kind of faith, being determined to put myself into the English system, and say *all that* our Divines said whether I had fully weighed it or not. It must be added that this very circumstance that I have committed myself against Rome, has the effect of setting to sleep men's suspicions about me, which is painful now that I begin to have suspicions about myself. (v. 7; To John Keble, 26 Oct. 1840)

I think I am getting to see my way more clearly still, but as I feel at present nothing will convince me and no one will have influence with me who take the line of saying that we are not in a state of near schism as we well can be. I can only say that it seems to get clearer to me that it is not the duty of individuals to return to Rome, but I have no hope at all till she renounces or at least mourns over her isolated position; though one may trust in the ways of Providence she is kept from renouncing it till the Roman Churches (or Greek if you will) are more worthy to receive her. And I see the minds of others separately travelling in the same direction. My grounds for holding this are. 1 The sentiment of the Fathers, to reject which is to stultify one's Creed from the foundations. 2. the fact that are left in that body which we receded from (which has it still while we fled out of that house naked as well as wounded) a body of customs and ways, an *ethos* which is most high and Christian, I mean the system of charity, Sisters of mercy etc, Confession – which alone keeps a Church from being hollow though it does not secure sincerity – reverence – the sacramental principle etc This is an atmosphere which the Catholic Church has and we have not. 3. Our divisions, we have ever had them since we left the Catholic Communion. The English Church is the mother of schism. (v. 7; To Frederic Rogers, 26 Dec. 1840)

[W]hile Rome is what she is, union is impossible – that we too must change I do not deny. (v. 8; To J. R. Bloxam, 23 Feb. 1841)

I lament as much as one can, our present state in the English [Church], in which high aspirations have so little means of exercise. . . . we must one and all *resign* ourselves, except where duty comes in, to the disorders with which our Church labours at this day. [v. 8; To Miss Mary Holmes, 8 April 1841)

That our Church is in a wrong position I cannot doubt; but my own feeling is rather to wait and see what Providence intends for us than to take active measures the effect of which may be in a wrong direction. (v. 8; To Robert Williams, 14 July 1841)

Grievous as are the defects of the English system, painful as is the position of Catholicly minded persons in it, still these persons do *remain* in it. (v. 8; To Miss Mary Holmes, 8 Aug. 1841)

[T]hat we have our difficulty I am far indeed from denying. Ours is that we are separated from the great *body of Christians*, . . . (v. 8; To Miss Mary Holmes, 6 Sep. 1841)

[I]f the Bishops will not let us use Church weapons *for* the Church, they will be used by the R C's against her. I do not ask them to *adopt* these arms – I only asked to be allowed to use them myself – I do not ask for sanction but sufferance. . . . But instead of that we have a new thing in the English Church – while the so called evangelical principles are left unnoticed in Episcopal charges, when all sorts of irregularities are committed as to the Church Services weekly, while (as at Bristol) a man in the pulpit alluding to Pusey says 'You have lately had the hell-born heresy of Puseyism here in person,' and another taking up a volume of the Tracts holds it out to his congregation saying 'I denounce the authors of this volume as agents of Satan," the Bishops employ themselves in a series of charges against us as Angels from heaven' preaching another gospel. And *the rest keep silence* – No one has dared to praise us simply, for 8 years . . . I think the Bishops are laying the seeds of future secessions. (v. 8; To Thomas Henderson, 8 Nov. 1841)

I have now been for a long while assuring persons that the English Church was a branch of the Church Catholic. If then a measure is in progress which in my judgment tends to cut from under me the very ground on which I have been writing and talking, and to prove all I hold a mere theory and illusion, a paper theology that facts contradict, who will not excuse it if I am deeply pained at such proceedings? When friends who rely on my word, come to me and say, 'You *told* us that the English Church was *Catholic*,' what am I to say to this reproach? (v. 8; To J. R. Hope, 24 Nov. 1841)

For two years and more I have been in a state of great uneasiness as to my position here, owing to the consciousness I felt that my opinions went far beyond what had been customary in the English Church. (v. 8; To Samuel Rickards, 1 Dec. 1841)

I fully think that *if* this Jerusalem measure comes into full operation, it will all but unchurch us. I cannot help *facts* – it is not my doing, it is an external fact. And if it takes place, I think it clear that, though one might remain where one was, oneself – yet we should have *no arguments* to prevent others going to Rome. (v. 8; To [sister] Harriet Mozley, 2 Dec. 1841)

I have very hard and continual work in putting out sparks, which might blow up into secessions. And as if this were not enough, even my *friends* are writing to me begging *me* not to turn Roman. . . . O that I could keep men (not young men exactly) from thinking of Rome – but I assure you, when the notes of the Church are crumbling away day after day, it is a very arduous matter. (v. 8; To Thomas Mozley, 13 Dec. 1841)

The truest friends of our Church are they who boldly say when her rulers are going wrong and the consequences – and (to speak catachrestically) they are most likely to die in the Church who are (under these black circumstances) most prepared to leave it. (v. 8; To R. W. Church, 25 Dec. 1841)

Of *course* preaching the doctrine of the Holy Catholic Church will lead men to Rome, *supposing* our Bishops declare we are *not* part of the Catholic Church, or that we do not hold the Catholic doctrines. . . . no serious movement towards Rome took place, in fact, till the year 1841, when the authorities of the Church had more or less declared themselves against Catholic truth. (v. 8; To William Dodsworth, 27 Dec. 1841)

Your question is just the difficult one of English Theology and as time goes on it will be more and more felt. . . . While the Catholic Church is broken up into fragments, it will always be a most perplexing question, what and where is the Church? and those who maintain the article of the Creed which declares the fact that there is a Church will be looked upon by hard headed dissenters and liberals as unreal and cloudy in their views I consider that according to the great Anglican theory, (by which I mean the theory of Laud, Bull, Butler, etc upon which alone the English Church *can* stand as being neither Roman nor Puritan) the present state of the Church is like that of an Empire breaking or broken up. . . . Our difficulties in faith and obedience are just those which a subject in a decaying Empire has in matters of allegiance. We sometimes do not know what is of authority and what is not – who has credentials and who has not – when local authorities are exceeding their power and when they are not; how far old precedents must be modified in existing circumstances, how far not. (v. 9; To James Cecil Wynter, 16 July 1842)

I am not at all surprised or hurt at persons being suspicious of my faith in the English Church. I think they have cause to do so. It would not be honest in me not to confess, when persons have a fight to ask me, that I have misgivings, not about her orders, but about her ordinary enjoyment of the privileges they confer when she is so separate from Christendom, so tolerant of heresy. (v. 9; To Edward B. Pusey, 24 Aug. 1842)

The laity say, *Whom* are we to believe? It is a most distressing state of things for those who *wish* to be quiet and dutiful, and a great triumph to unbelievers and worldly persons. How can that be practically a church, how can it *teach*, which speaks half a dozen things in the same breath? (v. 9; To Simeon Lloyd Pope, 4 Sep. 1842)

I have such a dreadful impression of our corruptions and heresies and unrealities, viewing us as a body, that the holiness of individuals, and the good that is doing in externals and on its surface, are insufficient to overcome this deep despondency . . . how can one turn a Church which has been so radically Protestantized into Catholic in a day? (v. 9; To C. H. J. Anderson, 21 Jan. 1843)

I suppose the Catholic theory is, that creeds, sacraments, succession etc are nothing without unity – St Cyprian of the Novatians, and St Austin [Augustine] of the Donatists. The only way I have ever attempted to answer this, is by urging that we really were, or in one sense were, in unity with the rest of the Church – but, as you know, I never have been thoroughly satisfied with my arguments, and grow more and more to suspect them. (v. 9; To John Keble, 6 Sep. 1843)

I cannot bear this universal expression of feeling against me from Bishops and other authorities, from the organs of religious parties, from the public voice, an expression which is as emphatically conveyed in the silence of one class of persons as in the clamour of another, conscious as I am of nothing to fall back upon. Were our Church in such sense Catholic that I could appeal to certain clear formularies of hers in my favour, I hope I should not mind any opposition – but I have nothing *within* the Church to stand upon – countenance of Bishops, popular feeling, prescription, authoritative statements, divines, or other resting place for the soles of my feet. . . . I inculcate a body of doctrine, which as a body is now universally reprobated and was never avowed at any time. (v. 9; To Charles Lewis Cornish, 29 Sep. 1843)

I think the English Church is showing herself intrinsically and radically alien from Catholic principles, so do I feel difficulties in defending her claims to be a branch of the Catholic Church. It seems a dream to call a communion Catholic, when one can neither appeal to any clear statement of Catholic doctrine in its formularies, nor interpret ambiguous formularies by the received and living sense past or present. Men of Catholic views are too truly but a party in our Church. (v. 9; To Henry Edward Manning, 14 Oct. 1843)

[A] series of thwartings such as I have experienced, (I do not mean, creates, which logically they cannot do) but realizes, verifies, substantizes, a[n impression] of the English Church very unfavourable to her Catholicity. If a person is deeply convinced in his *reason* that her claims to Catholicity are untenable, but fears to trust his reason, such events, when they come upon him again and again, seem to do just what is wanting, corroborate his reason experimentally. They force upon his imagination and familiarize his moral perception with the conclusions of his intellect. Propositions become facts. (v. 10; To James Robert Hope, 14 March 1844)

I found a portentously large body of Christians thrown into schism by the Council [of Chalcedon in 451] – at this day the Churches of Egypt, Syria (in part) and Armenia; and the Schismatics, not like the Arians of a rationalist, but with a theology of a warm and elevating character. I found that they appealed, as with much plausibility to certain of the Fathers, as St

Athanasius and St Cyril of Alexandria – that they professed to be maintainers of Antiquity – that they called their opponents (the Catholics) *Chalcedonians*, as we call RCs Tridentines, that their cause was taken up by the civil power, and created a contention between Emperors and the Church. Further I found there was a large middle party as well as an extreme. There was a distinct Via media, which indeed the Emperor took up – and there was a large body who went on for centuries without Bishops. . . . in a word I found a complete and wonderful parallel, as if a prophecy, of the state of the Reformation Controversy, and that we were on the Anti-Catholic side. . . . I had hitherto read ecclesiastical history with the eyes of our Divines, and taken what they said on faith, but now I got a *key*, which interpreted large passages of history which had been locked up from me. I found every where one and the same picture, prophetic of our present state, the Church in communion with Rome decreeing, and heretics resisting. Especially as regards the Arian controversy, how could I be so blind before! except that I looked at things bit by bit, instead of putting them together. . . . There were two parties, a Via Media, and an extreme, both heretical – but the Via Media containing pious men, whom St Athanasius and others sympathise in – there were the kings of the earth taking up heresy against the Church – there was precisely the same appeal to Scripture, which now obtains, and that grounded on a liberal interpretation of its text, to which St Athanasius always opposes the 'ecclesiastical sense' – There was the same complaint of introducing novel and unscriptural terms into the Creed of the Church, 'Consubstantial' 'Transubstantiation' being both of philosophical origin, and if Trent has opposed some previous Councils (which I do not recollect) at least the Nicene Council adopted the very term 'Consubstantial' which a celebrated Council of Antioch 60 or 70 years before condemned or discountanenced. (v. 10; To Mrs. William Froude, 5 April 1844)

[A] number of the Dublin Review appeared containing an article by Dr Wiseman ['The Anglican Claim of Apostolical Succession',

Aug. 1839] . . . I found it on careful attention to contain so powerful an argument, that I became (I may say) excited about it. . . . The argument in the Article in question was drawn from the History of the Donatists, and was directed to show that the English Church was in Schism. The fact to which the Monophysite controversy had opened my eyes, that antagonists of Rome, and Churches in isolation, were always wrong in primitive times, and which I had felt to be a *presumption* against ourselves, this article went on to maintain as a recognised *principle and rule* in those same ages. It professed that the *fact* of isolation and opposition was *always taken* as a *sufficient* condemnation of bodies so circumstanced, and to that extent that the question was not asked how did the quarrel arise? which was right, and which wrong? who made the separation? but the *fact* of separation was reckoned anciently as decisive against the body separated. This was argued chiefly from the language of St Augustine, as elicited in the Donatist controversy, and the same sort of *minute* parallel was drawn between the state of the Donatists and our own, which I had felt on reading the history of the Monophysites. . . . The system in which we have been placed is God's voice to us, till He supersede it – and those means by which He supersedes it must be more distinct than the impression produced on us by that system itself. (v. 10; To Mrs. William Froude, 9 April 1844)

I have most honestly attempted to do a service to the English Church, and my tools have broken in the work. (v. 10; to Charles Wordsworth, 2 Sep. 1844)

It is at this time above four years since a clear conviction rose in my mind from reading the early controversies of the Church that we were in loco haereticorum. ['in a state of heresy']. I saw the position of the Novatian, the Arian, the Nestorian, the Monophysite a very definite one. I saw their position, their characteristics, their acts, their fortunes; these were all substantially one and the same. We seemed to me faithfully to reflect them at this day; i.e. to be as like them as they are to each other. I saw they generally consisted of a two-fold variety, an extreme party and a moderate. I saw our own image reflected in the ancient via media. I saw the [image] of the Church of Rome reflected in the severe, uncompromising, and if you will imperious, peremptory conduct <behaviour> of the saints of the ancient Church, St Justin, St Cyprian, St Athanasius?, St Augustine, St Leo. But at first I saw still more strikingly the opposite fact; not merely that the Protestant bodied [embodied], 'that individuals, that numbers among ourselves, but, if it must be spoken, that our own communion, as such, was there, where heretical Churches were of old. It became far more certain to me that we were cut off from the Church than that the Church of Rome was departed from primitive doctrine. I saw more in the early Church <history> to convince me that separation from the great body of the Church, that separation from the see of St Peter was the token of heresy and schism, than that the additions which that great body which the see of St Peter has received upon the primitive faith were innovations. I was not so certain that they might not be developments, instead of corruptions as I was certain that we were not in a position to know, that our Church was not in a position to pronounce, whether they were corruptions or not. (If I must illustrate what I mean, I will take the Monophysite controversy which affected me most, though I think the Donatist furnishes a stronger instance in point. I felt on *what* principle do we receive Chalcedon *yet not* Trent?) illustrated by conduct of [the] American [Episcopal] Church being more unshackled than we which is obliged to receive Nestorians. One same argument which would prove us one Church with them, would prove our Dissenters one Church with us) . . . to receive a Council is to receive it *as* a Council; It is to hold that certain kinds of Councils are infallible, and certain actual Councils are true. Now I cannot make out in what sense the Councils of Nicaea, Constantinople, Ephesus, or Chalcedon are true Councils, in which that of Trent is not a true Council also. I seem to feel I must either go on to Trent or stop short of

Nicaea. . . . Again – I cannot make out about the separate books of the Canon – why I receive e.g. Esther and not Ecclesiasticus or Wisdom, . . . Again about separate doctrines. I cannot see why prayers for the dead are primitive, and not the Pope's Supremacy. Thus I am in the condition that I must either believe all or none. And so it really is. I see no resting place for the sole of my foot between all and none. (v. 10; "Draft," 30 Oct. 1844)

What Did Newman Think of Anglicanism After 1845?

I think that the only *body*, which has promises attached to it, is the Catholic Church – and if I think the Anglican Communion, as such, is not included in the Catholic Church, I think it has not any divine promise or power. (v. 21; To Edward B. Pusey, 25 Nov. 1864)

Now the Anglican Church is sui generis – it is not a collection of individuals – but it is a bed, a river bed, formed in the course of ages, depending on external facts, such as political, civil, and social arrangements. Viewed in its structure it has never been more than partially Catholic. If its ritual has been mainly such, yet its Articles are the historical offspring of Luther and Calvin. And its ecclesiastical organisation has ever been, in its fundamental principle, Erastian. To make that actual, visible, tangible body Catholic, would be simply to make a new creature – it would be to turn a panther into a hind. There are very great similarities between a panther and a hind. Still they are possessed of separate natures, and a change from one to the other would be a destruction and reproduction, not a process. It could be done without a miracle in a succession of ages, but in any assignable period, no. (v. 22; To Ambrose Phillipps de Lisle, 3 March 1866)

As to your question, 'whether I should have left the Anglican Church, if it had been twenty years ago what it is now –' it seems to me to admit of an easy answer. I left it because I was sure that it was not a portion of that Catholic Church which our Lord and

His Apostles established, as the source of teaching and the channel of grace till the end of the world. We are saved by grace, and grace is ordinarily supplied to us through the sacraments, and, excepting baptism, no sacrament exists outside the Church. If the Church of England is not part of the Catholic Church, it does not possess the sacraments of confirmation, penance, Eucharist, or extreme unction, to give to its people – and these are the ordinary means of grace. It cannot give them even though it professed to give them. Then, even as to its baptism, this is very doubtful. I joyfully believe that the rite is administered much more carefully, than it was thirty years ago by many clergymen, but I much doubt whether the majority administer it safely even now. (v. 22; To Miss Bristowe, 15 April 1866)

As to the wonderful revival of religion in the Established Church, I certainly think it comes from God. If so, it must tend, as it visibly does tend, to the Church's benefit. One cannot conceive the generation which is brought up under it, when they come to maturity and to power, resting satisfied with the Anglican system. If their fathers, the present generation, yearn for unity, and for communion with St. Peter, much more will their children. There is nothing to prove that the present race of Catholicizing Anglicans is in bad faith; and there is much to show on the other hand that they are in good faith. It is possible indeed that the next generation may go off into Liberalism – as Hale and Chillingworth, the disciples of Laud. But I rather hope that Holy Church will arrest and win them over by her beauty and sanctity, her gentleness, serenity, and prudence. (v. 25; To John Thomas Walford, S. J., 19 May 1870)

To my mind it is just one of the signs that the Anglican body is not the true Church that it gives such scope for essential difference in doctrine in its members and consequently to the existence of party action. It was an especial pain to me as an. Anglican to be considered one of a party. Disciples indeed! I have said in my Apologia 'I felt great impatience at our. being called a party, and would not allow that we were such.' (v. 25; To George Hay Forbes, 11 Aug. 1871)

Are Anglican Orders Valid?

As to my view of Anglican orders – I cannot *conceive* that they are valid – but I could not *swear* they are not – I should be most uncommonly surprised if they were – It would require the Pope ex cathedra to convince me – I would not believe in them, if you or a hundred Fathers of the Society guaranteed their validity, though of course, it would be a remarkable fact; but nothing but the Church's acting on it would convince me. I don't think the Church ever will act upon it, and for this reason, that, putting them at their best advantage they are doubtful, and the Church ever goes by what is safe. How do I even know that all the Anglican Bishops who continued the succession had received valid baptism? What can I, what need I say more? It is difficult to prove a negative – but it is not for us to prove that the Anglican orders are not valid, but for them to prove that they are. I don't think they will ever be able to prove this. (v. 24; To Henry James Coleridge, 6 Feb. 1868)

Catholics consider that a reasonable doubt in the validity of Orders is sufficient for treating them practically as invalid; and it is the universal sentiment among us that, not on one only, but on many grounds, there is a reasonable doubt about the Anglican. Some think them certainly invalid, others think them very uncertain; others not improbably, others probably valid; but one and all hold that there is a reasonable doubt about them. They will never be recognized by Catholics. (v. 24; To Arthur West Haddan, 14 July 1869)

Chapter Six

Conversion (to Catholicism)

What Was Newman's View of the Catholic Church in 1834?

Really, you must not suppose that I do not feel the force and influence of those parts of the Roman Catholic system, which have struck you. To express vividly what I mean, I would say, 'I would be a Romanist, if I could. I wish I could be a Romanist.' But I cannot – there is that mixture of error in it, which (though unseen of course by many many pious Christians who have been brought up in it,) effectually cuts off the chance of my acquiescing in it. I admire the lofty character, the beauty, the sweetness and tenderness of its services and discipline – I acknowledge them divine in a certain sense, i.e. remnants of that old system which the Apostles founded. On the other hand I grieve to think of our own neglect in realizing the Church system among us, which our Reformers intended to be ours, . . . The more I examine into the R.C. system, the less sound it appears to me to be; and the less safely could I in conscience profess to receive it. . . . I feel the Roman Catholic system to be irreverent towards Christ, degrading Him, robbing Him *practically* of His sole honor, hiding His bounty; – i.e. so far forth as it is Roman Catholic – *so far as* it differs from ours. Its high points are our points too, if it would but keep them, and not give up our jewels. But, while what is good in it is reverent, solemn, and impressive, its corruptions *practically* undo all this excellence. Surely we shall be judged according to our conscience, and if we have a clear sight of what is wrong in Rome, we must not follow our inclinations, because Rome has what is attractive in some part of her devotions. (v. 4; To Mrs. William Wilberforce, 17 Nov. 1834)

How Far Was Newman from the Catholic Church in 1837?

It only shows how deep the absurd notion was in men's minds
that I was a Papist; and now they are agreeably surprised. Thus I
gain, as commonly happens in the long run, by being
misrepresented – . . . I call the notion of my being a Papist
absurd, for it argues on utter ignorance of theology. . . . Any one
who knew any thing of theology would not have confounded me
with the Papists; and, if he gave me any credit for knowledge of
theology or for clearheadedness, he would not have thought me
in danger of becoming one. True it is, any one who by *his own
wit* had gone as far as I *from* popular Protestantism, or who had
been taught from *without,* not being up to the differences of
things, and trained to discrimination, might have been in danger
of going further; but no one who either had learned his doctrine
historically, or had tolerable clearness of mind, could be in more
danger than of confusing the Sun and the Moon. (v. 6; To [sister]
Jemima Mozley, 25 April 1837)

Were High Church Anglicans in 1839-40 Enticed to Catholicism?

[O]ur Church has not the provisions and methods by which
Catholic feelings are to be detained, secured, sobered, and trained
heaven-wards. . . . I am conscious that we are raising longings
and tastes which we are not allowed to supply – and till our
Bishops and others give scope to the development of Catholicism
externally and visibly, we *do* tend to make impatient minds seek
it where it has ever been, *in* Rome. (v. 7; To Henry Edward
Manning, 1 Sep. 1839)

Our practical difficulty is this – *we* are raising feelings and
aspirations and (till our Church is reformed) Rome alone finds
the *objects* for them. Thus we are educating persons for Rome
somewhat in the way that Evangelicalism does for Dissent. At
least this is what I fear when desponding. It is comparatively easy
to get up a Catholic movement, it is not easy to see what barriers

are to be found to its onward progress. (v. 7; To H. A. Woodgate, 20 Oct. 1839)

I have from the first thought that nothing but a quasi miracle, would carry us through the trial with no proselytes whatever to Rome . . . (v. 7; To William Dodsworth, 19 Nov. 1839)

Things are progressing steadily – but breakers ahead! the danger of a lapse into Romanism I think gets greater daily. I expect to hear of victims. (v. 7; To J. W. Bowden, 17 Jan. 1840)

I fear too that some persons will turn Roman Catholics, up and down the country; indeed how is this possibly to be helped as things are? they will be right in their major and wrong only in their minor – right in their principle, wrong in their fact – they seek the true Church, but do not recognize the Church in us. (v. 7; To J. W. Bowden, 21 Feb. 1840)

What Was the Initial Troubling Blow to Newman's Anglicanism?

Since I wrote to you, I have had the first real hit from Romanism which has happened to me . . . Dr [Nicholas] Wiseman's article in the new Dublin. I must confess it has given me a stomach-ache. You see the whole history of the Monophysites has been a sort of alterative, and now comes this dose at the end of it. It does certainly come upon one that we are not at the bottom of things. At this moment we have sprung a leak, . . . I seriously think this is a most uncomfortable article on every account, though of course it is ex parte. How are we to keep hot heads from going over? Let alone ourselves. I think I shall get Keble to answer it: – as to Pusey I am curious to see how it works with him. . . . there is an uncomfortable vista opened which was closed before. (v. 7; To Frederic Rogers, 22 Sep. 1839; the article was "Tracts for the Times: Anglican Claim of Apostolical Succession," in the *Dublin Review*, Aug. 1839, 139-180)

I do not deny that it requires considering and has a claim upon us for an answer. . . . There either is something in what Dr W[iseman] says, or there is not. If not, all will reject it – if there is, all will accept it, i.e. at length. . . . going by my own judgment, even granting, which I do not exactly see, that Dr W's argument is good on the other side, yet that same judgment tells me of arguments good on the other. (v. 7; To S. F. Wood, 29 Sep. 1839)

You should read the late article in the Dublin – it is the best thing Dr Wiseman has put out. It is paralleling the English Church to the Donatists; and certainly the parallel is very curious – . . . (v. 7; To J. W. Bowden, 4 Nov. 1839)

I have written an article . . . in reply to one of Dr Wiseman's in the Dublin, which has fidgetted me a good deal. It is the only formidable thing I have seen on the Roman side but I cannot deny it is good and strong, and calculated to do harm, considerable harm. I have done what I can by way of an answer. But it is a large subject. (v. 7;   To [sister] Jemima Mozley, 29 Nov. 1839)

Since I read DrW's [Wiseman] article I have desponded much – for, I said to myself, if even I feel myself pressed hard, what will others who have either not thought so much on the subject or have fewer retarding motives? (v. 7; To Edward B. Pusey, 15 Jan. 1840)

Was it "Thinkable" for Newman in 1839 to One Day Convert?

I really believe I say truly that, did I see cause to suspect that the Roman Church was in the right, I would try not to be unfaithful to the light given me. And if at any future time, I have any view opened to me, I will try not to turn from it, but will pursue it, wherever it may lead. I am not aware of having any hindrance, whether from fear of clamour, or regard for consistency, or even love of friends, which could keep me from joining the Church of

Rome, were I persuaded I ought to do so. . . . Considering then the exceeding weakness of individual judgment and the great risk of one's being swayed this way or that by impulses short of divine truth, I think I should never make up my mind to any overt act towards Rome, without giving up two or three years as a time of religious preparation towards forming a judgment. And next, I think I should not even then act, without having the sanction of one or two persons whom I most looked up to and trusted. I am far from saying that there is not a degree of conviction so strong as to supersede all advice from others, nay all delay. Nor would I deny that there may be supernatural guidances given in cases, of such a nature as to require prompt and unhesitating obedience. And if I felt either this conviction or this guidance, I should have to act in a way which others would call rash, and must leave my conduct in the hands of Him who had inspired it. But such dispensations of Providence seem to me rare . . . When one considers how very solemn a step it is to change our religion, what a responsibility we incur if wrong, what an obligation there is under ordinary circumstances to remain where God has placed us, it seems to me but reasonable to say that such a step should not be taken without the guidance of others, without a long season of deliberation, and serious exercises during it. It is surely a much less sin to *remain in*, than to *change to*, a wrong faith. (v. 7; To Robert Williams, 10 Nov. 1839)

What Was Newman's View About Conversion in 1841-1845?

I have no thought whatever of going over to Rome, or letting others – but I have a great wish to make our Church more Catholic in its tone, and to introduce into it the good points of Rome – and if the consequence is a more friendly feeling between the Churches, it may tend to the improvement of Rome herself. I am quite sure that both Churches have their excellences, and both are injured by being so much at enmity . . . (v. 8; To Richard Westmacott, 8 April 1841)

That my *sympathies* have grown towards the religion of Rome I do not deny; that my *reasons* for *shunning* her communion have lessened or altered, it will be difficult perhaps to prove. And I wish to go by reason not by feeling. (v. 8; To Charles W. Russell, 5 May 1841)

[I]t is not impossible that our Church *may* lapse into heresy. I cannot deny that a great and anxious *experiment* is going on, whether our Church be or be not Catholic – the issue may not be in our day. But I must be plain in saying that, if it does issue in Protestantism, I shall think it my duty, if alive, to leave it. This does not seem much to grant – but it is much, supposing such an event to be at our doors, for one naturally tries to make excuses then, whereas one safely pledges oneself to what is distant. I trust it not only is distant, but is never to be. But the way to hinder it, is to be prepared for it. I fear I must say that I am beginning to think that the only way to keep in the English Church is steadily to contemplate and act upon the possibility of leaving it. . . . At all events I am sure that to leave the English Church, unless something very flagrant happened, must be the work of *years*. (v. 8; To J. R. Hope, 17 Oct. 1841)

I think that it still may be, that the English Church is not part of the Church Catholic, but only visited with over-flowings of grace – and that God may *call* some persons on to higher things. They must *obey* the calling; but that proves nothing against those who do not receive it. I have no call at present to go to the Church of Rome; – but I am not confident I may not have some day. (v. 8; To Henry Wilberforce, 8 Nov. 1841)

If people are driving me quite against all my feelings out of the English Church, they shall know they are doing so. (v. 8; To J. R Hope, 8 Dec. 1841)

R[obert] Wilberforce . . . thinks I am turning R C . . . I think you will give me credit, . . . of not undervaluing the strength of the feelings which draw one that way – and yet I am (I trust) quite clear about my duty to remain where I am. Indeed much clearer than I was some time since. If it is not presumptuous to say, I trust I have been favored with a much more definite view of the (promised) inward evidence of the Presence of Christ with us in the Sacraments, now that the outward notes of it are being removed. And I am content to be with Moses in the desert – or with Elijah excommunicated from the Temple. I say this, putting things at the strongest. (v. 8; To S. F. Wood, 13 Dec. 1841)

The simple case then, much as I grieve to say it, is this: – about two years and a half ago I began reading the Monophysite controversy, and with great concern and dismay found how much we were in the position of the Monophysites. I am not saying there is anything *peculiar* in their history, but merely that it put me into a new train of thought. After that I turned my mind to the Donatists, and there the same truth, or a parallel one, came out in the strongest colours. In the Monophysite history it is that the Church of Rome, in the Donatist that that body which spreads through the world, is always ipso facto right. I am not measuring my words as if I were arguing, but giving you my line of thought. Since then whatever line of early history I look into, I see as in a glass reflected our own Church in the heretical party, and the Roman Church in the Catholic. This is an appalling fact – which, do what I will, I cannot shake off. One special test of the heretical party is absence of *stay* or *consistence*, ever crumbling ever shifting, ever new forming – ever self consumed by internal strife. Our present state, half year by half year, the opposition of Bishop to Bishop, is a most miserable and continual fulfilment of this Note of error. . . . Another is a constant effort to make alliance with other heresies and schisms, though differing itself from them. . . . This has led me anxiously to look out for grounds of remaining where Providence has placed me . . . It has also forced me back upon the *internal or personal Notes* of the Church; and with thankfulness I say that I have received great comfort there. But, alas, in seeking to draw out this comfort for the benefit of others, who (without knowing my state) have been similarly distressed, eager inquisitive sensitive minds have taken the alarm, and (though I acted with the greatest anxiety and tried to do what I could to avoid the suspicion) they are beginning to guess that I have not an implicit faith in the validity of the *external* Notes of our Church. . . . One obvious consequence is to be mentioned besides – a growing dread lest in speaking against the Church of Rome I may be speaking against the Holy Ghost. This is quite consistent with a full conviction of the degraded state of that Church whether here or elsewhere. . . . my fears slept for very many months, and have only lately been re-animated by our dreadful divisions, the Bishops' charges, and this Prussian affair, . . . You are the first person to whom I have drawn it out. . . . Of course this painful thought comes into my mind – whether, if Rome be the true Church, the divinely appointed method of raising her from her present degradation be not to *join* her. Whether either she or we *can* correct our mutual errors while separated from each other. (v. 8; To Robert I. Wilberforce, 26 Jan. 1842)

I wish to be guided not by controversy but by *ethos* – so that (please God) nothing would seem to me a reason for so very awful and dreadful a step as you point at, but the quiet growth of a feeling through many years. I may sincerely say that no one has exerted himself more than I have to make a case for the English Church and theory, from the Fathers – perhaps (following our divines) I have succeeded – but I mean that I have honestly set myself to it and spared no pains. I really think I have examined and replied to more objections than most people. I don't think argument will help me. (v. 8; To Robert I. Wilberforce, 1 Feb. 1842)

I advise you to be very much on your guard about the approaching visit of Dr Wiseman. You may be committed before you know where you are. Do consider that you are about to be submitted to temptation; that is, the temptation of acting, not on *judgment* but on *feeling*. Your feelings are in favor of Rome, so are mine – your judgment is against joining it – so is mine. Yet I would not trust myself among R[oman] Catholics without recollecting how apt feeling is to get the better of judgment – and I warn you of the same. I remind you, as I should wish to remind myself, of the necessity of keeping a strict watch over yourself. (v. 9; To Miss Mary Holmes, 8 Feb. 1843)

In June and July 1839, near four years ago, I read the Monophysite Controversy, and it made a deep impression on me, which I was not able to shake off, that the Pope bad a certain gift of infallibility, and that communion with the see of Rome was the divinely intended means of grace and illumination. I do not know how far I fully recognized this at the moment, – but towards the end of the same Long Vacation I considered attentively the Donatist history, and became quite excited. It broke upon me that we were in a state of schism. Since that [then], all history, particularly that of Arianism, has appeared to me in a new light, confirmatory of the same doctrine. In order to conquer this feeling, I wrote my article on the Catholicity of the English Church, as I have written other things since. For awhile my mind was quieted; but from that time to this the impression, though fading and reviving, has been on the whole becoming stronger and deeper. At present, I fear, as far as I can realize my own convictions, I consider the Roman Catholic Communion the Church of the Apostles, and that what grace is among us (which, through God's mercy, is not little,) is extraordinary, and from the overflowings of His Dispensation. I am very far *more* sure that England is in schism, than that the Roman additions to the Primitive Creed may not be developments, arising out of a keen and vivid realizing of the Divine Depositum of faith. (v. 9; To John Keble, 4 May 1843)

Do you know, though you need not say it, that I have taken to liking the Jesuits? (v. 9; To Henry Wilberforce, 9 June 1843)

There is no doubt at all that I am approximating towards Rome; nor any doubt that those who are very much about me see this, little as I wish it. (v. 9; To Mrs. William Froude, 28 July 1843)

My present views were taken up in the summer of 1839 upon reading the Monophysite and Donatist controversies. I saw from them that Rome was the centre of unity and the judge of controversies. (v. 9; To [sister] Harriet Mozley, 2 Oct.? 1843)

I think the Church of Rome the Catholic Church, and ours not a part of the Catholic Church, because not in communion with Rome, and feel that I could not honestly be a teacher in it any longer. This conviction came upon me last summer four years. I mentioned it to two friends in the autumn of that year, 1839. And for a while I was in a state of excitement. It arose in the first instance from reading the Monophysite and Donatist controversies; in the former of which I was engaged in that course of theological study to which I had given myself. . . . that wretched Jerusalem Bishoprick affair, *no personal matter*, revived all my alarms. They have increased up to this moment. . . . the various ecclesiastical and quasi-ecclesiastical acts, which have taken place in the course of the last two years and a half, are not the cause of my state of opinion; but are keen stimulants and weighty confirmations of a conviction forced upon me, while engaged *in the course* of duty, viz the theological reading to which I have given myself. (v. 9; To Henry Edward Manning, 25 Oct. 1843)

I am in no perplexity or anxiety at present. I fear that I must say that for four years and a half I have had a conviction, weaker or stronger, but on the whole constantly growing, and at present very strong, that we are not part of the Church. I am too much accustomed to this idea to feel pain at it. . . . At present I do not feel any such call. . . . It was the Monophysite and Donatist controversies which in 1839 led me to this clear and distinct judgment. (v. 10; To Edward B. Pusey, 19 Feb. 1844)

To remain in the English Church from a motive of expediency seems to me altogether unjustifiable both in a theological and a religious point of view. The English is either a true Church or it is not. If it is, it ought not to be left by any member of it, on any account – and if it is not, it ought to be left at all hazards. If a person doubts, whether it be or no, he is bound to remain in it, while he doubts. In no case is there room for expediency. (v. 10; To Charles John Myers, 25 Feb. 1844)

There was only one question about which I had a doubt, viz whether it would *work*, for it has never been more than a paper system. . . . One thing of course I saw clearly – that there was a great risk of Anglican principles running into Roman. . . . Nothing then but a strong positive difficulty or repulsion has kept me from surrendering my heart to the authority of the Church of Rome; a repulsive principle, not growing out of Catholic, Anglican, or Primitive doctrine, in the way in which I viewed that doctrine, but something antagonistic, arising from *particular doctrines* of the Church of Rome, particular historical views, etc etc. And this very circumstance led me to be violent enough against the Church of Rome – because it was the only way of resisting it. A bulwark or breakwater was necessary to the position of the English Church and theory. And in being violent, I was not acting on private judgment against so great a Communion, but I had the authority or rather the command of all our Divines, who, doubtless from the same constraining necessity have ever been violent against her also. To be violent against Rome was to be dutiful to England, as well as a measure of necessity for the English theory. . . . such were my feelings and views from 1833 to 1839. It was my great aim to build up the English system into something like consistency, to develop its idea, to get rid of anomalies, and to harmonize precedents and documents. I thought, and still think, its theory a great one. What then was my dismay . . . when in 1839 it flashed upon me in the course of reading the Fathers, which I had hitherto read with the eyes of our own Divines, that (not only was it a theory never realized) but a theory unproved or rather disproved by Antiquity? (v. 10; To Mrs. William Froude, 3 April 1844)

Unless anything happened which I considered a divine call, and beyond all calculation, I never should take any one by surprise – and therefore you need not alarm yourself, as if anything were happening. But if I judge of the future by the past, and when I recollect the long time, now nearly 5 years, that certain views and feelings have been more or less familiar to me and sometimes pressing on me, it would seem as if anything might happen. And I must confess that they are very much clearer and stronger than they were even a year ago) I can no more calculate how soon they may affect my will and become practical, than a person who has long had a bodily ailment on him (though I hope and trust it is not an ailment) can tell when it may assume some critical shape, though it may do so any day. (v. 10; To [sister] Jemima Mozley, 21 May 1844]

[F]or the last five years (almost) of it, I have had a strong feeling, often rising to an habitual conviction, though in the early portion of it after a while dormant, but very active now for two years and a half, and growing more urgent and imperative continually, that the Roman Communion is the only true Church – And this conviction came upon me while I was reading the Fathers and from the Fathers – and when I was reading them theologically, not ecclesiastically, in that particular line of study, that of the ancient heresies, . . . as far as I see, all inducements and temptations are for remaining quiet, and against moving. The loss of friends what a great evil is this! the loss of position, of name, of esteem – such a stultification of myself – such a triumph to others. It is no proud thing to unsay what I have said, to pull down what I have attempted to build up. And again, what quite pierces me, the disturbance of mind which a change on my part would cause to so many – the casting adrift, to the loss both of religious stability and comfort – the temptation to which many would be exposed of scepticism, indifference, and even infidelity.

. . . But it does strike me on the other side 'What if you are the cause of souls dying out of the communion of Rome, who have had a *call* to join it, which you have repressed? What, if this has happened already?' Surely time enough has been allowed me for wavering and preparation – I have fought against these feelings in myself and others long enough. . . . The time for argument is passed. I have been in one settled conviction for so long a time, which every new thought seems to strengthen. When I fall in with friends who think differently, the temptation to remain quiet becomes stronger, very strong – but I really do not think my conviction is a bit shaken. (v. 10; To John Keble, 8 June 1844)

[S]o it was in June or July 1839 reading the Monophysite controversy, I found my eyes opened to [a] state of things very different from what I had learned from my natural guides. The prejudice, or whatever name it is called, which had been too great for conviction from the striking facts of the Arian history, could not withstand the history of St Leo and the Council of Chalcedon. I saw that if the early times were to be my guides the Pope had a very different place in the Church from what I had supposed. When this suspicion had once fair possession of my mind, and I looked on the facts of the history for myself the whole English system fell about me on all sides, the ground crumbled under my feet, and in a little time I found myself in a very different scene of things. . . . towards the end of October, my attention was drawn to the subject of the Donatists, in the consequence of an article in the Dublin Review – The English explanations I found a second time unequal to the facts of the case – and for a time the great truth that the Anglican Church is in a state of schism had possession of my mind. (v. 10; "Memorandum in case of need," 28 July 1844)

What am I to say but that I am one who, even five years ago, had a strong conviction, from reading the history of the early ages, that we are not part of the Church? that I am one whose conviction of it now is about as strong as of any thing else he believes – so strong that the struggle against is doing injury to his faith in general, and is spreading a film of scepticism over his mind – who is frightened, and cannot tell what it may end in, if he dares to turn a deaf ear to a voice which has so long spoken to him – that I am one who is at this time in disquiet when he travels, lest he should be suddenly taken off, before he has done what to *him* seems necessary. For a long time my constant question has been 'Is it a dream? is it a delusion?' and the wish to have decisive proof on this point has made me satisfied – it makes me satisfied to wait still . . . (v. 10; To Edward B. Pusey, 28 Aug. 1844)

I do not say I have that certainty, but I am approximating to it. To judge from the course of my thoughts for five years, I am certain of reaching it some time or other. I cannot tell whether sooner or later. (v. 10; To Edward Badeley, 9 Sep. 1844)

It seems to me I have no call at present to take so awful a step, as you justly call it – but if I may judge by the past and present, I have very little reason to doubt about the issue of things. But the when and how are known to Him only from whom I trust both the course of things and the issue come. . . . I have a great dread of going merely by my own feelings, lest they should mislead me. . . . If you want to know plainly, I have little doubt where I shall be this time in two years, though my imagination cannot embrace the idea. (v. 10; To Miss Maria Rosina Giberne, 7 Nov. 1844)

I have no reason to suppose that anything is happening to me now, or will for I do not know how long. The pain I suffer from the thought of the distress I am causing cannot be described – and of the loss of kind opinion on the part of those I desire to be well with. The unsettling so many peaceable, innocent minds is a most overpowering thought, and at this moment my heart literally aches and has for days. I am conscious of no motive but that of obeying some urgent imperative call of duty – alas what am I not sacrificing! and if after all it is for a dream? (v. 10; To Mrs. William Froude, 12 Nov. 1844)

What a forlorn miserable prospect, humanly speaking, I have before me! but what hitherto has oppressed me, till all the complaints in the Psalms seemed to belong to me, has been the thought how I was perplexing, unsettling, frightening, depressing others . . . (v. 10; To Mrs. Elizabeth Bowden, 16 Nov. 1844)

I am going through what must be gone through – and my trust only is that every day of pain is so much from the necessary draught which must be exhausted. There is no fear (humanly speaking) of my moving for a long time yet. This has got out without my intending it, but it is all well. As far as I know myself my one great distress is the perplexity, unsettlement, alarm, scepticism which I am causing to so many – and the loss of kind feeling and good opinion on the part of so many, known and unknown, who have wished well to me. And of these two sources of pain it is the former is the constant, urgent, unmitigated one. I had for days a literal ache all about my heart, and from time to time all the complaints of the Psalmist seemed to belong to me. And, as far as I know myself, my one paramount reason for contemplating a change is my deep unvarying conviction that our Church is in schism and that my salvation depends on my joining the Church of Rome. I may use argument ad hominem to this person or that – but I am not conscious of resentment, or disgust, at any thing that has happened to me. I have no visions whatever of hope, no schemes of action, in any other sphere, more suited to me. I have no existing sympathies with Roman Catholics. I hardly ever, even abroad, was at one of their services – I know none of them. I do not like what I hear of them. And then how much I am giving up in so many ways – and to me sacrifices irreparable, not only from my age, when people hate changing, but from my especial love of old associations and the pleasures of memory. Nor am I conscious of any feeling, enthusiastic or heroic, of pleasure in the sacrifice – I have nothing to support me here. What keeps me yet, is what has kept me long – a fear that I am under a delusion – but the conviction remains firm under all circumstances, in all frames of mind. (v. 10; To Henry Edward Manning, 16 Nov. 1844)

What possible reason of mere 'preference' can I have for the Roman Church above our own? I hardly ever, even abroad, was at any of their services. I was scarcely ever for an hour in the same room with a Roman Catholic in my life. I have no correspondence with anyone. I know absolutely nothing of them except that external aspect that is so uninviting. In the Tablet and Dublin Review, in radical combinations and liberal meetings, this is how I know them. My habits, tastes, feelings are as different as can be conceived from theirs, as they show outwardly. No – as far as I know myself the one single over-powering feeling is that our Church is in schism – and that there is no salvation in it *for one who is convinced of this*. . . . this time three years the conviction came on me again, and now for that long time it has been clear and unbroken, under all change of. circumstance, place, and spirits. Through this time my one question has been 'Is it a delusion?' and I have waited, not because my conviction was not clear, but because I doubted whether it was a duty to trust it. I am still waiting on that consideration. . . . If I once am absolutely convinced that our Church is in schism, there is, according to the doctrine (I believe) of every age, no safety for me in it. (v. 10; To Edward Coleridge, 16 Nov. 1844)

For three full years I have been in a state of unbroken certainty. Against this certainty I have acted, under the notion that it might be a dream, and that I might break it or a dream by acting' – but I cannot. In that time I have had ups and down[s] – no strong temptations to move, and relapses again, though of course at particular moments the (if so be) truth has often flashed upon me with unusual force. . . . You must not suppose, I am fancying that I know *why* or *on what*, on what *motive*, I am acting – I cannot. I do not feel love, or faith. I feel myself very unreal. I can only say negatively, what I think does *not* influence me. But I cannot analyze my mind, and, I suppose, should do no good if I tried. . . . My sole ascertainable reason for moving is a feeling of indefinite *risk* to my soul in staying. This, I seem to ascertain in the following manner. I don't think I *could* die in our communion – . . . I am kept first from deference to my friends – next by fear of some dreadful delusion being on me. (v. 10; To John Keble, 21 Nov. 1844)

I have gone through a great deal of pain, and have been very much cut up. The one predominant distress upon me has been the unsettlement of mind I am causing. This is a thing that has haunted me day by day – and for some days I had a literal pain in and about my heart, . . . Besides the pain of unsettling people, of course I feel the loss I am undergoing in the good opinion of friends and well wishers – though I can't tell how much I feel this. It is the shock, surprise, terror, forlornness, disgust, scepticism, to which I am giving rise – the differences of opinion – division of families – all this makes my heart ache. . . . A clear conviction of the substantial identity of Christianity and the Roman system has now been on my mind for a full three years. . . . I am giving up everything. . . . I seem to be throwing myself away. Unless anything occurs which I cannot anticipate, I have no intention of an early step even now. . . . What keeps me here, is the desire of giving every chance for finding out, if I am under the power of a delusion. (v. 10; To [sister] Jemima Mozley, 24 Nov. 1844)

If I have a clear certain view that the Church of England is in schism, gained from the Fathers and resting on facts we all admit, *as facts*, (e.g. our separation from Rome) to rest on the events of the day is to put sight against faith. . . . as far as such outward matters go, I am as much gone over as if I *were already gone*. It is a matter of time only. I am waiting, if so be, that if I am under a delusion, it may be revealed to me though I am quite unworthy of it . . . (v. 10; To Edward B. Pusey, 25 Feb. 1845)

I would I knew how least to give you pain about what, I suppose, sooner or later must be. . . . I suppose Christmas cannot come again without a break-up – though to what extent or to whom I do not know. (v. 10; To Edward B. Pusey, 12 March 1845)

The unsettlement I am causing has been for a long while the one overpowering distress I have had. It is no wonder that through last Autumn it made me quite ill. It is as keen as a sword in many ways, and at times has given me a literal heartache, which quite frightened me. But in proportion as my course becomes clearer, this thought in some respects becomes more bearable. . . . I cannot master the *idea* of that being one Church, (if Church means *Kingdom*) which has two independent governments making war on each other. I cannot answer the question '*In what sense* are we one Church with Rome?' by the apostolical succession? then are the United States one Kingdom with England. A common *descent* is not a unity of polity. Again it has pressed most strongly on me that we pick and choose our doctrines. There is more, I suspect, in the first four centuries, or as much, for the Pope's supremacy, than for the real Presence, or the authenticity of certain books of Scripture. . . . the Fathers would have said that we were not the Church and ought individually to join the Church . . . (v. 10; To Edward B. Pusey, 14 March 1845)

As to my convictions, I can but say what I have told you already, that I cannot at all make out *why* I should determine on moving except as thinking I should offend God by not doing so. I cannot make out what I am *at*, except on this supposition. At my time of life men love ease – I love ease myself. I am giving up a maintenance, involving no duties, and adequate to all my wants; what in the world am I doing this for, (I ask *myself* this) except that I think I am called to do so? I am making a large income by my Sermons, I am, *to say the very least*, risking this – the chance is that my Sermons will have no further sale at all. I have a good name with many – I am deliberately sacrificing it. I have a bad name with more – I am fulfilling all their worst wishes and giving them their most coveted triumph – I am distressing all I love, unsettling all I have instructed or aided – I am going to those whom I do not know and of whom I expect very little – I am making myself an outcast, and that at my age – Oh what can it be but a stern necessity which causes this. . . . Suppose I were suddenly dying – one may deceive oneself as to what one should do – but I think I should directly send for a Priest – Is not this a test of one's state of mind? Ought I to live where I could not bear to die? . . . My resolution to move has grown so much stronger lately . . . Were persons never yet in a schismatical or heretical Church, and would not their trial, when they came to see their state, be exactly what mine is? Have Jews never had to turn Christians, and been cursed by their friends for doing so? Can I shock people so much as they did? Is the Church of Rome, can it be, regarded more fearfully than Jews regard Christianity, than Jews regarded St Paul? – was he not the prince of apostates? Has Nestorian, or Donatist, or Monophysite, never discovered that he was out of the Church, and had to break through all ties to get into it? Nay is not this the peculiar trial which happens in Scripture to be set upon a Christian . . . the quitting of friends and relations and houses and goods for Christ's sake? . . . What right have you to judge me? have the multitude, who will judge me, any right to judge me? who of my equals, who of the many who will talk flippantly about me, has a right? who has a right to judge me but my Judge? (v. 10; To [sister] Jemima Mozley, 15 March 1845)

I wished to have waited seven years from my first conviction – which would bring it to the Summer of 1846 – but really my mind is getting so much more made up, that I don't think I shall last so long. As a great secret I wish to say that my expectation is that some move will take place with the end of the year – but to what extent or whom it will embrace, I do not know. (v. 10; To Henry Wilberforce, 20 March 1845)

I can't help trusting that when I act I shall be much happier, both because the very fact of acting presupposes that my mind is made up – and next because doubt and suspence are so very depressing. I do trust I am undergoing the chief pain *before* I take any step – Also I trust that, much pain as you and others must feel, yet when it is over, you will find it less than you expect, and that things altogether will be more tolerable. (v. 10; To [sister] Jemima Mozley, 22 March 1845)

Now I will tell you just how things stand, and I am telling you more than any one in the world knows, except two friends of mine who are living here with me. My own convictions are as strong as I suppose they can be – only it is so difficult to know whether it is a call of *reason* or of *conscience*. I cannot make out if I am impelled by what seems to me clear, or by a sense of *duty*. You can understand how painful this doubt is. So I have waited on, hoping for light . . . My present intention is to give up my fellowship in October – and to publish some work or treatise between that and Christmas. I wish people to know *why* I am acting as well as *what* I am doing – It takes off that vague and distressing surprise 'What *can* have made him etc etc?' and also what I feel myself as good reasons may have to strengthen and satisfy others who mean to take the same step, but want reasons put out for them. And I think people have a claim on me, since I said one thing formerly, now frankly to say the other. (v. 10; To Miss Maria Rosina Giberne, 30 March 1845)

All that is dear to me is being taken away from me. My days are gone like a shadow, and I am withered like grass. (v. 10; To James Bowling Mozley, 2 April 1845)

If I move, it will only and simply be on the ground that I fear to die where I am. (v. 10; To Robert Francis Wilson, 11 April 1845)

I am very much more made up both in steady conviction and in preparation of my feelings, to change my place – but am suffering from fatigue of mind, partly from former distress, partly from other causes. (v. 10; To Mrs. William Froude, 10 June 1845)

At present I will but say that the conviction that I am acting rightly increases continually – and if I were left to myself, that is, if it were not for my necessary anxiety about others, I think I should have no question or doubt whatever. (v. 10; To Charles Crawley, 14 July 1845)

I have no desire at all to leave the English Church. . . . My reason for going to Rome is this: – I think the English Church in schism. I think the faith of the Roman Church the only true religion. I do not think there is salvation out of the Church of Rome. This of course does not interfere with my thinking an exception is made for those who are in involuntary ignorance; . . . (v. 10; To [brother] Francis William Newman, 7 Aug. 1845)

I suspect my own change will be soon before or after the publication of my book – but I can't tell. (v. 10; To Miss Maria Rosina Giberne, 24 Aug. 1845)

The nearest and dearest friends are, I think, (as they necessarily must) getting annoyed at me, and the stupid ungrateful feeling comes upon me in consequence that I am a trouble to anyone I address. All sorts of idle reports are afloat about me, and friends believe them as greedily as if they had never themselves laughed at the fictions of the Record or Morning Herald. And next it is of course unpleasant to me to be talking so constantly about myself. . . . when it [his *Essay on Development*] is out, I suppose a further step will take place very soon. (v. 10; To Mrs. Elizabeth Bowden, 31 August 1845)

I am convinced that, (to those who are enlightened see it) the Church of Rome is the only place of salvation. I do not think I can remain out of it, and yet remain in God's favor. (v. 10; To Simeon Lloyd Pope, 18 Sep. 1845)

[N]o reason for leaving our Church for the Roman comes home to me as sufficient, except this, – the conviction that such a step is necessary for salvation. As I have never held that 'all Roman doctrine' could be held in our Church, I have not myself been at all afflicted by recent decisions. The simple question to my mind is whether St Athanasius or St Augustine would have acknowledged us as a Church. (v. 10; To Edward Walford, 21 Sep. 1845)

Not only have I no doubts at all, but I have had a regularly increasing conviction, and am now more certain on the subject than I ever have been. To my reason it is as plain as day that we are not part of the great Catholic communion which the Apostles set up. . . . Considering then what the dreadful consequences are of being outside the Church, what can I do but obey a conviction . . . [?] (v. 10; To Robert Francis Wilson, 25 Sep. 1845)

[Newman was received into the Catholic Church at Littlemore on 9 October 1845 by Fr. Dominic Barberi, an Italian Passionist]

How Did Newman View His Conversion After 1845?

[D]uring the last half of that 10th year [1845] I was engaged in writing a book (Essay on Development) in favor of the Roman Church, and indirectly against the Anglican; but even then, till it was finished, I had not absolutely intended to publish it, wishing to reserve to myself the chance of changing my mind, when the argumentative views, which were actuating me, had been distinctly brought out before me in writing. (v. 13; To Frederick A. Faber, 6 Dec. 1849; Newman later commented on this letter, on 7 April 1863: "I had not finished my Essay on Development, when I became a Catholic. My convictions became too strong for my patience. Consequently the work is unfinished, and ends abruptly. I was received, and left it, where the argument stood, at the time of my reception.")

You are under a mistake in conjecturing I am not at rest. I have not had a moment either of doubt or anxiety, ever since I became a Catholic. . . . Do you not think, forgive me for saying it, you have sent me enough Protests? By your making them, I conjecture you are not at ease yourself – nor will you be my dear Sir, take my word for it, till you are a Catholic as I am. (v. 14; To Archdeacon Allen, 10 Nov. 1850)

I assure you solemnly that I have not had a single doubt of the truth of the Catholic religion and its doctrines ever since I became a Catholic. And I have an intense certainty that the case is the same with my friends about me, who have joined the Church with me. (v. 14; To R. B. Seeley, 31 July 1851)

I should be loth to think I was not converted logically. I was converted by the manifest and intimate *identity* of the modern RC Church with the Antenicene and Nicene Church . . . (v. 15; To Francis Richard Wegg-Prosser, 22 Feb. 1852)

One after another, moving not as a party, but one by one, un-willingly, because they could not help it, men of mature age, from 40 to past 50, in all professions and states, numbers have done what I have done. since the date of W.F.'s [William Froude's] letter; – such as Manning, R. Wilberforce, H. Wilberforce, Allies, Dodsworth, Hope Scott, Badeley, Bellasis, Bowyer, Monsell, Sir John Simeon, Dr Duke, Biddulph Phillips, Dean Madavori, Bishop Ives, the de Veres, H. Bowden, Mrs Bowden, Lady Lothian, Lady G. Fullerton, Lord H. Kerr, etc. I cannot help thinking it was dangerous for W.F. to have recourse to this argument. It is surely much easier to account for Keble and Pusey not moving, Catholicism being true, than for all these persons moving, Catholicism being not true. And, whereas it was the fashion at first to use this argument, as W.F. does in 1847 *against* us – I think it ought to have its weight *now* for us. It was the fashion then to say 'O, Newman is by himself. We don't deny his weight – but no one else of any name has gone – and are we to go by one man?' Times are altered now. . . . I do really think the character and variety of the converts to Catholicism of late in England form a most powerful argument, that there is such a thing as ascertainable truth in religion . . . (v. 16; To Mrs. Catherine Froude, c. Nov. 1854 or c. Nov. 1855)

I believe with all my heart and soul all that the Holy Roman Church teaches; and never have had one single doubt about any portion of her teaching whatever, ever since I became a Catholic. (v. 20; To the Editor of *The Lincolnshire Express*, 17 June 1862)

I have not had a moment's wavering of trust in the Catholic Church ever since I was received into her fold. I hold, and ever have held, that her Sovereign Pontiff is the centre of unity, and the vicar of Christ. And I ever have had, and have still, an unclouded faith in her Creed in all its articles; a supreme satisfaction in her worship, discipline, and teaching; and an eager longing, and a hope against hope, that the many dear friends whom I have left in Protestantism may be partakers in my happiness. (v. 25; To the *Globe*, 28 June 1862; cited in a letter to Samuel Walshaw, 11 April 1870)

Dr. Newman . . . owes it to truth to assure the Editor that he has never had, nor has, nor (as he believes) ever will have, any, either wish or intention, of leaving the Church of Rome and becoming a Protestant again. (v. 20; To the Editor of *The Record*, 29 June 1862)

Ever since I have been a Catholic, the regard and respect you speak of has been shown (I am not speaking in irony) only in one way; – in reports that I was coming back. Vivid manifestations, on my part, of my real state of mind have been the only method by which I have been able to clear the air, and destroy the popular anticipation. They have succeeded for a time; and then I have enjoyed a little peace. But my silence has encouraged its revival, and then I have had to make new manifestations. Hardly had I left Oxford, when the reports began. I had quarrelled with Dr Wiseman. I was suspended by ecclesiastical authority for my preaching. I had refused to be ordained. I had already come back to the Church of England, or at least my friends about me had done so. I had given up revealed religion altogether. I was an infidel. An Oxford friend of mine did not scruple in the Guardian to suggest this, that I was an infidel. There was something of a lull in these reports between 1852 and 1859, when they could not well stand their ground in the face of what I was then suffering or doing in the Catholic cause. Then they revived, and with a plausible minuteness of detail. I have had letters from strangers assuming I was a Protestant, or asking whether I was not returning to Protestantism, or telling me that it was only pride that kept me from returning, persons near conversion have been kept back by the assurance that I was on the point of returning; that I owned that Catholicism had its drawbacks as great as those of Protestantism; that I had recommended Protestants to stay where they were. It was stated that, if I did not return, yet I repented of going over, and was making the best of things; that I felt I never should have left the Established Church, if I had but waited; that I thought one religion as good as the other. All this so told upon some kind Protestants, that they wished to get me to their houses, by way of maturing and smoothing my change back again; and others have proceeded to discuss how I was to be treated, what was to be done with me, on my return. At length Catholics began to believe the reports also; to their own distress, and to my grave dissatisfaction. I felt that, if I were to die, it was certain to be maintained by numbers of men, and to go down in history, that I had died a Protestant. I could not, as a matter of conscience, allow such reports to continue without a decisive contradiction; nor could this be given, till they appeared in the Newspapers. At last they made their way into them; and the question then arose, what was the most effectual mode of contradiction. There was but one real way of putting them down, and I adopted it. It was to show that I regarded Protestantism, not merely with disapprobation, but with aversion and scorn. . . .

What I have said then in my letter in the Globe about Protestantism and the Anglican system, was, like these former statements, the deliberately chosen and studied means of effecting a necessary end. It was intended to force Protestants to put out of their minds the hope of my ever coming back to them. Tastes, sentiments, affections, are deeper, more permanent, more trustworthy, than conclusions in logic. Convictions change: habits of mind endure. Had I mildly and courteously said that my reason was antagonistic to Protestantism, I should have said what was true, but I should not have obliterated the general anticipation and instinctive suspicion that I should return to it. It would have been said that my words were dictated, nay written by someone else . . . (v. 20; To Charles Crawley, 21 July 1862)

I say to myself, if a mind can come to a solid immoveable conclusion, mine has done so – I have a clear anticipation that there is no possible argument which has a chance of interfering with my conviction that what is called the 'Roman communion' is a continuation of that ecclesiastical body to which St Cyprian belonged, and which the Apostles founded. . . . I say the same, and I suppose you would do so also, as to the question of the Being of a God. Surely these are points on which we have a right to be certain. (v. 20; To Daniel Radford, 15 Oct. 1862)

[T]he doctrine of the necessity of communion with the Holy See was *not* the consideration which made me a Catholic, but the visible fact that the modern Roman Communion was the heir and the image of the primitive Church. (v. 23; To Edward B. Pusey, 9 Aug. 1867)

As to your second question 'Did you ever regret leaving the Church of England?' I can answer sincerely 'Never, for a single moment.' I have been in the fullest peace and enjoyment ever since I have been a Catholic, and have felt a power of truth and divine strength in its ordinances, which exists, I believe, nowhere else. (v. 24; To Albert Smith, 8 Jan. 1868)

My main reason for becoming a Catholic was that the present Latin communion was the only one which answered to the early Church in all substantial matters. (v. 25; To J. F. Seccombe, 2 Jan. 1870)

You do not, cannot know, the reality which Catholicism is to the mind, which is enlightened to receive it. I have stood where you stand; you never have stood where I stand. Since I have been a Catholic, it is my happiness, unmerited and the gift of grace, never to have had a single doubt of the divine origin and truth of Catholicism; did I 're-consider', as you advise, I should be most cruelly unthankful to Him who has so blessed and prospered my search after Him. No one should inquire or reconsider, who does not doubt – did I ever doubt, which God forbid, then certainly I should be obliged to reconsider – but such reconsideration would not, I am sure, lead me back to any form of Protestantism – for I have long been convinced that so far only is Protestantism true, as it has retained some grains of that Revealed Truth which is in its fulness in the Catholic Church. If there is no Church there is no revelation. What shall judge between us, whether you are in a delusion or I, but the Last day? (v. 25; To Edward Bishop Elliott, 16 June 1870)

For myself, what made me a Catholic was the fact, as it came home to me, that the present Catholics are in all essential respects the successors and representatives of the first Christians, such a remarkable identity in position and character in ages so widely separated and so strikingly dissimilar, being at the same time the note of a supernatural origin and life. (v. 25; To an Unknown Correspondent, 19 June 1870)

'Have I found', you ask of me, 'in the Catholic Church, what I hoped and longed for?' That depends on what I 'hoped and longed for?' I did not hope or long for any 'peace or satisfaction', as you express it, for any illumination or success. I did not hope or long for anything except to do God's will, which I feared not to do. I did not leave the Anglican Church, as you think, for any scandals in it. You have mistaken your man. My reason was as follows: – I knew it was necessary, if I would participate in the grace of Christ, to seek it there where He had lodged it. I believed that that grace was to be found in the Roman communion only, not in the Anglican. Therefore I became a Catholic. This was my belief in 1845, and still more strongly my belief now, because in 1845 I had not that utter distrust of the Anglican Orders which I feel in 1870. . . . whether I have, since a Catholic, been treated well or ill, by high personages or confidential friends, does not touch the question of truth and error, the Church and schism. Be sure, if I can answer for myself in any thing, Anglican I can never be again. (v. 25; To Edward Husband, 17 July 1870)

I am as certain that the Church in communion with Rome is the successor and representative of the Primitive Church, as certain that the Anglican Church is *not*, as certain that the Anglican Church is a mere collection of men, a mere national body, a human society, as I am that Victoria is Queen of Great Britain. Nor have I once had even a passing doubt on the subject, ever since I have been a Catholic. I have all along been in a state of inward certainty and steady assurance on this point, and I should be the most asinine, as well as the most ungrateful of men, if I left that Gracious Lord who manifests Himself in the Catholic Church, for those wearisome Protestant shadows, out of which of His mercy he has delivered me. (v. 25; To Henry Thomas Ellacombe, 23 Aug. 1870)

I have never had a single doubt on the subject, thank God, since I have been a Catholic; and never the slightest, however transient, wish to return to the Church of England or regret at having left it. (v. 25; To Miss Alice Smith, 3 Nov. 1870)

[I]t is not at all the case that I left the Anglican Church from despair – but for two reasons concurrent, as I have stated in my

Apologia – first, which I felt *before* any strong act had been taken against the Tracts or me, namely, in 1839, that the Anglican Church *now* was in the position of the Arian Churches of the fourth century, and the Monophysite Churches of the fifth, and this was such a shock to me that I at once made arrangements for giving up the editorship of *The British Critic*, and in no long time I contemplated giving up St. Mary's. This shock was the *cause* of my writing [*Tracts for the Times*] Number 90 which excited so much commotion. Number 90 which roused the Protestant world against me, most likely never would have been written except for this shock. Thus you see my condemnation of the Anglican Church arose *not* out of despair, but, when everything was hopeful, *out of my study of the Fathers*. Then, as to the second cause, it began in the autumn of 1841, six months after Number 9o, when the Bishops began to charge against me. This brought home to me that *I had no business in the Anglican Church*. It was not that I despaired of the Anglican Church, but that their opposition *confirmed* the interpretation which I had put upon the Fathers, that they *who loved the Fathers, could have no place in the Church of England*. As to your further question, whether, *if* I had stayed in the Anglican Church *till now*, I should have joined the Catholic Church at all, at any time now or hereafter, I think that most probably I should *not*; but *observe, for* this reason, because God gives grace, and if it is not accepted He withdraws His grace; and since, of His free mercy, and from no merits of mine, He then offered me the grace of conversion, if I had not acted upon it, it was to be expected that I should be left, a worthless stump, to cumber the ground and to remain where I was till I died. (v. 25; To Mrs. Houldsworth, 3 July 1871)

Who can have *dared* to say that I am disappointed in the Church of Rome? 'dared,' because I have never uttered, or written, or thought, or felt the very shadow of disappointment. I believe it to be a human institution as well as divine, and so far as it is human it is open to the faults of human nature; but if, because I think, with others, that its rulers have sometimes erred as fallible men, I therefore think it has failed, such logic won't hold; indeed, it is the wonderful anticipation in Our Lord's and St Paul's teaching, of apparent failure [and real] success in the times after them which has ever been one of my strong arguments for believing them divine messengers. (v. 31; To Alfred Henry Spurrier, 11 Dec. 1886)

I will not close our correspondence without testifying my simple love and adhesion to the Catholic Roman Church, not that I think you doubt this; and did I wish to give a reason for this full and absolute devotion, what should, what can, I say, but that those great and burning truths, which I learned when a boy from evangelical teaching, I have found impressed upon my heart with fresh and ever increasing force by the Holy Roman Church? That Church has added to the simple evangelicism of my first teachers, but it has obscured, diluted, enfeebled, nothing of it – on the contrary, I have found a power, a resource, a comfort, a consolation in our Lord's divinity and atonement, in His Real Presence, in communion in His Divine and Human Person, which all good Catholics indeed have, but which Evangelical Christians have but faintly[.] (v. 31; To George T. Edwards, 24 Feb. 1887)

Do Converts Sometimes Become Obnoxious and Lack Humility?

Of course the circumstance that God grants a change of heart is a just ground of hope and rejoicing, whatever our past offences may have been. I do not think that such feelings are at all incompatible with the deepest and most lasting humiliation. . . . It seems to me that there is great danger of any one who has experienced such a change of views . . . becoming excited. She must not expect to have always the sunshine she now has – and the more she indulges her feelings now, the greater reverse perhaps is in store. . . . While God gives peace and joy, we have cause to be thankful, but let us rejoice with trembling. (v. 7; To Miss Mary Holmes, 10 June 1840)

Does God Provide Overwhelming Assurance to Converts?

Now is it not highly desirable in the case of anyone, that he should not change his religion merely on his *private judgment*? are you not, as all of us, *very* likely to be perplexed and deceived by argument? does Almighty God *commonly* require a man to go by private judgment? I think not. *Three thousand* souls were converted on the day of Pentecost; whereas when he asks of us *singly* to follow Him, He then usually gives overpowering evidence, as to St Paul. (v. 7; To W. C. A. MacLaurin, 26 July 1840)

[T]he *sole* reason we can have for leaving the Church in which God's Providence has placed us is a *call from God*; not a mere wish on our part to be nearer heaven. (v. 8; To Miss Mary Holmes, 15 Aug. 1841)

[I]t is a comfort to be assured that those who, when in religious perplexity, quietly commit their souls to God in well doing, who try to please Him and who pray for guidance, will gain, through His mercy a spiritual judgment for 'trying the spirits' and deciding between the claims of opposite arguments, quite sufficiently for their own peace and their own salvation. (v. 8; To Thomas Kirkpatrick, 6 March 1842)

With the convictions she has, it is her clear duty to submit herself to the Church at once; for who that knows he is external to it can for a moment delay, when he knows in his heart that the Catholic Church is the fold of Christ and the Ark of Salvation and that Rome is the necessary centre of it. She had better go to the nearest Priest. . . . She must frankly tell her husband who has a right to know what she is doing, and for what she can tell he will receive this in a far other spirit than you fear, and will understand she is called by God to do what at the moment will so much distress. I have known wonderful effects come of such straightforward courage and most unsuspected graces –

sometimes husbands or wives have themselves been converted, when the question of religion has thus been brought home to them. (v. 23; To Anselm Bertrand Gurdon, 2 Oct. 1867)

Should One Convert Quickly?

[T]o all great changes, a season of thought and preparation is a necessary introduction, if we would know what God's will is. Apply this to the case of a change of religion. . . . To any friend who asked me what to do, I should prescribe three years, during which his thoughts and prayers should be directed this one way, to learn God's will. It is a comfort in a matter of religion to follow not to originate. (v. 8; To Miss Mary Holmes, 8 Aug. 1841)

Should a Person Convert Merely to Alleviate Persisting Doubts?

Not that I deny, of course not, just the contrary, that you must come to the Church to be taught, and with the intention of submitting to her teaching – and I grant that if that was the way in which you could rid yourself of your doubts, viz from a belief that the Church knew, as God's oracle, what you did not, then you might safely let yourself be swayed by the desire of escaping from what is so painful – but there are those who believe in the Church simply from the wish to escape from doubt, and on them the doubts sometimes fall back, after they are in the Church. I have no definite cases before my mind – yes, as I write one comes into my mind – but at least I do not know of many such, but I see clearly there is a great risk of such cases. The question is, can I believe the Church have I reasons for believing the Church, so that I may fairly hope, with God's grace, that my faith will be a match for those difficulties, which I still feel? Now there are those who say (e.g.) 'Nothing can make me believe in eternal punishment.' Of course I should condemn such a sentiment – but, supposing they went on to say 'Nevertheless I will join the Church, for I will *simply* put the doctrine *out of my thoughts,'* I could not approve such a course of action. I think they ought to say 'I will wait till by God's grace I can feel it my duty to mortify and sacrifice this opinion or persuasion of mine to that word of His, which is truer than is, in this case, the thought of my heart.' (v. 25; To Richard Holt Hutton, 16 Feb. 1870)

Do Converts Typically Have Last-Minute Jitters and Qualms?

'A person fast drifting towards Catholicism,' but 'not seeing his way to become a Catholic at once' either has some definite obstacle in the way of faith, as a distinct holding off from some particular doctrine or doctrines, or has a general and indefinite want of faith, a dim belief amid remaining doubt, such as to warrant or oblige him to *wait* till he has clearer views. (1) If the former, that obstacle ultimately falls on the doctrine of the Pope's prerogatives – for if he believed that the Creed of the Pope could not be wrong, he would accept the difficult points in Catholicism on *faith* – in the Pope – Therefore, since he does *not* accept them, this shows that he does *not* apply the 'Feed My Sheep' to the Pope – or that he does *not* believe in the Pope's universal jurisdiction. . . . (2) On the other hand, if, according to the latter supposition, he merely has not a clear view, and doubts which way the truth lies, though he inclines to believe Catholicism and thinks he shall do so, doubting in some sense every thing, . . . We give to the Pope and to the Church an authority above the law of the land in *spiritual* matters. (v. 24; To Richard Frederick Clarke, 21 April 1868)

Are Non-Catholics Sometimes Cynical About Catholic Converts?

It would be interesting if we all were obliged to bear testimony to the Catholic Church, as you are doing – yet, do what we would, our Anglican friends would not believe that in our secret hearts we were not woefully disappointed. (v. 13; To J. M. Capes, 1 July 1849)

Do Protestants Hope that Famous Catholic Converts Will Return?

[T]hey are always hoping that Dr Manning and I may come back; and from wishing and hoping, they proceed to maintain that it is likely; and those who hear them say that it is likely, misinterpret them, on account of their own similar hopes and wishes, and say that it is to be expected. And then the next hearer says that it is a fact which is soon to be, for he has heard of the expectation on the best authority. And then the next hearer says that he has the first authority for saying that Dr Manning or Dr Newman is coming back in the course of the next few months. And then, lastly, someone perhaps puts into the newspapers that he knows a person who was told by Dr Newman himself that he had discovered the unreality or hollowness of Romanism, and meant to return in the course of April, May, or June, to the bosom of the Establishment. Thus only can I account for the most absurd, and utterly unfounded, reports which, ever since I have been a Catholic, have been spread abroad about the prospect of my return from the Mother of Saints to the City of Confusion. (v. 19; To an Unknown Correspondent, 18 April 1859)

Can we Know Who is Likely to Convert to Catholicism?

As to deciding, who are in invincible ignorance and who are not, it is a point quite beyond us. Our great mistakes when we try to determine who are likely to be converted and who not, when we compare our anticipations with the events, are enough to show how little we know the minds of others. One alone knows the soul; He who made it and will judge. We, on the contrary, only make ourselves ridiculous when we attempt it. Let us set about creating, and summoning to judgment with the Archangel's trumpet; and then we shall have a claim to the omniscience, which we are so disposed practically to attribute to ourselves. It is one thing to urge upon all Protestants the fearful peril of trifling with the grace of God; quite another thing, to assert that this or that person has actually done so. (v. 20; To A. J. Hanmer, 27 Sep. 1862)

Does God Use Curiosity to Bring in Converts?

It surprises me much to find that you are a convert. I do not recollect your saying so in any former letter. Truly do you say, that the ways by which souls arrive at the home of their true Mother are wonderfully various. That drawing of the heart to the Church, which you speak of, is very common, and most mysterious. It is wonderful the sort of innate curiosity which Protestants, who have no intention, and no ground of reason, to join the Church, feel when they come near Catholics. They cannot help asking questions, and showing an interest, as if from some inward impulse and sentiment, similar to that which is described in novels, when some unknown heir of a great family comes into the presence of his relations or is brought within the walls of his own castle. You speak of feeling drawn to the religion of Ireland by your love of Ireland; I felt something like this as regards the Fathers. After my conversion I had a sensible pleasure in taking down the Volumes of St Athanasius, St Ambrose ere in my Library – The words rose in my mind 'I am at one with you now.' I had a feeling of family-intimacy with them then, the want of which I suffered from before, without recognising it. (v. 21; To W. J. O'Neill Daunt, 13 Aug. 1864)

Must Converts Get Used to Catholic "Strangeness" at First?

The greatest trial a Convert has to sustain, and to women it is often greater than to men, is the strangeness at first sight of everything in the Catholic Church. Mass, devotions, conversation, all may be a perplexity to you, so I am not at all surprised at what you say about the Mass. You must be brave and determined, and resolutely beg of God's grace to carry you through your difficulties. Every nation, every body of people, has its own ways – Catholics have their own ways – we may not at first like them – and the question is where is religious *Truth*, where is *salvation*? – not is this habit, this fashion pleasant to me or not? (v. 24; To Miss Ellen Fox, 25 Feb. 1868)

Chapter Seven

Lay Participation

Do Laymen Have an Important Role to Play in the Church?

I am sure they may be made in this day the strength of the Church. (v. 14; To J. M. Capes, 10 April 1851)

[T]he Holy See ever has gone great lengths, and will go great lengths, in order to regain a *population*. Of course it is ever bound to uphold the faith in its integrity; but it never will deny, that, . . . the people are in their place essential to the Church and the deposit of faith, as the Hierarchy is essential in its own. (v. 20; To Edmund S. Ffoulkes, 29 Nov. 1861)

The same dreadful jealousy of the laity, which has ruined things in Dublin, is now at the bottom of this unwillingness to let our youths go to Oxford. I am far from denying that there are strong reasons against that step, but these are not at the root of the dread of it. Propaganda and our leading Bishops fear the natural influence of the laity: which would be their greatest, or (humanly speaking) is rather their only, defence against the world. (v. 21; To T. W. Allies, 30 Nov. 1864)

On both sides the Channel, the deep difficulty is the jealousy and fear which is entertained in high quarters of the laity. . . . Nothing great or living can be done except when men are self governed and independent: this is quite consistent with a full maintenance of ecclesiastical supremacy. St Francis Xavier wrote to St Ignatius on his knees; but who will say that St Francis was not a real centre of action? (v. 21; To Robert Ornsby, 2 Dec. 1864)

I am amused at my Most Revd and Rt Revd Lords. When they want to carry their point against Oxford, then the Laity are absolutely nothing at all, though it is a matter as close to them as the future of their sons; but, when the Laity have to do a thing for them in Parliament, then all at once they are of such great consequence and calibre, that their acts commit Pope, Cardinals, Apostolic Delegates, and whatever else is sacred and infallible in Holy Church. (v. 21; To William Monsell, 3 April 1865)

A great Prelate said to me years ago, when I said that the laity needed instruction guidance, tenderness, consideration etc etc, 'You do not know them, Dr N. Our laity are a peaceable body-they are peaceable.' I understood him to mean 'They are grossly ignorant and unintellectual and we need not consult or consult for them at all . . . at Rome they treat them according to the tradition of the Middle Ages, as, in Harold the Dauntless, the Abbot of Durham treated Count Wittikin. Well, facts alone will slowly make them recognize the fact of what a laity must be in the 19th century, even if it is not, if it is to cope with Protestantism[.] (v. 21; To Emily Bowles, 1 May 1865)

[T]here has been a tradition among the Italians that the lay mind is barbaric – fierce and stupid – and is destined to be outwitted, and that fine craft is the true weapon of Churchmen. When I say the lay mind, I speak too narrowly – it is the Saxon, Teuton, Scandinavian, French mind. (v. 23; To Henry Wilberforce, 16 April 1867)

As far as I can see, there are ecclesiastics all over Europe, whose policy it is to keep the laity at arms-length; and hence the laity have been disgusted and become infidel, and only two parties exist, both ultras in opposite directions. I came away from Ireland with the distressing fear, that in that Catholic country, in like manner, there was to be an antagonism, as time went on, between the hierarchy and the educated classes. You will be doing the greatest possible benefit to the Catholic cause all over the world, if you succeed in making the University a middle station at which clergy and laity can meet, so as to learn to understand and to yield to each other – and from which, as from a common ground, they may act in union upon an age, which is running headlong into infidelity. (v. 26; To George Fottrell, 10 Dec. 1873)

Do Popes Consult Laypeople Regarding Dogmatic Definitions?

[O]ut of the condescension of the Holy See, the Christian people at large were consulted on the *fact* of the *tradition* of the Immaculate Conception in every part of the Catholic world. The fact of the tradition, I conceive, was one chief ground of the Definition being possible. (v. 19; To Bishop Ullathorne, 13 May 1859)

To the unlearned reader the idea conveyed by 'consulting' is not necessarily that of asking an opinion. For instance, we speaking of consulting a barometer about the weather. The barometer does not give us its opinion, but ascertains for us a fact. In this sense of the word, surely, the Sensus Fidelium has a real place in the evidences (per modium unius) of Apostolical Tradition, and in the preliminaries of a dogmatic definition. I had not a dream of understanding the word, as used in the Rambler, in the sense of *asking an opinion.* I understood it to mean, that the Holy Father before defining the Immaculate Conception, proceeded (over and above the use of other more authoritative instruments of ascertaining the tradition of the doctrine,) to ascertain, through the Bishops of all Christendom, the sensus fidelium. (v. 19; To John Gillow, 16 May 1859)

He seemed to think that I had no right to commit myself to any opinion, till I knew what they thought upon the subject at Rome. Now on the contrary I think that all parts of the Catholic world should say their say on those matters in which they hav~ a right to have an opinion from their local interests, experience etc, and that, while it is the gain of the Holy Father to *hear* those many opinions *in order* that he may have the materials of pronouncing a judgment, it is the duty of all parts of the Church to submit to his voice when at length he speaks. But to assume that we are to keep silence *before* he speaks is to put the cart before the horse. (v. 20; To William Monsell, 27 Dec. 1863)

Do Laymen Have to Interpret and Apply Church Proclamations?

[A]ny declaration of the Pope's, if he were ruled infallible, would require explanation in the concrete in *another way* also – not only as to its application, but its interpretation. As lawyers explain acts of Parliament, so theologians have ever explained the dicta of Popes and Councils – and that explanation, when received generally, is the true Catholic doctrine. Hence, I have never been able to see myself that the ultimate decision rests with any but the general Catholic intelligence. And so I understand it to be implied in the 'Securus iudicat orbis terrarum.' (v. 25; To Robert Edmund Froude, 30 March 1870)

Was Newman's Thinking on the Laity Vindicated in Vatican II?

Did I tell you that I have given up [being editor of] the Rambler? . . . The July number is nearly entirely written by me. . . . Our Bishop interfered immediately after the May Number and asked me to resign it, which I at once promised him I would do. . . . I did all I could to ascertain God's will, and that being the case, I am sure good will come of my taking it – I am of opinion that the Bishops see only one side of things, and I have a mission, as far as my own internal feelings go, against evils which I see. On the other hand, I have always preached that things which are *really* useful, still are done, according to God's will, at one time, not at another – and that, if you attempt at a wrong time, what in itself is right, you perhaps become a heretic or schismatic. What I may aim at may be real and good, but it may be God's will it should be done a hundred years later. . . . When I am gone, it will be seen perhaps that persons stopped me from doing a work which I might have done. God overrules all things. Of course it is discouraging to be out of joint with the time, and to be snubbed and stopped as soon as I begin to act. (v. 19; To Henry Wilberforce, 17 July 1859)

[T]he voice of the Schola Theologorum, of the whole Church diffusive, will in time make itself heard, and Catholic instincts and ideas will assimilate and harmonize into the credenda of Christendom, and the living tradition of the faithful, . . . (v. 25; To William Maskell, 12 Feb. 1871)

Chapter Eight

Bible, Tradition, and Authority

How Fundamental is Revelation to Religious Truth?

[T]he mind cannot arrive at religious truth 1st without a revelation, 2nd without God's dispersing its prejudices in order to it's receiving that revelation. . . . till you have recourse to the Author of Nature himself for direction, humbly, sincerely, perseveringly, can you expect to possess real knowledge and true peace. (v. 1; To [brother] Charles Robert Newman, 14 April 1825)

[T]he mind cannot arrive at religious truth without a revelation. (v. 2; To [brother] Charles Robert Newman, 19 Aug. 1830)

Does Revelation Tend to be Unpredictable By its Very Nature?

A revelation implies the disclosure of something before unknown: nay, if, we consider the circumstances of the case, something otherwise indiscoverable. Now doubtless what is thus discovered *may* prove agreeable to our own experience, but *as* certainly it may turn out to be beyond its reach. We know how an enlarged view of a subject changes our ideas respecting it. . . . I venture confidently to say, that if the contents of a professed revelation on divine things are to be made the test of its genuineness, *no revelation could* be made us: for scarcely two persons can be got together, who will agree in their antecedent or self-originated ideas of God and his purposes towards man. Nay even, were the same method of proof applied to the sciences, we should have no system of mathematics, chemistry, astronomy or natural history. . . . It might then, I repeat, be most reasonably expected, that a revelation professing to give information on divine things, would contain many particulars beyond the reach of our present reason: many things, which from our ignorance (I do not say *the weakness of our faculties*) it is perhaps impossible now to prove to us; and which consequently it would be a pure mistake to bring in disparagement to its claims on our acceptance. (v. 1; To [brother] Charles Robert Newman, 14 April 1825)

What is the Relationship Between Revelation and Faith?

[T]he formation of a virtuous character depends on trial, this world is a world of temptation – and among these, the temptation to unbelief is one. Accordingly, the reception of revealed truth being a trial, it was never intended to force truth upon any one, but to give to those who *seek*. Hence, tho' the evidence for the Christian Revelation is more than sufficient for the proof of the fact, still it is not so great as it might have been. . . . it was left purposely (as it would seem) in the state it is – very strong but not overpowering, that men might not *be forced* to accept it as if they were mere machines, but in order to try what each man was made of . . . (v. 2; To [brother] Charles Robert Newman, 19 Aug. 1830)

Whether in nature then, or by the supernatural, all religion is a revelation – an acceptance of truths conveyed to us from a Personal God, but of course in theology we restrict the word 'revelation' to the communication of those truths which reason cannot reach, and the formal organ of those truths is the Church, but, I repeat, not the only organ to individuals. (v. 21; To Richard Holt Hutton, 18 June 1864)

This is the very meaning of Revelation. It is made to teach us something, which otherwise we should not know, – for our soul's good, for the education of our soul – for our preparation for heaven – It teaches us how to please God. How can we fancy we shall be saved unless we let Him guide us? and He guides us by propositions addressed to the intellect, such as I see down above 'our Lord died for sinners.' (v. 26; To Isy Froude, 9 April 1873)

Does Revelation Have Rational Evidences in its Favor?

[I]t was unlikely Providence should rest such important doctrines as those of Scripture upon *one kind of proof.* I reply 1st such a course is analogous to His other arrangements: we know historical facts only from moral [[i.e. *probable*]] evidence: we are informed of the presence of material objects only through our senses etc etc 2nd there is a fallacy in calling it *one kind of proof*: for it contains a vast, nay, infinite field of evidence; viz. miracles, prophecies, the establishment of Christianity etc etc[.] (v. 1; To [brother] Charles Robert Newman, 7 July 1825)

Can we Expect to Understand Revelation?

[I]f the fact of a revelation be granted, it is most extravagant and revolting to our reason to suppose that after all its message is not ascertainable and that the divine interposition reveals nothing. (v. 7; To [brother] Francis W. Newman, 22 Oct. 1840)

How Do we Come to Best Understand Scripture?

[T]he different books have such an intimate relation with each other, and throw on one another so much unexpected light, that life is not sufficient for a perfect view of the comprehensive subject they treat on – This knowledge is styled in Scripture 'the full assurance of understanding' [Col 2:2], and it is in vain to seek for it in reading comments and treatises though of the most excellent description. . . . And it is the study of Scripture, it is this painful and continued searching which gives us that 'inward witness' it so often describes, which is after all the great evidence for its divine origin – as we read, we see more and more of a majesty, a sublimity, a holiness, an awful grandeur, which while it affects the heart, subdues the will and convinces the understanding – Allow me to add, and that in order to remind myself not less than others, that we can expect nothing of these blessed advantages without constant and earnest prayer for divine grace that we may be able really to understand what we read. (v. 1; To Simeon Lloyd Pope, 18 Feb. 1824)

Are Church and Tradition Necessary to Understand the Bible?

[S]uppose it is objected that the principle of the Bible Society creates a certain indifference to the preservation of Ecclesiastical Order, or that it encourages the notion that the Bible may be rightly understood without the need of theological learning or a previous religious education. I may think these alleged effects of the institution *bad* – nay I may even allow that they in a degree exist – and yet in spite of them on the whole see cause to join the Society. (v. 2; Speech at the Bible Society Meeting, 29 May 1828)

[T]here is no *authorized* interpretation of Scripture in the Church, for the simple reason that none was ever given to her. When it is said that she interprets by the Fathers, (which is most true) it means that their doctrinal teaching is the *rule* of interpretation. (v. 16; To Mrs. Catherine Froude, 26 Dec. 1854)

[T]he Catholic believes in the word of God thro[ugh] His Church . . . (v. 19; To Charles Crawley, 17 March 1861)

I never should be surprised if the received popular views of Scripture would, as time goes on, undergo some modification, as they *have* done since the time of Galileo; but we are not *pledged* to those popular views, and, while we are too cautious to scandalize and unsettle the weak, we look for some determination of the Church to guide us, and we wait patiently for it. This is our position, very different from that of Protestants. (v. 20; To William Wilberforce, 4 Dec. 1862)

The Scripture writers then, according to the Schola, are always *true*; but then practically, this does not tell for so much, as seems at first sight. For (1) We must consider what is the *sense* of each passage. . . (2) The sense of Scripture is determined by the *Church*; now very seldom has she authoritatively interpreted any passage; . . . (v. 21; To William Wordsworth, 22 Oct. 1864)

2. Now to answer this question 'What did the sacred writers mean?' the answer always is they meant *that*, which the Church says that they meant. 3 Holy Church has not been divinely prompted to put forth a *general* comment on the *whole* of Scripture. This, I say, she has *not* done, though she has the gift enabling her to do it. 4. What she *has* done is this; – according to the circumstances of the time, or the emergencies of controversy, she has declared what was the sense which the sacred writers meant in *this passage* of Scripture or *that*. 5. I repeat, though she has the gift of being able to declare the sense which in every part of Scripture was intended or was not intended by its writer, yet she has not declared it. She has only given the sense of certain portions of Scripture, and we do not know the times and seasons when she will be guided to interpret other parts. Consequently a great deal of Scripture is left more or less to the judgment of divines, which is not, strictly speaking, infallible, even when it is unanimous, or again to the private judgment of individuals. . . . The great question then always is, What did the sacred writer *mean*? *not*, what does the bare letter say? and in order to solve this, what does the Infallible Church *say* that the sacred writer *meant*? (v. 21; To an Unknown Correspondent, 19 March 1865)

To myself, it seems a paradox that the Almighty should give to men a revealed doctrine without giving also a standard interpreter of it. It is in that case but a half or a quarter gift, or rather a gift reversing and undoing itself. As being a revelation it must be in one sense or other a new doctrine; and, Christianity especially, is marvellous, strange, unexpected, mysterious, as well as new, requiring large explanations, which could not be exhausted in the lifetime of Apostles, but, according to the shifting circumstances of times and places, would be required for this or that part of the revelation till the end of time. A Christian of the Apostolic age would go straight to an Apostle for information, if he was in doubt of what the revelation taught on the subject of baptism – or to one who personally knew an Apostle . . . I consider then that a standing authoritative interpretation of revelation is the complement of revelation in its very idea – and without which revelation virtually is not. Various Protestant Sects have felt this great incongruity – and have considered in consequence that there was given to the individual Christian an inward infallible light, which definitely interpreted the revelation as the Apostles meant it to be interpreted. (v. 23; To an Unknown Correspondent, 4 Feb. 1867)

Is the Canon of Scripture Based on Tradition Only?

[M]any books of the New Testament . . . are received on the custom of reading them in some Churches from the beginning, the testimony of one or two Fathers to one or two *verses* in them, and the fiat of the 4th century which formed the Canon. E.g. I speak without accurate investigation, but I believe St Paul to Philemon is received on a reference to it in Tertullian, . . . on a passage in Caius, and then by Origen and Eusebius. This is a favorable specimen – I think I am right in saying that not a single Latin Father for 3 centuries quotes the Epistle to the Hebrews, but Tertullian who gives it to S. Barnabas, Irenaeus and Hippolytus seem to have thought it not St Paul's, or not canonical – at all events it was not, I believe, received by the Roman Church in early times. I may be incorrect in these particular instances, but they serve as illustrations of what I think will be found to hold, viz that we receive great part of the Canon on less evidence than that produceable for prayers for the dead in Christ. The main evidence for both is the *reading* of the one and the *use* of the other in the Church from the beginning. (v. 6; To George Stanley Faber, 16 May 1838)

Are the Five Books of Moses (Pentateuch) of Late Origin?

There is an orderly growth of revelation, and a structure in the prophecies. Can any one believe that the books were all written after Ezra, or great part of them, so as to exhibit the scheme of progress intentionally? How is it, for instance, we do not find the doctrine of a future life in the Pentateuch, if it was garbled, interpolated, enlarged, at a late date? (v. 26; To R. W. Church, c. 24 March 1872)

Is There a Method to Proper Bible Interpretation?

[T]he sense of Scripture does not lie *in the bare letter,* but is that sense which the Sacred writer of each passage *intended* to be the sense. Thus it is that St Stephen 'fell asleep;' now this must not be interpreted in the letter, but in the sense which St Luke meant when he used the words; and he meant 'died,' or 'resigned his soul and body into our Lord's hands.' And so, when our Lord bids us 'hate' our parents, we have to ask His *sense,* and are not at liberty to put our own sense upon it. And so, when upon our Lord's ascension we are told that 'two *men* stood by the Apostles in white garments,' the question is what did St Luke mean to express by the word 'men'? And when we are told that 'a star appeared to the Wise men,' it has to be determined whether by a star St Matthew meant a real star or a meteor. And when he says that at the passion there was darkness 'over the universal earth,' we have to determine whether by this expression he meant the whole globe or Judea only. (v. 21; To an Unknown Correspondent, 19 March 1865)

Are Catholics Allowed to Interpret the Bible on Their Own?

[I]ndividuals . . . especially if they are learned and have the proper gifts of mind, have often a permission, or even a call, to interpret Scripture by their private judgment, provided they use the best lights which they can get, and ever profess themselves ready to submit all they may say in the way of interpretation to the judgment of the Church, should it ever be given. . . . This is the state of the case, and I think it immediately applies to most of the difficulties which you enumerate. I am not aware that the Infallible Church has ever told us what the Evangelists or other sacred writers *meant* in the passages of Scripture to which you refer. Therefore we must form our judgment on the matter as best we can, consulting commentators and divines, and making use of the sciences of History, Archaeology, Criticism and the like. (v. 21; To an Unknown Correspondent, 19 March 1865)

[T]he Church has not put forth any authoritative interpretation of Scripture, and doctors differ very much, and allowably, in the senses they affix to particular passages. (v. 24; To Miss Maria Rosina Giberne, 20 Aug. 1868)

How Are the Church Fathers Related to Bible Interpretation?

We are bound to interpret all Scripture by the unanimous consent of the Fathers . . . (v. 20; To Thomas Arnold, 11 Oct. 1862)

[T]he *Church*. . . refers us, as a standard of interpretation, to the consent of the Fathers; but it must be unanimous, which limits the application of this rule very materially, . . . (v. 21; To William Wordsworth, 22 Oct. 1864)

Does the Church Authoritatively Interpret Apostolic Tradition?

[T]he Church in all times is the *interpreter* of Apostolic doctrine. Thus, take the question whether our Lord was ignorant in His *human* nature or knew all things that man could know from the first – the Fathers differ on the point till the 6th century, when the Church settles the question in favour of His *knowledge*, by her infallible interpretation of Apostolic tradition. (v. 24; To Mrs. Helbert, 10 Sep. 1869)

[T]he rule of the Church is never to decree any doctrine to be of faith but what comes by tradition; but the infallible Church, while she always appeals to tradition, is the true judge and interpreter of it, not you or I. And therefore certainly, I say this, let *no one make a Catholic of you*, TILL you can say with me 'I believe all that the Church formally teaches to be the very word of God, revealed by His Son, transmitted by Him to His Apostles, and committed to the Church after them.' This you must believe. What the Church in Ecumenical Council declares or has declared is *final*; . . . (v. 24; To Mrs. Helbert, 28 Sep. 1869)

Is the Biblical Canon a Difficulty for Protestantism?

[T]he Canon was never formally settled; . . . there cannot be a more complete overthrow of the Protestant theory. . . . I do not think the Canon was settled till the fifth century really. Up to the end of the 4th the Latin Church did not receive the Hebrews, nor the Greek the Apocalypse. . . . What the Apocrypha is to the Pentateuch, Prophets and Psalms, such are the Hebrews, Apocalypse, St James, 2 and 3 St. John, 2 St Peter to the Gospels, Acts and Epistles. . . . there is clearer and earlier Catholic consent for the Church doctrines than for most of the books of the New Testament . . . (v. 7; To Mrs. William Froude, 8 Nov. 1840)

The books, comparatively deficient in evidence, which are received by Protestants, are the Epistle to the Hebrews, the Catholic Epistles of St James and 2nd St Peter, the 2nd and 3rd of St John, and the Apocalypse. I am not quite sure of St James being one of them. It was rejected by Luther, but, I fancy, on its internal evidence, as being contrary to his doctrine of justification by faith alone. Of the Hebrews and Apocalypse, the former was not received generally in the West, nor the latter in the East. As to the Old Testament, the books Protestants take, depend on the authority of the Jews, so that that of the Fathers is superseded by them. However, the book of Daniel (which Protestants acknowledge) was but doubtfully received, I think, by the Jews-

and is not found in the Septuagint Version. . . . Anyhow, the Jews are said to have looked doubtfully on the book of Daniel. (v. 16; To W. J. O'Neill Daunt, 16 March 1855)

Why is Tobit Considered Scripture by the Catholic Church?

Now as to the book of Tobit. First there is a difference between the edition in the Protestant Apocrypha and in the Catholic canon, e.g. in the Catholic edition there is nothing, I think, of the evil spirit being in love with Sara, or of *smells, perfumes*, driving him away. Next I do not think the style or tone are special, except as Daniel is special. The narrative style of Daniel is very different from that of the Pentateuch – and Tobit from that of Daniel – just as the miracles of Elijah and Elisha are different from those of Moses – and those of Moses from those of Our Lord. Further, is the history of Tobit on the whole stranger than the history of Samson? or consider that graphic account of Nabal's treatment of David Sam. XXV. . . . 'If the book of Tobit has errors the Church has erred, which says that it has no errors'. What are the specific errors of the book of Tobit? Is not the fish and its consequences the sole point in any attack which can be made upon it? And this difficulty I have in part at least removed. Is want of dignity and decorum an error? (v. 25; To Richard Holt Hutton, 27 April 1870)

What is the "Rule of Faith"?

'The Rule of faith' is an ambiguous expression, and I cannot answer your question till I know what you mean by it. It has been a received phrase from 'Scripture,' only during the last 150 years, as you will see drawn out in Tract 90. Before that time it was sometimes applied to Scripture, sometimes to the Creed, sometimes to both, sometimes to Tradition. In antiquity (as by Tertullian) it is the phrase for Tradition. (v. 9; To an Unknown Correspondent, 4 March 1843)

Christians agree in Christian doctrine, *not* because it is *eternal* and the object of their *moral sense*, but because it is actually *revealed*, and handed down to them by *tradition*. 'Consent' is the convenient witness and test *both* of moral truth *and* of revealed – but of moral, because it is seen and approved by the mind naturally; of revealed because it has been handed down by the Church to her children. . . . What comes from heaven as revelation, is attested first by miracles, next by the general voice of believers, or of the Church. Hence St Augustine says 'Securus judicat orbis terrarum.' (v. 26; To H. A. Woodgate, 23 Feb. 1872)

Is Sola Scriptura *("Scripture Alone") a True Principle?*

On what ground of reason or Scripture do you say that every one may gain the true doctrines of the gospel for himself from the Bible? where is illumination promised an *individual* for this purpose? where is it anywhere hinted that the aid of teachers is to be superseded? where that the universal testimony of the Church is not a principle of belief as sure and satisfactory as the word of Scripture? . . . Till you give it up, till you see that the unanimous witness of the whole Church (as being a witness to an historical fact, viz that the Apostles so taught), where attainable, is as much the voice of God (I do not say as sacredly and immediately so, but as really) as Scripture itself, there is no hope for a clearheaded man like you. (v. 5; To [brother] Francis William Newman, 23 Nov. 1835)

[Y]ou all along assume that Scripture is the standard of appeal but do not prove it. . . . It ought to be proved somewhere or other. (v. 6; To H. A. Woodgate, 23 Feb. 1838)

Nor . . . have I gone to the question whether individuals were even *intended* to find doctrinal truth for themselves from Scripture. I do not think they were. (v. 7; To Lord Adare, 28 Sep. 1840)

Father Newman presents his compliments to Sir Francis Goodrich, and feels much gratified at the news that he intends to honour him with his company . . . At the same time he fears Sir Francis may do so on a wrong impression. He has *never* intended to prove to Sir Francis the infallibility of the Roman Catholic church from the Holy Scriptures, . . . to do so would be to encourage a great yet common mistake on the part of Protestants as to the truth of the Catholic Church. Catholics never have held that their whole faith must be proved by Scripture. They do not consider that Scripture is the whole word of God, or sole rule of faith. Before then he could agree to do that, to which Sir Francis invites him, viz to prove the infallibility of the Roman Catholic Church from the Holy Scripture, he should wish to invite Sir Francis to prove first that nothing is revealed but what is contained in the Holy Scriptures. It will be a true satisfaction to him, if Sir Francis will condescend to call on him on March 4, with the intention of proving this previous proposition. (v. 13; To Sir Francis Goodricke, 26 Feb. 1850)

Does Prior Bias Influence Scriptural Interpretation?

The difficulty is this, *are* our notions so on the surface of Scripture that a plain person ought to see them there, at least when suggested to him? or again *how far* is the unpopularity of our notions among Scripture readers to be traced to Protestant blindness and prejudice? (v. 5; To Richard Hurrell Froude, 11 June 1835)

Should we Memorize Scripture?

If you have leisure time on Sunday, learn portions of Scripture by heart. The benefit seems to me incalculable. It imbues the mind with good and holy thoughts. It is a resource in solitude, on a journey, and in the sleepless night. (v. 1; To [sister] Harriet Newman, 13 Oct. 1823)

In What Sense is the Authority of Scripture Supreme?

The more I read of Athanasius, Theodoret etc. the more I see that the ancients did make Scripture the basis of their belief. . . . Scripture, according to the Fathers, is the authentic record and document of this faith. . . . Now this *theologia* [Greek in original], I say, the Fathers do certainly rest upon Scripture, as upon two tables of stone. . . . when they met together in Council, they brought the witness of Tradition as a matter of fact – but, when they discussed the matter in council, cleared their views etc etc. proved their point, they always went to Scripture alone. (v. 5; To Richard Hurrell Froude, 23 August 1835)

Is the Bible Materially Sufficient for Salvation?

That the Bible *contains* in it all things necessary to salvation, is undoubtedly true . . . (v. 2; Speech at the Bible Society Meeting, 29 May 1828)

The 6th Article says that Scripture contains all that is to be '*required* that it should be believed as an article of *the Faith*,' and 'thought requisite or necessary to salvation.' (v. 6; To George Stanley Faber, 11 April 1838)

The Tracts *nowhere* say that anything need be believed in order to salvation which is not contained in or can be proved from Scripture. (v. 9; To an Unknown Correspondent, 4 March 1843)

Is the Bible Formally Sufficient for Salvation?

I am still of opinion that the *great* evil of our want of theological knowledge is its resulting in differences of opinion. Men may say what they will about going by Scripture not tradition – but nature is stronger than systems. . . . As to Scripture being practically sufficient for making the Christian, it seems to me a mere dream – nor do I find it anywhere said so in Scripture – nor can I infer logically that what is confessedly *the* sole oracle of doctrine, is therefore also of *practice* and *discipline*. (v. 3; To E. B. Pusey, 5 Dec. 1832)

Is the Bible Inspired?

There has been, indeed, a distinct and strong tradition, both popular and devotional, in favour of its inspiration in the highest sense, and that tradition is still in vigour . . . What the Schola is unanimous in, (as far as I know,) is this: that there is *nothing* in the Scriptures but what is *true*. (v. 21; To William Wordsworth, 22 Oct. 1864)

[T]he words of Scripture have a power which no abstract or catechism can give. (v. 21; To Miss Mary Holmes, 9 May 1865)

Can the Bible Possibly Have Numerical Errors?

As to Luke ii, 2 it would be no shock to my feelings to find the Evangelist mistaken in a *secular* date. Why is a sacred writer to be inspired in profane history, when it does not actually come in his way? Where were the registers of Proconsulates and Procuratures kept? Why should the Roman annals be more familiarly known by him than the motions of the heavenly bodies? (v. 18; To Edmund O'Reilly, S. J., 25 May 1858)

As to Luke ii in so obscure a point of history, upon which ancient authorities and chronologists differ, it is enough to say that it is not of that vital importance to the inspiration of St Luke . . . [to] make it of consequence to decide upon it . . . (v. 18; To W. H. Scott, 7 June 1858)

Can Biblical Manuscripts *Possibly Contain Error?*

The veracity of Scripture is not compromised, though it be allowed that passages have crept into the text which do not belong to it. Thus a Catholic is not bound to receive the text of the Three Heavenly Witnesses [1 Jn 5:7-8]. (v. 21; To William Wordsworth, 22 Oct. 1864)

What is Oral Tradition?

Traditions are unwritten – so, to ask for a list of traditions in written works is a contradiction in terms. (v. 24; To Charlotte Wood, 18 Jan. 1869)

Does the New Testament Preclude Oral Tradition?

[T]he New Testament is not *Christianity*, but the *record* of Christianity. What if the Apostles have left no writing behind them, and their disciples have composed the gospels from the memory of their conversations, does it follow they cannot have had a divine commission? (v. 1; To [brother] Charles Robert Newman, 25 Aug. 1825)

I see he accuses me of allowing, or of having, no *experimental* knowledge of Scripture, because I say we receive it from the early Church. How strange he should not see that we receive it *both* from within *and* without! He should recollect the words of the Samaritans 'Now we believe, *not for thy saying*, for we ourselves have heard Him, and know that this is indeed the Saviour of the world.' John iv, 42. Yet a few verses before it is said 'Of that city many of the Samaritans believed in Him, *for the word of the woman* giving testimony, He told me all things whatsoever I have done.' In like manner the Church, (as the woman) is our original witness – and, as we act upon her word, and receive the gospel doctrine through her, whether in Scripture or by tradition, (for the doctrine is powerful in either channel, through which it comes to us) we gain an experimental knowledge of its truth, but we *begin* with the Church. This again is another incidental omission of your friend's, as if the doctrines of religion did not convert the heart *whether* they come to us through reading Scripture or the teaching, preaching, tradition, of missionaries, priests, and fellow Christians. He should recollect that the first conversions were made before the New Testament was written, and, even, after it was written, still without its aid[.] (v. 25; To C. Hussey Walsh, 22 April 1870)

Is Oral Tradition Superior to Written Tradition?

Men live after their death – or, still more, they live not in their writings or their chronicled history but in that unwritten memory exhibited in a school of pupils who trace their moral parentage to them. As moral truth is discovered, not by reasoning, but [by] habituation, so it is recommended not by books b[ut by] oral instruction. Socrates wrote nothing – authorship [is the] second-best way. (v. 2; To Samuel Rickards, 20 July 1830; "unwritten memory" is in Greek in the original and translated in a footnote. Brackets are in the original: i.e., as the portion appears in vol. 2)

Are Oral and Written Tradition Fundamentally Different?

As to tradition, I should speak thus: – *facts* of whatever kind are only known (except by miracle) in two ways – by senses and by testimony. Past facts cannot be known by senses and therefore are by testimony. Tradition resolves itself into testimony. A written or printed book is the testimony of a stranger – and believed because others bear witness to its trustworthiness. Tradition is the succession of testimonies, of each age to the next, of which the last link touches *you*. To say we believe by tradition is only to say we are told by persons *who* have been told by others who etc – Josiah would not have known the book of the Law to be divine by himself. He found it in a miraculous place, or the priests etc or Jeremiah would inform him. I do not think the difference of oral or written tradition alters the case – in either case it is testimony of a particular person, in oral, of the person who speaks to you – in written, of the person who wrote (i.e. perhaps some hundred years before) or (if you resolve this again) of the persons you have known, who testify to the supposed date of the writer. . . . we know facts by miracle or tradition, i.e. *including* in tradition its last link, *testimony made to us* personally, which last link often is *all*, i.e. in cases where the witness has *seen* the facts and does not take his account from a prior witness. (v. 6; To H. A. Woodgate, 23 May 1838)

How Should we Regard Extrabiblical Tradition?

Why may I not believe a thing not in the Bible, if I do not force the belief on others? . . . I claim the right of private judgment in matters *not* of 'the Faith'. Things may be true, [though] not declared in Scripture, e.g. the canonicity and inspiration of its books as they have come down to us. Again, I conceive that though the whole *faith* is in Scripture, yet *ordinances* need not [be] shown to be there. (v. 6; To George Stanley Faber, 11 April 1838; approximates Catholic belief, but not identical to it)

What is the Relation of Tradition to Church Authority?

[T]he line he would have you take is contrary to your duty to the Holy Catholic Church as imposed on you as a Christian in the article of the Creed, a duty not determined by private judgment, but by the voice of all saints in all times. (v. 9; To Thomas Mozley, 26 Sep. 1842)

It seems to us false, and we must ever hold, on the contrary, that the object of faith is *not* simply certain articles, A B C D, contained in dumb documents, but the whole word of God, explicit and implicit, as dispensed by His living Church. (v. 23; To Edward B. Pusey, 23 March 1867)

Till a point is actually *defined* by the Church, there will ever be confusion. It does not follow that a truth was not held, that there *was* confusion. (v. 24; To Edward B. Pusey, 4 July 1869)

What are Creeds?

My idea is this that the Apostles, without any reference to system, put down the *heads* of what they taught and called it the Creed. Their wording of it might vary at different times and places as our Lord varied His Prayer – but taken as a whole it was the same everywhere. . . . The descent into hell might have been an *original* article of the Creed of Aquileia. Accordingly I take the doctrine guaranteed by the Consensus omnium in early times to be the matter of which the Creed is a kind of form – and as to the doctrine of the Eucharist, I conceive it is maintained under 'the Church' or 'the Communion of Saints' – i.e. I conceive that the Creed was a help to the memory – and that when primitive teachers came to that Article 'the Church' or 'the Communion of Saints', *then* they brought in the Eucharist. . . . I conceive the Church cannot insert a new article in the Creed. The tone of the Athanasian Creed seems to me decisive of this – 'This is the Catholic Faith etc etc.' (v. 6; To Henry Edward Manning, 6 June 1838)

I have been accustomed to consider the Creed as the brief heads of the whole *tradition*, not a tradition in formal articles but a tradition of doctrine . . . (v. 9; To Edward B. Pusey, 1 Aug. 1842)

How Sure is the Deposit of Faith?

The faith is the foundation – it was laid in the beginning and no one can alter it. (v. 7; To Miss Mary Holmes, 10 June 1840)

Did the Jews Pass Down the Notion of Tradition to Christians?

[T]he Jews *had* tradition, first in Moses' words about writing on their foreheads, teaching their children, etc. vid Ps 79.1. etc. next there was the great post-captivity Tradition as evidenced first in the interpretations of the Septuagint – next by the Apocrypha – third by the Rabbinical and Christian writers – the doctrines of the atonement, our Lord's divinity etc. seem to be thus clearly handed down. (v. 6; To H. A. Woodgate, 23 Feb. 1838)

Were the Apostles Ignorant of Tradition Until Pentecost?

[Y]ou must not say the Apostles were quite ignorant till the day of Pentecost – Our Lord spent 40 days teaching them the things which belong to the Kingdom of God – moreover before the end of the 40 days, they chose another Apostle, . . . which implies a good deal. (v. 6; To H. A. Woodgate, 23 Feb. 1838)

Can One Possibly be Saved by Conscience Without Revelation?

[T]o all men (to speak generally) light enough is given for practical religious purposes – enough to lead them to heaven, and to condemn them if they do not employ themselves in disciplining and changing their moral nature. For all have a natural conscience, which at once exhorts them to virtue and by an instinctive vigor extracts from even the worst religious systems those better parts and real truths which relate to the being, providence, and moral governance of God. No one is vicious but by his own fault: for conscience and God's Spirit set him right on his first starting, till he blunts the one and quenches the other. (v. 2; To [brother] Charles Robert Newman, 19 Aug. 1830)

Is Conscience an Autonomous Authority?

I sincerely trust that my conscience, enlightened by the Bible, through the influence of the Holy Spirit, may prove a faithful and vigilant guardian of the principles of religion. (v. 1; To Walter Mayers, Jan. 1817)

What is Heresy and How Should it be Viewed?

[H]eresy . . . is not so much a positive doctrine, as the holding [of] a particular doctrine to the exclusion of other doctrines. (v. 7; To [brother] Francis W. Newman, 22 Oct. 1840)

I do not see that I am called upon to state what I mean by the *heresy* of Lutheranism and Calvinism. Heresy has its external Notes like the Church. Any novel doctrine, any doctrine which meets with general condemnation is a heresy. (v. 8; To J. R. Hope, 24 Nov. 1841)

[T]he presence of a heresy is always a sufficient reason for demanding an anathema. (v. 8; To T. D. Acland, 25 Nov. 1841)

No one is a real heretic who is not *wilfully* so. (v. 31; To Catherine Ward, 12 Oct. 1848)

Those who contradict opinions *everywhere received* are heretics – the Reformers professed to do this. It required then no Council or Pope to make them heretics. The (historical) principle and watchword of the Reformation was that *doctrine* was to be reformed, that doctrinal error was universal. Both could not be right; either Rome or England was heretical. (v. 13; To Mrs. Martha Lockhart, 5 Nov. 1849)

Alas, I fear great multitudes *have* fallen [from baptismal grace], and they have no second sacrament, of Penance, to restore them. But if souls fall into sin, are they therefore to be hated and avoided? Among these mortal sins is heresy – no one is really a heretic who is in invincible ignorance – and *I* cannot be certain who are invincibly ignorant, who not. Thus there are *two* reasons why I should not dream of avoiding a member of the Church of England, first, because he may *not* be formally and really a heretic, secondly because, tho' he were, he is to be loved and reclaimed by love, not by repulsion. When persons indeed are formal apostates, or set up new heresies, are the authors of new divisions, and found new schools, the case if different. Such persons were especially shunned in the early Church – but even this is a matter of *discipline*, and for wise reasons the rule of the Church is not so severe on such matters as it was. (v. 13; To Mrs. Wootten, 30 March 1850)

As to the severe view we take of heresy in the abstract, this arises out of the nature of the case. As rebellion is the correlative and antagonistic sin to the fact of a ruler, as want of natural affection is the critical sin of a mother *as such*, so a denial of revealed truth is the characteristic, disorganizing, disintegrating sin of a soul to which revelation comes. That is, if it comes and only when it comes – that is, not when it only seems to come, when a man is asleep, or deaf, or ignorant invincibly; then it has the *look* of heresy, the outward shape, the position, or is what is called *material* heresy, but is without the guilt. 'Whoso sheddeth man's blood, by men etc.' [Gen 9:6] No one would take this to be a justification of putting to death an involuntary homicide. How is wilful deliberate opposition to what a man knows to be a revelation, or might know, if he chose, more excusable than wilful murder? You recollect the present Pope has pointedly excepted from sin those who are ignorantly in heresy. (v. 25; To Richard Holt Hutton, 24 Feb. 1870)

Chapter Nine

Doctrine of the Church (Ecclesiology)

Is There Such a Thing as One Visible, Institutional Church?

St. Paul . . . calls the Church 'a pillar and ground of the truth;' . . . when I find that Scripture speaks of 'a pillar and ground,' and enforces discipline; that the Apostles made use of an exact organization in preaching the Gospel, and, moreover, that in matter of fact almost every Christian body that ever existed has attempted it, it does not seem hazardous to enlarge upon the advantages of it. (v. 4; To the Editor of *The Record*, 14 Nov. 1833)

Somehow I cannot deny that some clear notes are promised in Scripture to the Christian Church . . . a 'city set on a hill,'[Mt 5:14] our 'eyes seeing our teachers' [St. Irenaeus, *Against Heresies*, V, 1] etc. (v. 9; To John Keble, 6 Sep. 1843)

If your Lordship asks me *why I* maintain that my communion is *the* Church, the answer (to me) is so plain, that I do not know what can be said against it. I felt its force when I was a Protestant, and have done my utmost to overcome it, but in vain. The reason is this: – the Church is a *kingdom* – so our Lord says. . . . Is it an *invisible* kingdom? no Anglican will say so. Well then if it be a visible kingdom, *where* is such a kingdom, visible and yet spiritual, all over the earth except the Catholic Church? (v. 15; To Lord Charles Thynne, 18 Jan. 1852)

There is but one Church, that which, not only is, but also is even called Catholic, and ever has been so called, for the guidance of all who seek her. No other body has the promises; in no other is there salvation; and in proportion as souls begin to understand this, do they become answerable for the light vouchsafed to them. (v. 21; To Lavinia Wilson, 29 Nov. 1864)

St Paul says that the Church is the pillar and ground of the Truth. He says that there is *One* Body as there is *One* Faith. Our Lord has built His Church on Peter. (v. 22; To Lady Chatterton,   29 March 1866)

As to your first question, 'Are you indeed *one* in doctrine in the Roman Catholic Church?' the only true answer is, that we are and ever have been *one*, and that is one of the special notes of our being the True Church. It is one which has had a special effect on intellectual men not Catholics, when they have happened to become intimate with Catholics and to witness the action of the Church. Our faith is one. This great fact, however, is quite consistent with another – viz. that in those things which are not of faith, there has been considerable difference of opinion, among Catholics, and often serious and bitter quarrels. . . . Religion is so deeply interesting and sovereign a matter, and so possesses the whole man, when it once gains its due entrance into the mind, that it is not wonderful, that, as worldly men quarrel fiercely about worldly things, so, through the weakness of human nature, particular theologians have had unchristian disputes about Christian truths. Such have been the quarrels of some of the religious orders with each other; and I cannot deny that, from the existing events of the day, there have arisen undue contentions about points not essential, at this time also. But the Holy See, and the Bishops of the Church, and the School of Theologians are not committed to these extravagances. (v. 24; To Albert Smith, 8 Jan. 1868)

I do think communion with Rome is *necessary* for a person being in the Visible Church. Indeed, did I not think so, I never should have left the Anglican Church[.] (v. 24; To Edward B. Pusey, 24 May 1868)

It is the duty of every one whom God enlightens to see that the Catholic Church, that is the Church in communion with Rome, is the only true Church, the one fold of Christ, and Ark of Salvation . . . (v. 24; To Gilbert Simmons, 28 June 1868)

I do not see how any one can doubt, looking at the matter dispassionately, that the Church now (as ever) in communion with Rome is the Church set up by the Apostles. Some persons believe it to be the Church *because* it is in communion – this proposition, that Rome is the centre of unity, I believe as a *doctrine*, taught by the Church, and indisputable – but, while I quite allow another to be brought into the Church on the ground that union with Rome is the logical differentia of the Church, I was not so brought myself but by the visible identity of the ancient Church and the present Roman communion. In the same way that I hold the See of Rome to be the centre of unity on the word of the Church, so I should believe that See infallible, . . . (v. 24; To Sir John Simeon, 8 May 1869)

Now the very reason I became a Catholic was because the present Roman Catholic Church is *the only Church* which is like, and it is very like, the primitive Church, the Church of St Athanasius . . . It is almost like a photograph of the primitive Church; or at least it does not differ from the primitive Church near so much as the photograph of a man of 40 differs from his photograph when 20. *You know that it is the same man.* (v. 24; To Mrs. Helbert, 30 Aug. 1869)

In Scripture, we are told that to become interested in the promises, we must *join* the Church. The first Christians are represented as continuing in the *fellowship* of the Apostles – and those who were to be saved are said to have been added by Almighty God to His *Church*. The Apostles were visible men – the Church was a visible body, St Paul speaks of the Church as 'the pillar and ground of the Truth,' [1 Tim 3:15] thereupon it was a visible teaching body. If a man commit a fault against another, that other is directed by our Lord to 'tell it to the Church,' [Mt 18:17] – therefore the Church was a visible body. And the earliest Fathers as the Martyrs St Ignatius and St Cyprian, both of them in the clearest way speak of the Church as a visible body. Therefore the Church is the Ark of salvation, and it is necessary to join a visible body. I can understand a man doubting, *which* is the Church, at first sight, but not his doubting that it is a duty to join the Church, if he can find it. As to the question 'Which is the Church of *Christ*?' Of course it would puzzle any one – but there *is* a question which would puzzle no one. In the Creed we profess belief in 'the *Catholic* Church' – Now then go into any town, and ask for 'the Catholic Church,' and you know whither you would be directed. This is no accident – the early Fathers insist on it – they say that no sect *can* take the title of 'the Catholic Church.' Fourteen hundred years ago St Cyril of Jerusalem says to his Catholic hearers 'When you go into a strange place do not ask for 'the Church,' for you will be sent to some sect – but ask for "the Catholic Church", and you will be directed right.' (v. 25; To S. S. Shiel, 25 Jan. 1870)

Is the Church Infallible in Her Dogmas?

I conceive you are right in what you say of the Church Catholic never having been in any essential error. (v. 6; To H. A. Woodgate, 23 May 1838)

I believe the One Church is infallible in doctrine, and to be obeyed in all things . . . (v. 10; To Robert Francis Wilson, 25 Sep. 1845)

As to my own opinion, I should have fancied the doctrine of infallibility was implicit in every act of the Holy See and of the Church, as the necessary *account* of those acts – as, if a man said, '*Why* is a dead fish heavier than a live one,' he implies the *fact*. Catholics never say that *all* doctrines must have been passed in *Council* etc. The very idea of tradition is something unwritten, which happens to be consigned to Decrees and Canons when it is, in this or that particular, doubted. No one ever doubted that infallibility is a doctrine of the Roman Church. If the doubt arose and grew among us, the Church would be sure to be down upon it. (v. 13; To Frederick A. Faber, 20 Oct. 1849)

1. There must be ever in the world a continuation of the Primitive Church. 2 that continuation is infallible. 3. It is no other than the Roman. 4. What the Roman says is to be received. (v. 14; To Francis Richard Wegg-Prosser, 10 Sep. 1851)

My own proof of it would be such as this: – that our Lord set up a Church in the beginning which was to last to the end; that it was to retain His revelation faithfully; that the present Catholic Church is that destined continuation of it; that therefore prima facie it teaches now in substance what it taught then; that its early vague teaching is to be explained and commented on by its later and fuller; and, as to Infallibility, that, to say the least, there is nothing in its early teaching of a *positive* nature to hinder the interpretation of the early teaching on that point which is contained in its later teaching. (v. 18; To J. M. Capes, 10 August 1858)

[Y]ou know I suppose that the Decrees of Trent are not de fide, only the Canons. (v. 21; To Edward B. Pusey, 8 Jan. 1865)

I heard yesterday . . . that you had given up the doctrine of the infallibility of the Church. Though it is so short a time since you told me to say on your authority that you had no intention of giving up Catholicism as soon as you left Birmingham, I fear my informant is not mistaken. (v. 21; To Thomas Arnold, 4 June 1865)

The Church (or Pope) can determine the sense of the depositum – she can declare its implicit meanings – she can declare what contradicts it – she can declare what in its nature subserves it (i.e.

pious opinion) or is prejudicial to it, (i.e. what is erroneous, false, near heresy, savouring of heresy, etc) – she can declare its concrete manifestations, as that the inspiration originally given at Pentecost is carried out in the *particular* Epistle to the Hebrews (i.e. that it is canonical) or that certain five truths of the depositum are contradicted in the Augustinus of Jansen (i.e. a dogmatic fact.) – but all these enunciations are to be received by Catholics BECAUSE they *directly* relate to the depositum, *not* as being mere utterances of the Church or Pope. Next, I have said, 'they are to be received; –' but *how* received? as *infallible*? I have no difficulty in so receiving them myself, but I have yet to discover that it is de fide, or that there is a consensus scholar, that they *are* infallible. . . . *I* do not deny that in all these enunciations the Church is infallible and certain; – and is to be believed fide, not humana sed divina – divina *et* ecclesiastical. But while on the one hand I would destroy the distinction between infallible and certain, divine and ecclesiastical, as unintelligible, so on the other I would deny that the Church's infallibility stretches beyond those matters which are related to, which bear upon, the depositum. E.g. Muzzarelli, I suppose, would say, You are bound to believe under pain of damnation that 'the Pope's temporal power is necessary towards the spiritual in these times', because in saying so he is infallible or at least certain – but, according to my present information, I am not bound so to believe, unless 1. the Church in Council or at least ex Cathedra Petri said it – and 2. said it, with the *profession* that it came from tradition from the Apostles, and with the other formal requisites of a definition. Till this was done, I should not think the Church or Pope infallible or certain in saying it, because it did not *intrinsically bear upon* the depositum or was *in* the depositum implicitly (according to my apprehension) and it had not the extrinsic proof of it, arising out of the Church's authoritative declaration, that it *did* bear upon or was implied in the depositum. And if, to go back a step, as to what I have said above, it be asked me *why* I believe that the Church is infallible in her declarations as to what *subserves*, *prejudices*, and concretely *exhibits* the depositum, I answer that I do so on the general principle, that in all creatures nature is sufficient for herself, or is gifted with a self-conservative power – and thus that the Church has a true divine instinct as to what is good or bad for the depositum, which in fact is her life, as well as her charge. (v. 22; To Henry Ignatius Dudley Ryder, 16 July 1866)

[S]he is infallible in greater questions of morals – that is, . . . she will *always be protected* from all acts seriously infringing on that moral law, . . . (v. 24; To Mrs. Helbert, 20 Oct. 1869)

We can but leave the matter to God, and rest confidently in His protection of His Infallible Church and the guidance of the Holy Ghost. (v. 25; To Francis Diederich Wackerbarth, 28 June 1870)

I had always thought, and think still, that the infallibility of the Church is an *inference* (a necessary inference) from her prerogative that she is the divinely appointed Teacher of her children, and of the world. She cannot fulfil this office *without* divine help – that is, she never can be *permitted* to *go wrong* in the truths of revelation – This is a negative proposition – the very idea of infallibility is a negative. She teaches by human means, she ascertains the truth by human means – of course assisted by grace, but so is every inquirer; and she has *in kind* no promise of invincible grace, which a Father or a divine, or an inquirer has not – but she has this security, that, in order to fulfil her office, her *outcome* is always true in the matter of revelation. She is not inspired – the word has sometimes been used, and in Councils especially – but, properly speaking, inspiration is positive, and infallibility is negative; and a definition may be absolute truth, though the grounds suggested for it in the definition, the texts, the patristic authorities, the historical passages, are all mistakes. In saying this, I think I speak with Bellarmine and Fr Perrone. Perhaps I am used to only one school of theology, but I never heard of any view besides that which I am drawing out[.] (v. 25; To Alfred Plummer, 3 April 1871)

I can only advise you, as I have ever advised others in these days of difficulty, to have recourse to the Revelation of God, whatever it be, and there find your peace. If He has appointed a Prophet in His Church for His people, you must not set up another contrary to him. The Church is infallible because God has made it so. (v. 31; To Frederick Baker, 3 June 1890)

How is an Infallible Church Similar to a Prophet?

Now when you once fix your mind on this principle steadily, that, if God has spoken, He must have His organ or Prophet, I think you will see at once that the Catholic (or Roman Catholic) Church is that Prophet. Consider what is meant by the word Prophet, what *is the idea* which it conveys. I am not asking you to go by taste, or imagination, or feeling, or previous notions, or whatever is often included under the name and the exercise of *private* judgment in deciding what 'Prophet' means, but use the judgment not of a private person, not of yourself, but of all mankind, use what may be called *public* judgment, in determining this question, *what must a prophet be like*. Now surely it is no private judgment, but it is a mere explanation of the word to which all will assent to say that a Prophet must come *from* God, must *say* that he comes from God, must *know* what he has to tell, must be able to answer all questions which are put to him on the subject of his message, must be *firm and resolute* against all opposers or corrupters of it. He must be up to his office, up to emergencies, and consistent in his view of his duty. Has any so called Church any claim to answer such a description, (which I say is involved in the very idea of a prophet) but the Church of Rome? Is not the question reduced to this – either the Church of Rome is God's organ or He has none? And is not this conclusion arrived at without any private judgment at all? for my description of a prophet is nothing private . . . (v. 15; To William Pope, 15 April 1853)

Is Infallible Proof Required to Accept an Infallible Church?

First, I should say that *the word of God must* be infallible; if then God *has* spoken, what He has said must be true, and His organ of communication must be infallible. This I suppose you would allow, and then your question becomes this –, not, can the Infallibility of the Church be demonstrated, but can there be a demonstration (such as may legitimately be demanded) 1. that God has spoken, 2. that God has spoken by the Church. Now, as to the former of these two propositions, if an inquirer be an orthodox Protestant Christian, whether High Church or Low Church, he has no doubt at all about answering it in the affirmative. He will say that there is *sufficient* proof that the Bible is the word of God, and therefore true. But if I were to ask him 'do you think the proof *infallible*?' he would not perhaps know what to answer, he might say yes, or he might say no – but any how he would say that it was *sufficient* – and, if I could convince him that it would not be sufficient, *unless* it were infallible, he would have no hesitation in saying that in that case the proof *was* infallible; – so sure would he be of it. . . . I know well that the argument as you put it 'An infallible Church must have an infallible proof' is very common with Protestants; I have used it myself before now; but I think it should be held by those only who are not Protestants, but go much further. For surely it is to say with Hume that Revelation is incapable of demonstration, or that it is more likely than [that] testimony should be false than miracles true. If you ask me my own answer to the question, I shall feel only this reluctance in giving it, that it involves a great deal of definition and discrimination which I could not get through on a sheet of paper. I should have to determine what is meant by an infallible proof ere etc. Therefore I will only say this, that I agree with High Church and Low Church Protestant so far, as to be unable to see any metaphysical or a priori difficulty in holding on *moral* evidence and with a *moral* conviction that 'God is *infallible*, His word is *true*, and there is an *existing organ*, instrument, or record of His word –,' – and that I think the onus probandi lies with those who do feel it. (v. 31; To Frank Scott Haydon, 14 April 1858)

Your letter certainly puts forward an objection to religious evidence as far-spreading as it is deep; nor am I the person to undervalue it, though I utterly disallow its force for the purpose to which you put it. Thus to feel towards it implies no inconsistency, as I hope will appear from the answer I shall make to it. You ask, 'Must there not be an infallible evidence for the existence of an Infallible Church?' I would rather word the question thus, – 'Can I be certain that God is true, and that God has spoken?' And I prefer to throw it into this shape, because I then understand what I mean better, while I keep to the real point which is necessary in the argument for Catholicism. . . . You would question whether it is possible, from the nature of the case and antecedently, that we should have an infallible proof that God has spoken, or spoken this or that; you question whether there is not an antecedent impossibility of an infallible proof even in mathematics. I am disposed to agree with you here; but then, I make a distinction between the *judgment* of the mind as to the cogency of a conclusion, and the *state* of mind consequent upon that judgment. The 47th proposition of Euclid book 1st is certainly open to the objection, that the proof involves a grasp of previous propositions, which I cannot trust my memory to have accomplished. In my *judgment* then it is not absolutely demonstrated, 'without the taint of probability;' but *certainty* is not this judgment, it is a *state of mind,* and in spite of my *judgment* in disparagement of the *proof,* I suppose I am *certain,* without any sort of apprehension lest I should be mistaken, that the proposition in question is *true.* At the same time I consider it will be granted me, that the state of mind, which we call certainty depends ultimately on the will, which *could* so act upon the mind, as to lead it (morbidly) to use that microscopic objection as an occasion of *doubting* the truth of the proposition in question. In like manner, when I say that the existing proof, of a certain person or body being the oracle of that God who can neither deceive nor be deceived, is sufficient for certainty, I mean no more than that certainty is the state of mind to which that proof *legitimately* leads, and will lead unless an act of will is interposed to hinder such a result. How often do we say, 'I cannot prove it, but I firmly believe it, I am sure of it;' that is, 'though I cannot draw out a proof which is clear of all logical objection, I feel I possess one which is sufficient in reason for my accepting a certain conclusion.' Am I not certain that England is an island? am I not certain that I shall die? yet let me try, if I can, to make out a demonstration for either proposition. I may surely then take it as a *law* of the human mind that 'proof, speculatively incomplete, is sufficient (not only for practical, but) for speculative belief; or again, that 'objection and doubt are not correlatives.' (connatural?) Am I to go on to doubt of the truth of the laws of the human mind? If so, there are no laws of *reasoning* inclusively. Am I to go on, till I am sceptical of my own scepticism, and, though I condescend *practically* to follow what is probable or what is safest, to be allowed rationally to entertain *speculative* doubts whether I live or feel? . . . I assume then the being and presence of a Moral Governor of mankind, and I look at every thing which comes to me as coming from Him. The question simply is, What are the laws of thought, of belief, of conduct, under which my mind lies? Whatever they are, they are His imposing. I have only to ascertain them. He might have willed, that, as the Angels, I should need no middle terms at all; and now that He teaches me by means of inferences, I may see clearly that it is His will, that is, that it is a law of my nature, that they need not be infallible ones. I may have clear intimations, from a diligent scrutiny into the phenomena of human life and the course of the world, that He does not mean doubt to be the necessary consequence of logical imperfection. That is, it may be my duty to do in religion, what I continually do in matters of this world. . . . I do not know what others will think of such a view of the matter; for myself I can only say, that in matter of fact, from this abiding conviction that God is over us, though I am as keenly sensitive as any one to objections, I have at no time had any tendency to religious doubt. . . . Now I will suppose a powerful sceptical philosophy to bring out forcibly the 'taint of probability' attaching to mathematical demonstrations. In such a case surely it would not be preposterous in any one who felt it embarrass him in the prosecution of that science to repel doubt by a strong act of the will, and to make an act of faith in the conclusions of Euclid or Newton and that on the broad principle that objection is not necessarily the parent of doubt. And in like manner I think it possible to have such evidence that the Church is the oracle of the Almighty, as to make it a duty towards Him to accept her as such, under the conviction that He would not have invested her with evidence of such quality, though not demonstrative, unless He had meant thereby to signify to us the objective truth of a conclusion, to which proof at least points; and this, something in the way that I understand the signs and signals of my superior, whom I know well, though they are not drawn out into formal sentences. (v. 18; To Frank Scott Haydon, 24 April 1858)

Must we Believe All Dogmas that the Church Teaches?

It is quite true that the Catholic Church claims your absolute sub-mission to her in matters of faith – Unless you believe her doctrines as the word of God revealed to you through her, you can gain no good by professing to be a Catholic – you are not one really. At the same time she does not ask your confidence without giving reasons for claiming it – and one mode of proving her divine authority among others, certainly is . . . to see whether certain of her doctrines are not *like* truth, or reasonable, or scriptural, or conformable to the state of the world. . . . you must think it enough to prove her doctrines *to a certain point* – and then your argument will be this, '*Since* I have been able to prove the Catholic doctrines *so far*, I will take the whole on faith –' just as you trust an informant who has in other matters already shown he has a claim to be trusted. (v. 14; To Mrs. Lucy Agnes Phillips, 5 June 1851)

This I trust I may say, that if there be a man in the whole Church, who from faith, obedience, and love towards her would rejoice and exult in sacrificing any opinion of his own at the bidding of his Ecclesiastical superiors (if I dare speak of myself), I am the man. I have ever detested the spirit of shuffling and concealment of opinion, . . . (v. 15; To the Editor of *The Tablet*, 14 Sep. 1852)

I had no wish at all to say or hold any thing whatever but what the Church said and held . . . (v. 15; To Nicholas Cardinal Wiseman, 14 Nov. 1852)

[I]t became me, of all men first, to set an example of submission. No good ever came of resisting the appointed Pastors of the flock. It is they who are the guardians of doctrine, they who have to give an account of souls; they who are answerable, if the Church suffers. I will never be so rash, as not to leave them their responsibility, pure and simple, having this duty only in regard to it, viz. to help them with my prayers. When I became a Catholic, I sent a message to Dr Baggs, that, at the word of the Bishops, I would put into the fire my then out-coming book on Development of Doctrine; and now, had I been writing on those subjects which most deeply interest and distress me at this time, I trust I should have been equally ready to suppress my own convictions at the bidding of the Church. (v. 20; To William G. Ward, 28 Dec. 1862; this portion sent also to Bishop Ullathorne two days later)

[T]he act of faith, as we consider, must ever be partly explicit, partly implicit; viz 'I believe whatever God has revealed, whether I know it or not;' or 'I believe *whatever* has been and whatever shall be defined as revelation by the Church who is the organ of the revelation;' or again 'I believe in the Church's teaching, whether explicit or implicit,' . . . This rule applies both to learned and to ignorant; for, as the ignorant, who does not understand theological terms, must say 'I believe the Athanasian Creed in that sense in which the Church puts it forward,' or 'I believe that the Church is veracious –' so the learned, though they do understand the theological wording of that Creed, and can say intelligently what the ignorant cannot say, . . . still have need to add, 'I believe it because the Church has declared it,' and 'I believe all that the Church has defined or shall define as revealed,' and 'I absolutely submit my mind with an inward assent to the Church, as the teacher of the whole faith.' (v. 23; To Edward B. Pusey, 22 March 1867)

Do not let any one fancy she can be a Catholic, unless she can promise deliberately to receive all that the Church holds or *shall* hold as revealed truth. Many there are, who are received hastily, and fall away. (v. 25; To Helen Bradley, 28 April 1871)

[W]hile you have a clear consciousness that you reject any dogma of the Catholic Church you cannot go to confession with the hope of gaining absolution. (v. 25; To John Pym Yeatman, 25 May 1871)

What Are Catholics Free to Not *Believe?*

I hardly know what you ask for, when you want a definition of the word 'Submission'. To submit to the Church means this, first that you will receive as de fide whatever she proposes de fide; that you will submit to the decisions of Schola Theologorum, when unanimous in matters of faith and morals, as being so sure that it is forbidden to contradict them – that you obey the commands of the Church in act and deed, though as a matter of policy prudence etc. you may think that other commands would be better. You are not called on to believe de fide any thing but what has been promulgated as such – You are not called on to exercise an internal belief of any doctrine which Sacred Congregations, Local Synods, or particular Bishops, or the Pope as a private Doctor, may enunciate. You are not called upon ever to believe or act against the moral law, at the command of any superior. You are not bound to put yourself under the direction of any Priest, except as a matter of counsel, not of precept – and so on. (v. 20; To William Robert Brownlow, 25 Oct. 1863)

All we can say is that *so much* actually *is* de fide; and then allow a large margin of doctrine, which we accept as de fide implicitly, so far forth as God by His Church shall make it known. All one can say is, that till God illuminates the Church on a point, the children of the Church are obliged, and so are at liberty, to go by their best judgment . . . (v. 21; To Edward B. Pusey, 4 Jan. 1865)

Can we be Absolutely Certain of Church Doctrines?

The absolute certainty of faith in the truth of what the Church conveys to you from God, is the reward, through divine grace, of those souls who, before receiving it, have exercised their mental powers to the best; and you must throw yourself, in regard to it, on the Power, Love, and Faithfulness of Him who calls you. (v. 17; To Mrs. Catherine Froude, 20 May 1856)

What is the Difference Between Doctrines and Articles of Faith?

I do not see how a doctrine can be called 'an article of Christian faith' till it has been proposed by the Church. Since then certain books of the Canon were not so proposed in the earliest times, I do not see how they were articles of Christian faith in those times. Next, till they were so proposed, they might, I conceive, be 'doubted or denied without heresy' – certainly without formal heresy. The argument you maintain from the parallelism of the circumstances of the doctrine of the Canon and that of the Immaculate Conception seems to me correct. (v. 16; To W. J. O'Neill Daunt, 31 Aug. 1855)

Are Dogmas and Theological Opinions Two Different Things?

And so again as to theological *opinions*. There have always been over-earnest persons, who have advocated one or another of these opinions; as if they were dogma. But dogma is one thing, and opinion is another; – there are a number of persons in 1864 as well as in former times, who confuse the two. When a writer puts forward an opinion of his own, though it be a true one, as vital, he seems to me to be committing a great offence against the Catholic faith itself. . . . there is a spirit afloat, not less now than at other times, on the surface of society, in publications of the day, and in public transactions, with which I wish to have nothing to do – a spirit of arbitrary assumption in matters on which the Church has determined nothing. (v. 21; To Fanny Margaret Taylor, 10 March 1864)

[B]efore the Church decides, there may be two opposite *beliefs*, while, when she *has* decided, there is one *faith* . . . (v. 22; To the Earl of Denbigh, 1 April 1866)

Here I think you confuse theology with dogma. Dogma for the most part deals with propositions, theology is fertile in terms. Theology is for the learned and is scientific and difficult. Dogma is not scientific, not obscure and is for high and low. What can be simpler than the propositions 'there is One God,' or the Holy Ghost is God, or 'Jesus Xt is God,' 'Jesus Xt is man.' These are dogmas. Of course when such propositions are compared together, there at once issues mystery, questioning, argument, definition, science, theology; and that, according to the intelligence of the individual, that is, *just according to his capability* for *understanding* theology. Theology then is the answer or the correlative to the inquiring mind. But a child or a village old woman may take in the whole of dogma, without having to believe even one mystery, because such a one takes each proposition by itself without comparison. So much as to propositions; but as to terms, which the young, the poor, the uneducated, nay unread laymen generally need not, are not called on to, understand, these belong to theology, such as sanctification, regeneration, justification, transubstantiation and the like. (v. 23; To an Unknown Correspondent, 4 Feb. 1867)

The words then of Councils etc on the subject of the Pope's powers are (to a certain degree) vague, as you say, and indefinite; even for this reason, viz. from the strong reluctance, which has been ever felt, to restrict the liberty of thinking and judging more than was absolutely necessary, as a matter of sacred duty, in order to the maintenance of the revealed depositum. It has always been trusted that the received belief of the faithful and the obligations of piety would cover a larger circuit of doctrinal matters than was formally claimed, and secure a more generous faith than was imperative on the conscience. (v. 23; To Edward B. Pusey, 22 March 1867)

In all times the debates in the Schools have been furious, and it is in this way, out of the collision of flint and steel, that the light of truth has been struck and elicited. Controversialists have ever accused each other of heresy – and at times Popes have interfered; and put forth Bulls to the effect that, if any one called another a heretic out of his own head, he should lie under the censure of the Church. (v. 23; To Henry Wilberforce, 21 July 1867)

How Authoritative are Ecumenical Councils?

Of course what the General Council speaks is the word of God-but still we may well feel indignant at the intrigue, trickery, and imperiousness which is the human side of its history – and it seems a dereliction of duty not to do one's part to meet them. (v. 23; To J. Walker of Scarborough, 10 Nov. 1867)

We are all in great anxiety about the definitions of the Council. Of course in it cannot go beyond the will of God, but the spirit of many of the prime leaders is to me simply intolerable, and is *not* according to God's will surely. (v. 25; To Edward Bellasis, 2 March 1870)

That I deeply deplore the policy, the spirit, the measures of various persons, lay and ecclesiastical, who are urging the definition of that theological opinion, I have neither intention nor wish to deny; just the contrary. But, on the other hand, I have a firm belief, and have had all along, that a Greater power than that of any man or set of men will over-rule the deliberations of the Council to the determination of Catholic and Apostolic truth, and that what its Fathers eventually proclaim with one voice will be the Word of God. (v. 25; To the editor of *The Standard*, 15 March 1870)

[W]hatever the Council, as a Council determines, of course I will unreservedly accept[.] (v. 25; To Sir Rowland Blennerhassett, 24 March 1870)

. . . holding, as I do, the absolute divinity of any formal dogma, which an Ecumenical Council, as a Council, declares . . . (v. 25; To Sir John Simeon, 24 March 1870)

I suppose in all Councils there has been intrigue, violence, management, because the truth is held in earthen vessels. But God over rules. I do not see that the Vatican Council or the Council of Florence, is worse than the 2nd General Council in this respect, or than the 3rd. And the Fathers of the 4th may be said to have turned round at the word of a Pope[.] (v. 25; To J. J. Ignaz von Döllinger, 9 April 1870)

I certainly think this agitation of the Pope's Infallibility most unfortunate and ill-advised – and I shall think so even if the Council decrees it, unless I am obliged to believe that the Holy Ghost protects the Fathers from all inexpedient acts, (which I do not see is anywhere promised) as well as guides them into all the truth, as He certainly does. (v. 25; To W. J. O'Neill Daunt, 27 June 1870)

[T]he definition, if valid, has been passed under the Presence and Aid of the Holy Ghost . . . (v. 25; To Ambrose Phillipps de Lisle, 24 July 1870)

I have always inclined to the notion that a General Council was the magisterial exponent of the Creed, just as the judges of England are the legal expounders of the statutes of our realm. (v. 25; To Georges Darboy, Archbishop of Paris, end of 1870?)

What is the Relation of Popes to Ecumenical Councils?

[I]t is quite true, and Gallicans acknowledge it that without the Pope's confirmation the doctrinal decree of an Ecumenical Council does not stand – it is not Ecumenical without the Pope, but it does not *therefore* follow that the Council is confined to matters of discipline and cannot define doctrine *with* the Pope. 'Articles of faith not matters of discussion' – no, not when they are articles of faith – but before they are defined, they are discussed in two ways – 1. the testimony of the Bishops is asked and the authoritative declarations, of the Fathers and former times. 2. the expedience of defining is discussed. . . . I don't believe at all that a General Council can decree any thing which the Divine Head of the Church does not will to be decreed. (v. 24; To Sir John Simeon, 8 May 1869)

Is the Church Indefectible?

The Holy Church nowhere, whether in England or elsewhere, can do wrong – she is the immaculate Spouse – then only can you say the Church has gone wrong when everywhere and in Council assembled she has done it. Else it is but the deed of her children here or there. (v. 6; To S. F. Wood, 23 March 1838)

I suppose we may safely say that the Church is never to be lost, but is always to be a home of the flock of Christ. (v. 8; To William Dodsworth, 2 Jan. 1842)

I conceive that the fundamental proof of Catholicism, (i.e. the basis according to *my* conception of Catholicism,) is the promise that the Primitive church shall continue to' the end, the likeness of the (Roman) Catholic church to the Primitive, and the dissimilarity of every other body . . . (v. 14; To Francis Richard Wegg-Prosser, 24 Sep. 1851)

[T]here is a Power in it [the Church] stronger than Popes, Councils and Theologians – and that is the Divine Promise, which controls against their will and intention every human authority. 'Hitherto shalt thou go and no further,' . . . (v. 23; To Emily Bowles, 27 Aug. 1867)

[T]here is a depth and a power in the Catholic religion, a fulness of satisfaction in its creed, its theology, its rites, its sacraments, its discipline, a freedom yet a support also, . . . This is the true secret of the Church's strength, the principle of its indefectibility, and the bond of its indissoluble unity. It is the earnest and the beginning of the repose of Heaven. (v. 24; To Sir Frederic Rogers, 2 Feb. 1868)

We believe our Orders to have been transmitted without break, *because* we are the Church of God. We believe that God will not fail His Church . . . (v. 25; To an Unknown Correspondent, 1 May 1870)

How Did Church Government Originate?

[A] system of Church government was *actually established* by the Apostles, and is thus the *legitimate* enforcement of Christian truth. (v. 2; To Simeon Lloyd Pope, 15 Aug. 1830)

Does the Church Extend Back to Apostolic Times?

The more *obvious* reasons for believing the Church to come from God are its great notes, as they are called – such as its antiquity, universality, its unchangeableness through so many revolutions and controversies, its adaptation to our wants. (v. 14; To Mrs. Lucy Agnes Phillips, 5 June 1851)

What is Apostolic Succession?

[I]f there was a Present Christ, there must be a Guardian and Keeper of the Presence – if there was a sacrifice there must be a Priest. Thus the Apostolical Succession is cogently implied in the doctrine of the Presence of Christ in the Holy Eucharist. (v. 18; To A. Lisle Phillipps, 30 July 1857)

Anglicans claim to belong to the Church because their orders are good: but we claim to have good orders because we are the Church. We rest the fact of our being the Church, not on our Orders, but on our uninterrupted visible existence, on the continuity of body, system, claim, profession, doctrine, the see of Peter etc etc. and we say that, since we are the Church, *therefore* God has watched over us to preserve our Orders from any material damage. (v. 24; To Frederick George Lee, 21 Nov. 1869)

Is the Catholic Church Our Authoritative (Orthodox) Guide?

[T]he Catholic Church is God's *guide* to you. How ignorant we are! do we not *want* a guide? is the structure of Scripture such as to answer the purposes of a guide? How can a bare letter, written 2000 years ago, though inspired, *guide* an individual now? Everything has its use – God uses it according to its use – Is it the use of a written Word to answer doctrinal questions starting up to the end of time? as little surely, as it is the use of a spade to saw with, or a plough to reap with. If then Divine Mercy has given individuals, you and me, a revelation, *how,* in what *channel,* does

He bring it home to us? Even the Jews, whose doctrinal system was so simple, had a visible church. (v. 14; To Mrs. Lucy Agnes Phillips, 5 June 1851)

The Church, putting aside her divine guidance, putting aside her collection of great intellects, even merely from experience finds what is true and what is false, by fruits and consequences of doctrines, and hence has even set right in points of detail her Saints and Doctors. (v. 15; To Edward Healy Thompson, 7 Oct. 1853)

I suppose, though in *matter of fact* faith requires the proposition and authority of the Church, yet, speaking abstractedly and simply, we may say that it is *not* necessary. We rely, not on the word of man, but on the word of *God. However,* thro' *whatever* instrument, He speaks to us, *if* He speaks to us, we are bound to believe. The voice of the Church is but the particular mode under our Dispensation, and the usual and ordinary under it, in which the word of God is proposed to us. If Almighty God spoke to Abraham, Abraham was bound to believe, and (by divine grace) did believe, without the voice of the church.' And so at this day, a saint may have communications from God, so certainly from Him and no deceit, that he is bound to believe them, tho' no one else is. (v. 15; To W. J. O'Neill Daunt, 13 Dec. 1853)

What a Bishop says is law to those over whom he has jurisdiction . . . It seems to me as subverting all ecclesiastical authority, if that authority cannot stigmatize a statement with its ipse dixit. The question of its *arguments* being good or bad is not the point when it is a question not of doctrine, but of discipline. If the competent authority says that certain statements contain certain doctrines confessedly wrong (this is quite distinct from the case of infallibility, dogmatic facts, and internal assent) I think it is the duty of all who are under that authority to acquiesce. (v. 20; To Henry Bittleston, 28 Oct. 1862)

I am far from asserting that the instrument of revelation, or the oracle of the Authority on which we believe, must necessarily be the Church. The Church is the ordinary, normal Oracle; it is the only visible authority to which we appeal, the only authority which signs and seals a doctrine as the common property of Christians or an Article of the Faith, but still to individuals accidentally there are various instruments or organs of that Divine Authority from whom alone extra or super or praeter natural truth can primarily come, and the Scriptures constitute one of those channels – nay, I will say a Greek poem or philosophical treatise may be such – nay even the Koran. (v. 21; To Richard Holt Hutton, 18 June 1864)

[N]o one can become a Catholic without the intention of submitting and assenting with a real internal assent to any future definition which she may make with reference to it in time to come. For a belief in her as the living present interpreter of the Apostles is fundamental to the Catholic system, as involved in the article 'I believe the Holy Catholic Church.' (v. 21; To William Wordsworth, 22 Oct. 1864)

[T]he Church is the infallible interpreter of the old Apostolic doctrine. (v. 22; To Lady Chatterton, 10 Sep. 1865)

I have not a shadow of a misgiving that the Catholic Church and its doctrine are directly from God – but then I know well that there is in particular quarters a narrowness which is not of God. (v. 22; To Sir Frederic Rogers, 18 Jan. 1866)

[W]riters as Veron and Chrissman and Denzinger, in laying down what was *de fide*, never pretended to exclude the principle that it was *de fide* because the Church taught it as such, and that she could teach other things as *de fide* by the same right as she taught what she now teaches as such. This is our broad principle, held by all of whatever shade of theological opinion. While it would be illogical not to give an inward assent to what she has already declared to be revealed, so it is pious and religious to believe, or at least not to doubt, what, though in fact not defined, still it is *probable* she might define as revealed, or that she *will* define, or seems to *consider* to be revealed. . . . We embrace and believe what we find universally received, till a question arises about any particular point. (v. 23; To Edward B. Pusey, 23 March 1867)

I was converted simply because the Church was to last to the end, and that no communion answered to the church of the first ages but the Roman communion, both in substantial likeness and in actual descent. And as to faith, my great principle was 'Securus judicat orbis terrarum.' So I say now – and in all these questions of detail I say to myself, 'I believe whatever the Church teaches as the voice of God' . . . (v. 23; To Henry Wilberforce, 21 July 1867)

The Church is the *voice* of our Lord. (v. 24; To Miss Mary Holmes, 7 Oct. 1869)

Do you understand and believe that the Church is the Oracle of God in such sense that she can declare and interpret authoritatively every part of that body of doctrine which our Lord gave to His Apostles? (v. 25; To Fanny Pearson, 31 Oct. 1870)

I never have had one single doubt since I was a Catholic, that the Catholic Church is the one appointed Oracle of Truth and Ark of Salvation . . . (v. 25; To William Maskell, 12 Feb. 1871)

A Catholic believes that the Church is, so to call it, a standing Apostolic committee – to answer questions, which the Apostles are not here to answer, concerning what they received and preached. As the Church does not know more than the Apostles knew, there are many questions which the Church cannot answer – but it can put before us clearly, what the Apostles (being in heaven) cannot, what their doctrine is, what is to be believed, and what is not such. (v. 25; To Richard Holt Hutton, 20 Oct. 1871)

Is the Catholic Church Universal?

[T]he *nationalism* of all religions but the Catholic is one of the very evidences of Catholicism. . . . No religion has been a sojourner upon earth as the Catholic – finding a place in republics *or* despotisms – in the north and the south. (v. 15; To Catherine Anne Bathurst, 23 June 1853)

The Catholic Church is so called by the whole world [;] no other body has succeeded in obtaining its own recognition as the Catholic Church: no one calls the Anglican 'the Catholic Church' but its own members, i.e. some of them. (v. 21; To H. D. Forbes, 9 May 1865)

I do not think you have read aright my remarks in the Apologia, on Dr Wiseman's article on the Donatists. I think I expressly say that it did *not* strike me and I had known it for years. What did strike me was a passage he quoted from St Augustine which contained a maxim going far beyond the purpose of the controversy – Securus judicat orbis terrarum – 'the Christian commonwealth judges without misgiving.' That is the maxim, (as I also feel now,) on which all depends. The Christian commonwealth is one organized body – from time to time local disturbances rise in it – branches of it rise up separately from the rest, and claim to be heard in matters of discipline or doctrine- they appeal to the Fathers – so did the Donatists, so did the Arians, the Monophysites, the Protestants, the Anglicans – but the Christian State, Commonwealth, Kingdom judicat securus, has the right, the power, the certitude of deciding the rights and the wrongs of the matter. How do we know that Pius ix is true Pope? Securus judicat orbis terrarum. How shall we know that the coming Council is a true Council – but by the after assent and acceptance of it on the part of that Catholic organization which is lineally descended, as one whole, from the first ages? – How can we interpret the decisions of that Council, how the Pope's decisions in any age, except by the Schola Theologorum, the great Catholic school of divines dispersed all over the earth? This is why I am a Catholic – because our Lord set up the Church – and that one Church has been in the world ever since – because in every age bodies have fallen off from her, and have shown in the event that that falling off was death – that they tended to lose all definite faith, *as* bodies, (I don't mean *individuals* in them, as Dr Pusey) but as bodies – the Arians came to nought, and the Donatists . . . This is one of the great facts by which God meant the learned and unlearned to be guided – not by explorations into history, which are beyond most of us . . . (v. 24; To Mrs. Helbert, 20 Oct. 1869)

Securus judicat orbis terrarum means 'The Christian world judges with security' – that is, 'when all Christians agree together in a judgment, that is a sure warrant that its judgment is right. –' In consequence, it need not go back, to Scripture, or antiquity, in proof of a point in dispute, if it is in all its members of one way of judging. This saying of St Augustine's is in the teeth of the Anglican maxim, 'Nothing is true but what is to be found in the Antenicene church.' (v. 25; To Miss Maria Rosina Giberne, 15 Oct. 1870)

Is There Salvation Outside the Catholic Church?

We . . . hold with all our hearts that the Catholic Church is the sole communion in which there is salvation. But we know too, that there is such a state of mind as invincible ignorance, and the present Pope in one of his Allocutions has expressly recognised it. He has said too, if my memory is correct, that no one can decide who is in invincible ignorance and who is not – indeed, it seems plain, that it would require a particular revelation in order to be able to do so. (v. 20; To Sophia Ryder, 4 Sep. 1862)

[Y]ou are now in that Ark of God, out of which, (as St Jerome says) no one can be saved . . . (v. 21; To Helen Douglas Forbes, 4 Oct. 1864)

I believe too Extra Ecclesiam nulla salus, and, as I think the head and heart of that Ecclesia is Rome, I think that to be in communion with Rome is to be united to the Church of the promises, of grace and of salvation. But then, as Manning has brought out in his Letter to you, till baptism is forfeited by deliberate conscious rebellion of thought, it remains, what it really is in itself, an introduction into the Catholic Church, that Church of which Rome is the head. (v. 21; To Edward B. Pusey, 25 Nov. 1864)

I believe he lived and died in perfect good faith – and without a doubt that he was in the Catholic Church – and this belief is my great consolation. (v. 21; To W. J. Copeland, 16 May 1865; referring to Isaac Williams, who lived and died as an Anglican)

[F]ar be it from men to assert that they have wilfully shut their eyes upon light which has been granted them and which would have led them into the Catholic Church and thereby have forfeited heaven . . . (v. 25; To an Unknown Correspondent, beginning of 1871?)

No one is really a Catholic, who does not believe that the Church is the Oracle of revealed Truth and the fold of Christ, in which, and in no other body of men, is salvation lodged. (v. 25; To John Pym Yeatman, 10 July 1871)

The prime, I may say the only reason for becoming a Catholic, is that the Roman Communion is the only True Church, the Ark of Salvation. This does not mean that no one is saved who is not within that Church, but that there is no other Communion or Polity which has the promises, and that those who are saved, though not in the One Church, are saved, not by virtue of 'the Law or Sect which they profess', as the 39 Articles say, but because they do not know better, and earnestly *desire* to know the truth, and in con- sequence are visited by a superabundant mercy of God which He has not promised and covenanted. I think I have heard the late Mr. Keble say, 'If the Roman Church is the True Church, really, *I do not know it* – really *I do not see it'*. There are numbers, I joyfully believe, in the Church of England, such;- aided by God's grace, and I trust in the event justified and saved, not, however, by virtue of the Church of England, which is a human work and a political institution, but by grace extending beyond the True Church, to 'the children of God who are scattered abroad.' [Jn 11:52] (v. 26; To Miss Rowe, 16 Sep. 1873)

What are the Shortfalls of Contradictory Religious Opinions?

We find one man of one opinion in religion, another of another; and may thus be led hastily to conclude that opinions diametrically opposite to each other may be held without danger to one side or the other in a future state; but contradictions can no more be true in religion, than in astronomy or chemistry – and there is this most important distinction, to those who believe in revelation, between scientific and religious opinions, that, whereas errors in the former are unattended with danger to the person who maintains them, he who holdeth not 'the faith,' (I am not now determining what that faith is) such a one is said to be incapable of true moral excellence, and so exposed to the displeasure of God. . . . the generality of men have not made up their religious views in this sincere spirit... This is not the frame of mind in which they can hope for success in any worldly pursuit, why then in that most difficult one of religious truth? (v. 1; To [brother] Charles Robert Newman, 12 Dec. 1823)

Is Schism a Bad Thing?

Many times before now in the course of the last 300 years has a hope of concord arisen among Christians, but as yet it has ever come to nothing. When was a great schism ever healed? Why should ours cease, if that between the East and West has continued so long? And if a growth in sanctity be the necessary condition of it in both parties, what stipulation can be more costly, more hopeless? No. I feel that both parties must resign themselves to dying in their estrangement; but that is no reason they should not, though they be a few against many, both pray and labour against it. (v. 8; To Ambrose Lisle Phillipps, 16 April 1841)

If a person is *quite sure* he is in a schismatical body, he cannot expect to gain grace, to gain any thing but condemnation, by remaining in it. (v. 10; To Miss Maria Rosina Giberne, 1 June 1845)

It grieved me bitterly that you should have separated yourself from the One True Fold of Christ; . . . nothing which has taken place justifies our separation from the One Church. (v. 25; To Hyacinth Loyson, 24 Nov. 1870)

Who Tends to Jettison Orthodoxy in Order to Foster "Unity"?

[T]he maintainers of the Modern System will give up the formal Catholic doctrines in a *choice of difficulties* between doing so and excluding from their society those who seem spiritually minded. Next I by no means mean that all *do*, but that they *tend* to do so, that the Evangelical literature as a whole does . . . the Evangelical System . . . has become Rationalistic in Germany, Socinian in Geneva – Socinian among English Presbyterians and Arian among Irish – Latitudinarian in Holland – it tends to Socinianism among our own the Evangelical party. (v. 6; To Lord Lifford, 12 Sep. 1837)

How Shall we Regard Denominationalism and Sectarianism?

[T]he disunion of Christians in discipline and form of worship is a grievous evil, implying in some quarter or other a plain disobedience to Christ's command . . . fervently trusting that we may meet each other in that eternal Church of God, where schisms and differences and errors shall be at an end, when we shall not be forced to argue, to controvert, to protest, to stand apart, but where we shall have entirely one heart and one soul and shall have all things common. (v. 2; Speech at the Bible Society Meeting, 29 May 1828)

I cannot understand any communion between the Lutherans and Calvinists and ourselves except by reconciliation or formal admission. Even of our own members we require the submission to confirmation, a rite at once of professional acknowledgement, before they are admitted to the Holy Communion. (v. 8; To T. D. Acland, 25 Nov. 1841)

No two clergymen, next door to each other, return the same answer to the question 'What shall I do to be saved?' – with this consciousness, with what face can I say, 'Believe the Church, hear the Church'? . . . As you say, this is a great triumph to the Roman Catholics – but not only so, it inclines people to them. Many persons say to themselves 'We are more certain that the discord and variety of opinions which surround us is from beneath, than that the Creed of Pope Pius is not from above.' It needs to be no theologian to be sure that 'a house divided against itself cannot stand.' [Mk 3:25] (v. 9; To Simeon Lloyd Pope, 4 Sep. 1842)

What is Rigorism or an Overly Dogmatic Catholic Outlook?

Let me observe then, that, in former years *and now*, I have considered the theological differences between us as unimportant in themselves, that is, such as to be simply compatible with a reception, both by you and by me, of the whole theological teaching of the Church in the widest sense of the word 'teaching;' and again, now and *in former years too*, I have considered one phenomenon in you to be 'momentous,' nay portentous, viz. that you will persist in calling the said unimportant, allowable, inevitable differences (which must ever exist between mind and mind,) not unimportant, but of great moment. In this utterly uncatholic, not so much opinion, as feeling and sentiment, you have grown in the course of years, whereas I consider that I remain myself in the same temper of forbearance and sobriety which I have ever wished to cultivate. Years ago you wrote me a letter, in answer to one of mine, in which you made so much out of such natural difference of opinion between us, as exists, that I endorsed it with the words 'See how this man seeketh a quarrel against me!' Now you are running on, as it appears to me, into worse excesses. Pardon me if I say that you are making a Church within a Church, as the Novatians of old did within the Catholic pale, and as, outside the Catholic ale, the Evangelicals of the Establishment. As they talk o£ 'vital religion' and 'vital doctrines,' and will not allow that their brethren 'know the Gospel' or are 'Gospel preachers' unless they profess the small shibboleths of their own sect, so you are doing your best to make a party in the Catholic Church, and in St Paul's words are '*dividing Christ*' by exalting your opinions into dogmas, and shocking to say, by declaring to me, as you do, that those Catholics who do not accept them are of a different religion from yours. I protest then again, not against your tenets, but against what I must call your schismatical spirit. I disown your intended praise of me viz that I hold your theological opinions 'in the greatest aversion,' and I pray God that I may never denounce, as you do, what the Church has not denounced. (v. 23; To William G. Ward, 9 May 1867)

It is no trouble to believe, when the Church has spoken; the real trouble is when a number of little Popes start up, laymen often, and preach against Bishops and Priests, and make their own opinions the faith, and frighten simple-minded devout people and drive back inquirers. (v. 23; To Edward B. Pusey, 21 July 1867)

[W]hat is extraordinary is that the battle should pass from the Schools (which, alas, are not) to Newspapers and Reviews, and to *lay* combatants, with an appeal to the private judgment of all readers. This is a deplorable evil – and from all I have heard

Ward has hindered various people from becoming Catholics by his extreme views, and I believe is unsettling the minds of I can't tell how many Catholics. He is free to have his own opinion, but, when he makes it part of the faith, when he stigmatizes those who do not follow him as bad Catholics, when he saves them only on the plea of invincible ignorance, when he declines to meet those Catholics who differ from him and prefers the company of infidels to theirs, when he withdraws promised subscriptions from missions on the plea that the new missioner to whom the money has to be paid has not correct views of doctrine, when the spontaneous instinct of his mind is rather that Protestants should not be converted than converted by certain Catholics who differ from him, what is he (as I have told him) but a Novatian, making a Church within a Church, or an Evangelical preacher, deciding that the Gospel is preached here, and is not preached there. . . . The Jesuits, who agree with him, do not insist on their view as the only allowable view in the Catholic Church – they say it is the right view – of course they do – everyone thinks his own view right – but they do not dream of calling all who differ from them material heretics. . . . I see arguments here, arguments there – I incline one way today, another tomorrow – on the whole I more than incline in one direction – but I do not dogmatise – and I detest any dogmatism when the Church has not clearly spoken. And if I am told 'The Church *has* spoken,' then I ask where? and if, instead of having any thing plain shown me, I am put off with a string of arguments, or some strong words of the Pope himself, I consider this a sophistical evasion, . . . (v. 23; To Henry Wilberforce, 21 July 1867)

Are they not doing the Holy See a grave disservice, who will not let a zealous man defend it in *his own way*? but insist on his doing it in *their* way or not at all, or rather at the price of being considered heterodox and disaffected, if his opinions do not run in a groove –? (v. 23; Memorandum of Mgr Nardi's Visit, 24 Aug. 1867)

Should the Presence of Sinners in the Church Alarm Us?

[W]hen I speak of a pure Church, I would not be supposed to imply the expectation that the time will ever come when all the members of a Church will be members of Christ's invisible kingdom; *no rules can do this*, of course; and we know, on our Lord's own authority, that the tares will ever be mixed with the wheat while the present state of things lasts. Certainly it is an officious diligence which would attempt literally to pluck up the tares at all risks; and I cannot help thinking that it has been the mistake of many religious men of this day to indulge too sanguine hopes of the possibility of a pure Christian Society. (v. 4; To the Editor of *The Record*, 21 Oct. 1833)

That there have been great sins and great abuses in a vast communion or (as it may be called) Commonwealth consisting of many millions of men (200 millions at present) for a period of years, is not wonderful, and is undeniable – the 'net' according to the Scripture image, was to 'gather of every kind –' and those abuses will even serve as matter to justify the deep prejudices and suspicions of a portion of our countrymen who require of Catholics a sinlessness which they have not themselves – but they will have no effect on the candid and dispassionate beholder, whatever be his cast of opinions. (v. 13; To Thomas Ragg, 2 July 1849)

I do not believe there ever was a time when the gravest scandals did not exist in the Church, and act as impediments to the success of its mission. Those scandals have been the occasion of momentous secessions and schisms; in the earlier times, of the Novatian, the Donatist, the Luciferian; in latter of Protestantism and Jansenism. . . . It is also a fact, that, in spite of them still, the Church has ever got on and made way, to the surprise of the world; as an army may fight a series of bloody battles, and lose men, and yet go forward from victory to victory. . . . And it is a further fact, that our Lord distinctly predicted these scandals as inevitable; nay further, He spoke of His Church as in its very constitution made up of good and bad, of wheat and weeds, of the precious and the vile. One out of His twelve Apostles fell, and one of the original seven deacons; Thus a Church, such as we behold, is bound up with the very idea of Christianity. (v. 20; To Lady Chatterton, 10 June 1863)

If a divine system, when committed to men, becomes at once mixed up with human weakness and *corruption*, (as the parables and other portions of the New Testament seem to predict of the gospel dispensation,) it is not wonderful that defects, which are *short* of sin yet repulsive to the beholder, much of extravagance, of fanaticism, of ignorance, and of bad taste, also should be grafted upon or infused into it. Christianity was intended for whole populations; now a popular religion is necessarily deformed by the errors and bad taste of the multitude. As the religion of barbarous times will ever be fierce and superstitious, as the religion of the schools will ever tend to be subtle and pedantic, so the religion of a nation will ever partake of the peculiar faults of the national character. The most sublime truths take a vulgar shape and bear a forbidding aspect, when reflected back by the masses of human society – nay, often cannot be made intelligible to them, or at least cannot be made to reach them, till thrown into words or actions which are offensive to educated minds. The Church cannot countenance any such mistatement of the truth, much less any degradation or depravation of it – yet, when it has actually taken place, she may find it quite impossible to root out the tares without rooting out the wheat with them – and is obliged to let them grow together till the harvest. At least, she is obliged to be patient, and waits her time – hoping that an evil will at length die of itself – or again that some favorable opportunity may occur, when she may be able to do what she has no means of doing at present. (v. 20; To Lady Chatterton, 16 June 1863)

As to your not being able to see the splendours of the Church, as some persons represent them, I do not wonder – for 'the King's daughter is all glorious *within* –' the best of us have sin enough. The Bride of Christ is holy, but each of her children has a bad side as well as a good (if a good) and he wears his bad side outside. Do not forget the parable of the tares – of the net – and that 'many are called, few chosen.' Of course there is, and has ever been, an abundance of evil – and that in Popes as well as in others . . . (v. 24; To Mrs. Helbert, 30 Aug. 1869)

Never, thank God, have I had a single doubt about the divine origin and grace of the Church, on account of the want of tenderness and largeness of mind of some of its officials or rulers. And I think this will be your experience too. Bear up for a while and all will be right. (v. 25; To Lady Simeon, 18 Nov. 1870)

Does the Bible Teach the Concept of Excommunication?

St. Paul says to Titus (iii., 10), 'A man that is an heretic, after the first and second admonition, reject.' Here the Church officer is expressly bidden to reject those who profess false doctrine. Is this done? No; but why not? Truly, the omission of the practice has brought its curse with it in the present latitudinarian spirit which it has introduced into the Church. Again, to the Thessalonians (2 Thessalonians iii., 14, 15), 'If any man obey not our word by this epistle, note that man, and have no company with him, that he may be ashamed. Yet count him not as an enemy, but admonish him as a brother.' So much on the general duty. Next, let us observe *the kinds of offences* which are to be visited by ecclesiastical censure. They are threefold. First Heresy; e.g. 2 John, 10, 11; Titus iii., 10; 2 Thessalonians iii., 14, 15; as above cited. Secondly, Gross Sin; e.g. 1 Corinthians v., 7-13, 'Now I have written unto you not to keep company, if any man that is called a brother to be fornicator, or covetous, or an idolator, or a railer, or a drunkard, or an extortioner, with such an one, no, not to eat,' etc.; and 2 Timothy, iv., 15. Lastly Schismatical or otherwise disorderly proceedings; e.g. Romans xvi., 17, 'I beseech you, brethren, mark them which cause divisions and offences contrary to the doctrine which ye have learned; and avoid them.' and 2 Thessalonians iii., 6; 1 Timothy vi., 5. Further, there are two modes of excommunication insisted on in Scripture; one to be exercised by the spiritual authority, and the other by its individual members. The latter consists in *separation from* an offender (2 John, 10, 11; Romans xvi., 17; 2 Thessalonians iii. 14, 15, as above); bring a duty incumbent on every Christian, quite independently of the command of the Church; just as it is the duty of every one to abstain from offences himself. There is no difference in the manner of the respective Scripture injunctions to keep from sin and keep from notorious sinners. The duty of *ecclesiastical* excommunication is more solemn, and its effect is much greater, than that of merely separating the guilty individual from the intercourse of his brethren. (v. 4; To the Editor of *The Record*, 31 Oct. 1833)

The principal objections which have been adduced against a system of ecclesiastical discipline are these: – That there is a difficulty in drawing the line between those who should and those who should not be punished; that it is uncharitable to excommunicate; that it leads to spiritual pride in those who are within the pale of the Church; and especially in its pastors who are the officers of the discipline; further, that there is scarcely any warrant in Scripture for the exercise of it. To take the alleged Scripture argument first. It is maintained, there are only one or two passages in which the duty of excommunication is enforced; whereas St. Paul continually notices, without enjoining punishment on, offenders in the Churches to whom his Epistles are addressed, e.g. 1 Corinthians xi., 20-34; 2 Corinthians xi., 13; xii. 21; Galatians i., 7, etc. Now this negative argument is poor indeed against the plain fact, that the Corinthians *are* told, though but once, to 'put away the wicked person;' and Titus, though but once, to 'reject a heretic.' Those who wish to know and do

Christ's will are not in the habit of reckoning the number of times they must be told it before they need obey. The very utmost that can be said is, that we do not know *why* St. Paul is not always introducing the subject. (v. 4; To the Editor of *The Record*, 11 Nov. 1833)

Is Excommunication a "Spiritual" Thing?

Excommunication is as much a spiritual act as administering the Eucharist and Ordination. (v. 5; To Arthur Philip Perceval, 20 March 1835)

Is Christianity Difficult and a "Narrow Way"?

To objections of difficulty I answer, that Christian obedience is a course of difficulty from beginning to end; and to assume that it is necessarily not difficult, is nothing less than to maintain that the way of life is not narrow. (v. 4; To the Editor of *The Record*, 11 Nov. 1833)

What is the Principle of Unity in the Church?

I cannot but think that the very essence of the Episcopal System, is the referring every thing to *one head* – in order to ensure unity. (v. 4; To Thomas Martyn, 7 Feb. 1834)

Is Ordination of Priests or Pastors Necessary?

Adherence to Episcopal ordination is the *safest course* for the security of the validity of the sacraments and of the existence of Church fellowship. (v. 9; To an Unknown Correspondent, 4 March 1843)

Must Bishops Always be Obeyed?

Some of the Bishops, as Norwich, are driving fast at a denial of the Creed, which is heresy – and when a bishop is heretical, man, woman, or child has licence to oppose him. The faith is prior and dearer to us than the visible framework which is built upon it. (v. 6; To Miss Maria Rosina Giberne, 3 Dec. 1837)

[T]hough I have full liberty abstractedly to speak against individual heretical Bishops, yet I should be very cautious of even doing that; because men have not subtle minds enough to make the distinction; – the only way (I conceive) in which it is allowable is in the *way of appeals to the Body of the Church to disown those* individuals; thus you uphold the Church (viz the body) while you censure what at first sight seems identical with it. (v. 6; To S. F. Wood, 23 March 1838)

[W]e must obey our own Bishop – *the case of heresy of course is the exception.* . . . The truth is, St Ignatius's words weigh exceedingly with me. 'He who trifles with his Bishop, trifles with the Bishop Invisible'. – I could not myself oppose my Bishop except in a case of heresy. (v. 8; To Thomas Mozley, 29 Oct. 1841)

[W]hile I will pay unlimited obedience to the Bishop set over me while he comes in Christ's name, yet to one who come in the name of man, in his own name, in the name of mere expedience, reason, national convenience and the like, to the neglect of that creed . . . I should not be bound to pay any at all. (v. 8; To Thomas Kirkpatrick, 6 March 1842)

What is the Nature of a Bishop's Authority?

A Bishop's word is to be obeyed, not as doctrine, but as a part of discipline – only in Synod do they prescribe doctrine. (v. 8; To J. R. Hope, 17 October 1841)

You will find St Ignatius always contemplates in theory *one* Bishop when he is speaking of those *under* the Bishop. The Apostles are a Council to *Christ* – but singly they are each a perfect type of Christ. In like manner St Cyprian's language is, that the Episcopal power is shared by *all* Bishops *fully*. His expression is 'in solidum', which means like *joint tenure* or *partnership*, where each has full enjoyment of all prerogatives and the whole responsibility. Dioceses are unknown, – there are no local distinctions, in the *idea* of the Church. (v. 10; To [sister] Jemima Mozley, 19 April 1844)

Are Bishops the Primary Authorities in Their Own Domains?

All such local matters it [Rome] leaves to the local Bishops – it never acts without the local bishops. They ever have the formal initiative. It puts a veto on their proceedings, or does not, – but it does not originate – and, if it is *obliged* to speak, it speaks according to the strictest rule of ecclesiastical principle and tradition. In the late question about Oxford the Pope personally *wished* going to Oxford to be prohibited – and he *showed* his wish . . . the Pope never acted without the local Hierarchy – then, *when* the Bishops had *decided*, the Pope came out with a tremendously strong Rescript. (v. 24; To Edward B. Pusey, 24 May 1868)

Did Newman Think that Vatican II Would Clarify Vatican I?

I firmly believe that all this will work for good, tho' not perhaps in my day. If you look into history, you find Popes continually completing the acts of their predecessors, and Councils too – sometimes only half the truth is brought out at one time – I doubt not a coming Pope, or a coming Council, will so explain and guard what has been now passed by [the] late Council, as to clear up all that troubles us now. (v. 25; To Lady Simeon, 26 April 1871)

All this is the consequence of Luther, and the separation off of the Teutonic races – and of the imperiousness of the Latin. But the Latin race will not always have a monopoly of the magisterium of Catholicism. We must be patient in our time; but God will take care of His Church – and, when the hour strikes, the reform will begin – Perhaps it has struck, though we can't yet tell. (v. 25; To Emily Bowles, 30 April 1871)

[O]ther definitions are necessary, and were intended, and will be added, if we are patient, to reduce the dogma to its proper proportions and place in the Catholic system. This is just what took place in the history of the 5th century, as regards the doctrine of the Incarnation. (v. 25; To Lady Simeon, 15 Oct. 1871)

Chapter Ten

The Papacy / Papal Supremacy and Infallibility

How Powerful Was the Pope in the 5th Century?

. . . very remarkable at [the Council of] Chalcedon – [was] the great power of the Pope (as great as he claims now almost) . . . (v. 7; To Frederic Rogers, 12 July 1839)

Does the Pope Have Supreme Authority in the Church?

The Council of Chalcedon is the fourth <A.D. 452> Ecumenical Council, which it is generally considered the English Church receives. Our Divines consider its opponents heretics, as denying that Jesus Christ has come in the flesh.' Eutyches was condemned then, who said there was but one nature in our Lord. Now I cannot bring together all the strange things I found in its history. I found the Eastern Church under the superintendence (as I may call it) of Pope Leo. I found that *he* had made the Fathers of the Council unsay their decree and pass another, so that (humanly speaking) we owe it to Pope Leo at this day that the Catholic Church holds the true doctrine. I found that Pope Leo based his authority upon St Peter. I found the Fathers of the Council citing out 'Peter hath spoken by the mouth of Leo', when they altered their decree. . . . There was Pope Julius [r. 337-352] resisting the whole East in defence of St Athanasius, the Eusebians at the Great Council of Antioch [341] resisting him, and he appealing to his own authority (in which the historians support him) and declaring that he filled the see of St Peter. (v. 10; To Catherine Froude, 5 April 1844)

[W]e see how preposterous it is to talk of the Pope's 'usurped power'. As to his exercising power over the *whole* Church, he only does what all Bishops have a right to do, except they are restrained by definite provisions. As to his claiming power over other Bishops, he only does it by usage, by Prescription, by the canons, as the Archbishop of Canterbury. If he goes beyond these warrants he acts unjustifiably – while he can appeal to them, he is blameless. What he possesses, is either what he retains or what he has received. And in saying this, I am not going to question whether his power is by divine right or not. Even though it has been brought about by natural and human means, it may be the fulfilment of the prophetic promise to St Peter as recorded in xvi of St Matthew. A further conclusion seemed to follow from what has been said. If the ecumenical authority of the Pope has been created, not by his exaltation but by the canonical depression of other Bishops, and is no assumption, but the result of a voluntary arrangement, it follows that while it is lawful as being in their own power, it must necessarily be gradual as being the consequence of their positive acts. Canons are not framed, nor do usages obtain, in a day – nor do dispositions and ordinances which are the subject of them. The Papacy then could not but be of slow growth, and if it were the subject of prophecy in Matthew xvi, there is still greater reason for saying so. All then that we look for in antiquity, is tendencies and beginnings of its greatness, and these are found abundantly. This is the further conclusion which I meant, and with reference to it I will bring this long letter to an end. I write from memory, and therefore may make some mistakes in detail, though I am correct on the whole. St Clement of Rome, . . . who is mentioned by St Paul, wrote a pastoral letter which is extant to the Church of Corinth. St Ignatius addresses the Church of Rome as the Church 'which presides' or 'is the first see in the country of the Romans'. Dionysius of Corinth in the second century speaks of its alms and benevolences as extending all over the Church. St Irenaeus in the same century calls it the Church with which all others must concur. Pope Victor at the same time threatened the Churches with excommunication. Tertullian, Origen, and St Cyprian use language in the third [century] like Irenaeus's. Pope Stephen repeats towards St Cyprian the threat of Pope Victor. Pope Dionysius is appealed to against Dionysius Bishop of Alexandria in a matter of doctrine by the Alexandrians, entertains the appeal, requires an explanation of him, and receives it, and the Roman civil government submits the deprivation of Paul, Bishop of Antioch, to the decision of the see of Rome. In the fourth century St Athanasius and his friends appeal to Rome, and St Jerome professes in a matter of doctrine and in the choice of a patriarch of Antioch, to rule himself by its decision. Moreover in every case the view whether of doctrine or discipline taken by the see of Rome, ultimately prevailed, and, if success is the token of truth, is the true one. It is the Pope who has determined the rule for observing Easter, and for treating the baptism of heretics, who has confirmed or pronounced the condemnation of Arianism, Apollinarianism, Pelagianism, and the other numerous heresies which distracted the early Church. He appears to exercise an infallibility which in after ages he has more distinctly claimed. All these things being considered, I was forced to admit that the doctrine of the papacy was a primitive one . . . Nor is it anything to the purpose that the Pope's power was withstood in early times, e.g. by St Cyprian – for when a doctrine or ordinance has to be developed, collision or disturbance seem previous conditions of its final adjustment. Nor is it to the purpose that certain passages such as those which I have referred to above from writers of the first centuries *may* otherwise be explained – for the question is which of the two interpretations is the more likely – and the event seems to suggest the true interpretation, as in the case of a prophecy. (v. 10; To Mrs. William Froude, 19 May 1844)

What I believe about the Pope, I believe, as I believe any other doctrine, – because the Church teaches it – but, for me, the Church directs me to the Pope not the Pope directs me to the Church. I do not then rest my faith in the Pope on St Clement's

Epistle – but *believing* on authority of the Church that the Successor of St Peter *has* such over the whole Church, beginning with this and taking it for granted, I see in St Clement's Epistle a remarkable confirmation of that doctrine. (v. 22; To F. C. Burnand, 5 Nov. 1865)

There is nothing which any other authority in the Church can do, which he cannot do at once – and he can do things which they cannot do, such as destroy a whole hierarchy, as well as create one. (v. 23; To Edward B. Pusey, 22 March 1867)

[A] Universal Church cannot, by the laws of human society, be held together without a head. When did a simple republic last? The Greek republics were small – so were the Italian. Rome was at first a single city – but even then, in difficult times was obliged to have a dictator, and when it became an empire, had a permanent Ruler. If then it was in the designs of Providence to establish a spiritual Kingdom or universal Empire, it was in His designs to have a Pope, unless all was to be carried on by miracle. And so again, if doctrine was to be perpetuated. If one and the same faith, one and the same sacraments, the same worship, were to be the characteristics of Christianity in all lands, this could not be without a central authority. Law implies a territory which is subjected to it – and how can law be preserved and enforced without an Executive Government. And in matter of fact what has kept the religion together with the same faith, worship, and observances, is the Roman See – and, wherever Christians have left Rome, they have fallen under the power of the State and had as many sorts of worship and rules of faith as there are States, and, if they have *not* been ruled by the State, then they have not been ruled at all, and have had no consistency and no permanence, but have been like bubbles on the face of society, rising and breaking. (v. 25; To Anna Whitty, 9 Sep. 1870)

The essential doctrine is that all parts of the Church should form one visible body, that no part should be independent of the rest.

The Pope is the means by which this unity is effected. Union implies governance – governance implies a governor. (v. 25; To Mrs. Houldsworth, 5 April 1871)

Does the Pope Possess the Gift of Infallibility?

There is great virtue in a Pope – it is something to fall back on. It is a present avenger of the champions of truth. St Athanasius found it so in his day – and lesser and little men have found it ever since. . . . the infallible, keensighted, unwearied, undaunted tribunal in the background, undaunted amid all worldly troubles and reverses, to inspire a salutary awe . . . (v. 13; To Henry Wilberforce, 1 Jan. 1849)

'The infallibility of the Pope' is to be looked on as a doctrine to be received on faith, as the doctrine of the Holy Trinity or Incarnation (and with the same *historical* difficulties, rid my Essay on Development) by those who are to enter the Church on *other* grounds . . . such as prima facie similarity between modern and ancient Church, . . . (v. 13; To A. J. Hamner, 21 Nov. 1849)

The (Roman) Catholic church then, being proved to be the organ of revelation, or infallible in matters of faith, will *teach* the Pope's Infallibility, as far as it is a doctrine, just as it teaches the Divinity of our Lord, or original sin – and its teaching must, as regards the one doctrine and the other, be received on faith. . . . To *defend* the church's doctrines, when she is proved to be the divine *oracle*, is a very different thing from *proving* those doctrines nakedly by themselves. . . . The difficulty in the way of receiving the Papal Infallibility is, that certain Popes seem to have erred, and to have been recognized by the church as erring. See what a number of distinctions are obvious at once, in explanation of this difficulty, e.g. 'err' – granted, *but* not in matters of *faith* – or 'err' granted, but not *ex cathedra*; 'seemed to err,' granted, but the church has never so recognized etc etc. I mean the force and edge of the objection is not at first sight *decisive*. . . . Because so little is this doctrine the basis of our system, that any Catholic may in fact *deny* it – and this is bringing the matter to the shortest issue, viz for me to give up the doctrine to you. – As a controvertist, (though not in my own belief,) I *grant to you* that the Pope is not infallible. Now what will you say? (v. 14; To Francis Richard Wegg-Prosser, 24 Sep. 1851)

It still does puzzle me why, if you cannot *prove* the Pope's Infallibility, you will not take it, *so far* as it approaches to be a point of faith, on faith. If the Church is infallible, she is infallible in this – if she has said the Pope's infallibility (i.e. that the Pope is the seat of her infallibility) is a point of faith, or proximum fidei, or cannot be denied with- out temerariousness, or *whatever* she has said, weaker or stronger, still surely you may be sure she cannot have said wrongly – and you may enter the Church saying 'I will give up all theories of mine own, and whether I am Gallican or Ultramontane, or developmentist or what else, it shall be as the Church shall teach me – and when she has not expressly spoken, I will go as near as possible by what I think she feels and will say, if occasion calls for it.' To enter the Church *stipulating* for Gallican views, is to me unpleasant. (v. 15; To Francis Richard Wegg-Prosser, 20 Feb. 1852)

[I]t is not religious to insist on a *particular* difficulty being cleared up, *before* you acknowledge the Roman Church to be the true church. If you have *other* reasons, if you *can* have other reasons for believing in the divinity of the R.C. Church, you must take the doctrine of the infallibility of the Holy See on faith *as* the church takes it, viz as part of 'the faith,' or as certain, or as all but certain, or as probable etc. You must be able to say 'Whatever I find the church holds about the Roman See, that will I hold.' If you cannot say this, certainly you have not faith in the R.C. Church. . . . I took the Papal Infallibility (not indeed as a difficulty, as you do, yet not as a striking proof, but) in a measure on faith. (v. 15; To Francis Richard Wegg-Prosser, 22 Feb. 1852)

Ultramontane as I am, . . . (v. 16; To Henry Wilberforce, 12 March 1855)

You need not believe any thing that the Pope says, except when he speaks ex cathedra. (v. 17; To Mrs. Catherine Froude, 20 May 1856)

I have availed myself of your suggestions to leave out one passage and to modify another [in the *Apologia pro vita Sua*]. But I do not see my way to withdraw the statement that the Pope in Ecumenical Council is the normal seat of Infallibility . . . (v. 21; To Charles Russell, 5 May 1865)

No one says that St Clement's Epistle is inspired – if so, it would be part of Scripture, and might be put into the Canon. The general view of the infallibility of the Pope is this:- viz. not that his *writings* are all gospel, but that when he utters PROPOSITIONS ex cathedra whether affirmative or condemnatory (certain conditions being necessary to constitute the idea of 'ex cathedra') those propositions i.e. the sense of them as he means them, are true, and true because they are merely a development of what our Lord formally spoke and delivered to the Apostles in the beginning. (v. 22; To F. C. Burnand, 5 Nov. 1865)

As to the Infallibility of the Pope, I see nothing against it, or to dread in it . . . (v. 22; To Edward B. Pusey, 17 Nov. 1865)

As to writing a volume on the Pope's infallibility, it never so much as entered into my thoughts. I am a controversialist, not a theologian. And I should have nothing to say about it. I have ever thought it likely to be true, never thought it certain. I think too, its definition inexpedient and unlikely; but I should have no difficulty in accepting it, were it made. And I don't think my reason will ever go forward or backward in the matter. (v. 22; To William G. Ward, 18 February 1866)

Applying this principle to the Pope's Infallibility, (N B this of course is mine own opinion only, meo periculo) a man will find it a religious duty to *believe* it, *or* may safely *dis*believe it, in *proportion* as he thinks it probable Or improbable that the Church might or will define it, or does hold it, and that it is the doctrine of the Apostles. For myself (still to illustrate what I mean, not as arguing) I think that the Church *may* define it (i.e. it possibly may turn out to belong to the original depositum), but that she *will* not *ever* define it; and again, I do not see that she can be said to hold it. She never can simply *act* upon it (being undefined, as it is), and I believe never has; – moreover, on the other hand, I think there is a good deal of evidence, on the very surface of history and the Fathers in its favour. On the whole then I hold it; but I should account it no sin if, on grounds of reason, I doubted it. (v. 23; To Edward B. Pusey, 23 March 1867)

If I were a layman, I should say, 'I hold (if so) the Temporal Power to be necessary at this time, but I do not see why I need *commit* myself to the opinion – nor have I any wish to exalt it into a quasi dogma by assenting to it solemnly at the very time I am assenting solemnly in the Address to real dogmas.' For the same reason I should object to 'Infallibility' being brought into the doctrinal profession about the Pope. (v. 23; To F. R. Ward, 24 May 1867)

I am not denying the Pope's Infallibility – but questions arise, as to what are the conditions of his exercising the gift . . . (v. 23; To Edward B. Pusey, 10 July 1867)

That there is a party who would push for the Pope's Infallibility, and be unscrupulous in doing so, I can easily believe too – but this to me personally is no trouble – for they cannot go beyond the divine will and revealed truth. The result would be God's, did they succeed, whatever faults or offences they committed. . . . Whether the Bishops on the other hand will be disposed to take the Pope's infallibility as part of the original faith, I cannot divine

– I know too little about them – I shall be surprised, however, if they did. (v. 23; To Edward B. Pusey, 21 July 1867)

For myself I have never taken any great interest in the question of the limits and seat of infallibility. . . . I have only an opinion at best (not faith) that the Pope *is* infallible, and a string of arguments can only end in an opinion, and I comfort myself with the principle 'Lex dubia non obligat –' What is not taught universally, what is not believed universally, has no claim on me – and, if it be true after all and divine <[[though not universally held]]> my faith in it is included in the implicita fides which I have in the Church. (v. 23; To Henry Wilberforce, 21 July 1867)

Though I myself consider the Pope's formal definitions of faith to be infallible, I rejoice to see a pamphlet which has the effect of reminding the world that his infallibility is not a dogma, but a theological opinion. . . . I hold the Pope's Infallibility, not as a dogma, but as a theological opinion; that is, not as a certainty, but as a probability. You have brought out a grave difficulty in the way of the doctrine; that is, you have diminished its probability, but you have only diminished it. To my mind the balance of probabilities is still in favour of it. There are vast difficulties, taking facts as they are, in the way of denying it. (v. 24; To Peter le Page Renouf, 21 June 1868)

I can have no possible objection to your introducing any statements on controverted points in your letter to me, if only you say (what I suppose *you* would say too) that you know I hold that, *supposing* the *Church* declared and defined those controverted points in one particular way, i.e. defined that the Pope speaking ex cathedra was infallible, or that the Augustinian or the Dominican view of Predestination was not the true one, . . . I should receive such doctrine as part of the original faith. (v. 24; To Edward B. Pusey, 16 Aug. 1868)

I have ever more than inclined to hold the Pope's Infallibility – but as a matter of expedience, I wish nothing done at the Council about it. (v. 24; To Edward B. Pusey, 14 Nov. 1868)

I have ever held the Pope's Infallibility, that is, held it as a theological opinion, the most probable amid conflicting historical arguments. (v. 24; To Peter le Page Renouf, 30 Nov. 1868)

I have myself ever professed to hold the Pope's Infallibility as a theological opinion – but, as so holding it, of course I imply there are other opinions on the subject, and, though it would be no hard matter to me to accept it as a dogma, yet it isn't a dogma - and Dr A or B or Fr C. or D. cannot proprio motu make it so. (v. 24; To J. Walker of Scarborough, 15 Dec. 1868)

If anyone says to you 'this is of authority or that –' 'the Pope, for instance, is certainly infallible,' you have to ask 'do you hold it as an article of faith?' and again, 'Do *all Catholics* hold it as a matter of faith?' and the answer will be sure to be in the negative. Therefore, *supposing* the Archbishop says that the Pope is infallible in formal teaching, he has quite a right to say so, as I have myself, but he never will say that it is part of THE FAITH, for the Church has never so pronounced. I believe in the infallibility of the Pope myself – that is, as an opinion. I think there are very strong reasons for holding it – but I quite recognize the right of others not to hold it. I think it could be made an article of faith by a General or Ecumenical Council; and if such a Council should so determine, I should *formally believe as certain*, what I now believe in my own private judgment *as an opinion*, viz that our Lord and Saviour so determined, and gave the privilege of infallibility to St Peter and his successors. . . . If the Pope's infallibility were to be determined now, I should say after the event, that doubtless there were good reasons for its being done at this time and not sooner. And I can *see* such reasons; for instance, in the present state of the world, the Catholic body may require to be like an army in the field, under strict and immediate

- 202 -

discipline. I tell you frankly, that, in *my own mind*, I see *more* reasons for wishing it may *not* be laid down, by the Council, than for wishing it should be; but I know that I am fallible, and I shall have no difficulty in accepting it, if the Council so determine – and then there will be a point of private judgment less – but till then it *is* a point of private judgment. (v. 24; To Mrs. Helbert, 30 Aug. 1869)

There is an Essay of the Archbishop of Malines, a Redemptorist, on the Pope's Infallibility – very moderate, as I thought, and good – and agreeing with Fr Ryders pamphlet – and the view I should take myself, though *I* don't want it *defined*. But that is the view *on which* it will be defined, if it is. I don't know whether I am right, and write under correction of the Bishop of O. viz those theologians, as the French, who deny the Pope's Infallibility and lodge the gift in the Church, *enlarge the subject matter.* Ultramontanes, who uphold the Pope's Infallibility, *contract* the subject matter. Ward burns the candle at both ends – upholding the Pope's Infallibility *and* enlarging the subject matter. *This* it is that I dread – and, though there will be sharper and deeper wits than mine to see prospective dangers, yet I should be sorry if, while striving (perhaps in vain) to hinder the definition of the Pope's infallibility, men like the Bishop of O. allowed the *extended* subject matter to be defined. (v. 24; To William Monsell, 3 Sep. 1869)

I have ever held the Pope's Infallibility as an opinion, and am not therefore likely to feel any personal anxiety as to the result of this Council. Still I am strongly opposed to its definition – and for this reason. Hitherto nothing has been ever done at Councils but what is *necessary*; what is the necessity of this? There is no heresy to be put down. It is a dangerous thing to go beyond the rule of tradition in such a matter. In the early times the Nicene Council gave rise to dissensions and to confusions which lasted near a century. The Council of Ephesus opened a question which it took three centuries to settle. Well, these Councils were

NECESSARY – they were called to resist and condemn opposition to our Lord's divinity – heresies – They could not be helped. But why is the Pope's infallibility to be defined? even, if denying it were a heresy, which no one says, how many *do* deny it? do they preach their denial? are they making converts to it? . . . I am against the definition, because it opens a long controversy. You cannot settle the question by a word – whatever is passed, must be a half, a quarter measure. . . . Hitherto, I *personally* may be of *opinion* that the Pope is infallible by himself . . . Hitherto, the Pope has always acted, (for greater caution,) with the Bishops . . . then comes the question in *what matters* is the Pope infallible? – after this – when, under what conditions, is the Pope infallible? when e.g. he writes a letter? . . . it will be a great work to go through this question well. You have to treat it doctrinally – and then again historically, reconciling what you teach with the verdict of history. Then again recollect that this doctrine is a retrospective doctrine – it brings up a great variety of questions about *past* acts of Popes – whether their decrees in past ages are infallible, or whether they were not, and which of them, and therefore whether they are binding on *us*. If anything could throw religion into confusion, make sceptics, encourage scoffers, and throw back inquirers, it will be the definition of this doctrine. (v. 24; To Catherine Froude, 21 Nov. 1869)

As to myself, I should say that I have never felt any difficulty in the Pope's infallibility as a theological opinion. (v. 24; To Robert Charles Jenkins, 21 Nov. 1869)

I have long held the Infallibility of the Pope myself as a private or theological opinion – but I never have attempted to bring anyone into the Church by means of it, for I hold it principally because others whom I know hold it, as I may hold many doctrines which are not defined by the Church, as being pious to hold or agreeable to general sentiment. But if I am asked to defend it logically and prove it – I don't profess to be able – and I don't expect it will ever be made an article of faith. It did not bring me into the Church. . . . though I hold the Pope's Infallibility as most likely, and as having the suffrages of most people in this day, I cannot defend it in a set argument, and never would use it as the instrument of bringing inquirers into the Church. (v. 24; To J. F. Seccombe, 14 Dec. 1869)

As to the Pope's infallibility, I have no difficulty about it myself, and have no objection to others (if they can) making it *the* argument by which they enter the Church, for there must be a liberty to such things, but for myself, though it were defined de fide by the present Ecumenical Council, that would only change it in my mind from an opinion to a dogma, and not tend to make it a reason before being a Catholic for being a Catholic. For though *as a Catholic* I believe that the Pope's power is *de jure divino*, I never thought so till I was a Catholic, or at least not so firmly believed it as to make it a fulcrum for changing my religion. (v. 25; To J. F. Seccombe, 2 Jan. 1870)

As to myself personally, please God, I do not expect any trial at all . . . If it is God's will that the Pope's infallibility should be defined, then it is His blessed Will to throw back 'the times and the moments' [Acts 1:7] of that triumph which He has destined for His Kingdom; and I shall feel I have but to bow my head to His adorable, inscrutable Providence. (v. 25; To Bishop Ullathorne, 28 Jan. 1870)

I have ever held the infallibility of the Pope myself, since I have been a Catholic – but I have ever felt also that others had a right, if they pleased, to deny it – and I will not believe, till the event takes place, that a Council will make the belief obligatory. If it takes place, I shall say that Providence has ways and purposes for His Church, which at present are hid from our eyes – but that [it] is His Blessed Will for a time to check the successes of His Church upon the external world. (v. 25; To Lady Chatterton, 3 Feb. 1870)

[W]hile I think the Church might define doctrines to be true, which it has not yet defined, I hold strongly the distinction between dogma and theological opinion – and I am strongly opposed to the present attempt to make the Pope's infallibility a dogma, because I see no cause, that is, no sufficient motive, for doing so – and because I think we have difficulties enough on our hands, without burdening ourselves with a whole load of historical objections. (v. 25; To Richard Holt Hutton, 16 Feb. 1870)

I think it impossible that the violent party, the zealots, as I believe they call them, can have their way – whatever is passed dogmatically in the Council will come very short indeed of their hopes. I could desire nothing to be done, but whatever is done will be very neutral in character. (v. 25; To Lady Chatterton, 11 March 1870; the book referred to is *A few Specimens of 'Scientific History' from 'Janus,'* London 1870)

If it be God's will that some definition in favour of the Pope's infallibility is passed, I then shall at once submit – but up to that very moment I shall pray most heartily and earnestly against it. (v. 25; To David Moriarty, Bishop of Kerry, 20 March 1870)

I will not believe that the Pope's Infallibility can be defined at the Council till I see it actually done. Seeing is believing. We are in God's Hands – not in the hands of men, however high-exalted. Man proposes, God disposes. When it is actually done, I will accept it as His act; but, till then, I will believe it impossible. (v. 25; to Ambrose Phillipps de Lisle, 7 April 1870)

I will not believe that the Pope's Infallibility will be defined by the Council till it is actually done and over – when this is so, then of course, with every Catholic, I will accept it. (v. 25; To Thomas Joseph Brown, Bishop of Newport, 8 April 1870)

Men are illogical, when they conclude, as the newspaper which you send me, that because I disapprove of the actions of certain Catholics, therefore my faith is unsettled as regards the Catholic Church. No one denies that the Bishop of Orleans, in spite of his burning words against these same acts, has a firm faith in the Catholic Church; no one calls him restless. Why, then, am I restless because I wrote a strong, but a most confidential, letter to my own bishop, and to him alone, as a matter of sacred duty? (v. 25; To Samuel Walshaw, 11 April 1870)

Whoever is infallible, I am not; but I am bound to argue out the matter and to act, as if I were, till the Council decides; and then, if God's Infallibility is against me, to submit at once, still not repenting of having taken the part which I felt to be right, any more than a lawyer in Court may repent of believing in a cause and advocating a point of law, which the Bench of Judges ultimately give against him. . . . Hardly any one even murmured at the act of 1854 [the papal proclamation of Mary's Immaculate Conception], half the Catholic world is in a fright at the proposed act of 1870. (v. 25; To Robert Whitty, S. J., 12 April 1870)

I have nowhere and never 'protested against the dogma of the Infallibility of the Pope.' (v. 25; To Edward Husband, 20 July 1870)

[T]he definition is what the Church has acted on for some centuries, and a very large body of Catholics have long held. God will bring His chosen people through all difficulties. (v. 25; To Madame Jacques Blumenthal, 30 July 1870)

You must not fancy that any very stringent definition has passed – on the contrary it is very mild in its tenor, and has been acted on by the Pope at least for the last 300 years. And as, during those centuries, in spite of his Infallibility being firmly held at Rome, he has done nothing extravagant, now also, when it is declared authoritatively, we may reasonably expect that all things will go on quietly as before. (v. 25; To Lady Chatterton, 4 Aug. 1870)

I have ever held the Pope's Infallibility, since I have been a Catholic, thinking it very difficult to deny it historically, in spite of the difficulties against it, and, I repeat, I think things will go on as heretofore, even though this doctrine turns out to be legitimately defined. (v. 25; To Lady Chatterton, 6 Aug. 1870)

At present I wait to see what the minority will do. If they do nothing, I shall consider it a moral unanimity in favour of the definition. (v. 25; To Emily Bowles, 12 Aug. 1870)

Did the Bishops of the minority openly or tacitly yield now, and allow the doctrine, which has been the subject in dispute, to be circulated, proclaimed, and taken for granted among Catholics, then I should think that the majority represented the whole episcopate, and that the doctrine was really defined. As at present advised, I should in that case think the definition the voice of the Church, and to come to us with a claim of infallibility. (v. 25; To William Clifford, Bishop of Clifton, 12 Aug. 1870)

I had ever held it . . . The church has *acted* for 300 years on what is now defined. (v. 25; To Emilie Perceval, 15 Aug. 1870)

[S]upposing that protest came to nothing, supposing its subscribers did not act in a body, and did not carry it out in their own dioceses, then I should think that the definition was valid. The bar to moral unanimity would be removed, or at least the Catholic world would have become of one mind, and I should believe on the 'securus judicat orbis terrarum'. (v. 25; To Frederick Rymer, 15 Aug. 1870)

Since I have believed the matter of it for many years, (as I have at various times stated in print) it is not a point which concerns me very nearly. (v. 25; To John Pym Yeatman, 15 Aug. 1870)

[T]hey both implied that, putting the validity of the Acts of the Council aside, the fact of Pope and so many Bishops taking one side, if backed up by the faithful, would practically make the doctrine de fide – and that we must trust in God – and so I think myself. (v. 25; To Ambrose St. John, 21 Aug. 1870)

For myself I have never had any difficulty in receiving it, though for the sake of others, and for many further reasons, I earnestly trusted and prayed that it might not be defined. (v. 25; To Anna Whitty, 31 Aug. 1870)

As to this particular doctrine (Papal infallibility), I am not at all sure it will increase the Pope's power – it may restrict it. Hitherto he has done what he would, because its limits were not defined – now he must act by rule. I can't prophesy how it will be. Again, if terrible times are coming, this increase of his spiritual authority may be absolutely necessary to keep things together. (v. 25; To Anna Whitty, 9 Sep. 1870)

There has ever been a great deal of disturbance after any new definition of faith. If there was none at Trent, it must be recollected it went on for 20 years, and good part of the trouble went before it, and the rest during it. The *Reformation* created the trouble – in our case, alas, an unscrupulous Church faction has created the trouble. We were going on quite well when they meddled. However, God overrules all things. If the whole Church accepts the late definition, then it will stand on its proper ground, universal acceptance (according to St Augustine's maxim, 'Securus judicat orbis terrarum –' 'The judgment of the whole Church has no chance of being wrong') At present it is a great shame to hurry people on. I believe very little is added to the faith of the Church by the definition. The Pope cannot do what he will more than before. (v. 25; To Mrs. Margaret A. Wilson, 24 Oct. 1870)

The doctrine of Infallibility has now been more than sufficiently promulgated. Personally I have never had a shadow of doubt that the very essence of religion is protection from error, for a revelation that could stultify itself would be no revelation at all. (v. 25; To Georges Darboy, Archbishop of Paris, end of 1870?)

As little as possible was passed at the Council – nothing about the Pope which I have not myself always held . . . (v. 25; To Catherine Froude, 2 Jan. 1871)

As to Dr Dollinger and others [who rejected papal infallibility], the case is quite tragic. I wish he could see, as I do, that as little as possible has really been passed at the Council. (v. 25; To Alfred Plummer, 15 Jan. 1871)

It has long been my belief that the Pope had the infallibility which he was proclaimed to have last July . . . there is no doubt that the Ultra party did not effect what they wished. I am quite sure that Mr Ward, for instance, wished a great deal more than he got. (v. 25; To Mrs. William Maskell, 31 Jan. 1871)

[N]othing has been passed, (as I think,) but what I have ever held myself, about the Pope's Infallibility . . . (v. 25; To William Maskell, 12 Feb. 1871)

I deeply grieve about Dollinger [who rejected papal infallibility] . . . Of course there are propositions which the Church could not impose on us – as that God was not good – but I marvel that he should so set his judgment against so very vague a definition as that which passed the Council – In the first place it says that the Pope has the Church's infallibility, but that in- infallibility has never been defined or explained – then it says that the Pope is infallible, when he speaks ex cathedra, but what ex cathedra is has never been defined. [v. 25; To Alfred Plummer, 12 March 1871)

I almost held the Pope's Infallibility and the Immaculate Conception as an Anglican . . . (v. 25; To George Hay Forbes, 11 Aug. 1871)

I have never myself had a difficulty about the Pope's Infallibility . . . (v. 25; To Malcolm MacColl, 11 Nov. 1871)

I am quite sure that, if I said in print a hundred times that I accepted the doctrine, the world would go on saying that I did not. They have thus treated me ever since I was a Catholic[.] (v. 26; To William Monsell, 20 Jan. 1872)

I have long held it, but as thinking the historical evidence in its favour not so strong that the Church would think it safe to pass it. Consequently I can quite understand a man saying 'there is not evidence strong enough for my believing it (*on* evidence)' but I cannot understand a man logically saying 'there is evidence sufficient for my rejecting it (when the Church has affirmed it)'. (v. 26; To J. H. Willis Nevins, 12 June 1872)

I have for these 25 years spoken *in behalf* of the Pope's infallibility. The other day a review (I forget what) observed with surprise that even in my article on la Mennais in 1838 I had tacitly accepted the Pope's infallibility. I think I have spoken for it in my Essay on Development of Doctrine in 1845. In 1850 I have introduced the Pope's Infallibility several times into my lectures at the Birmingham Corn Exchange. In 1852 I introduced it most emphatically and dogmatically into my lectures delivered at the Rotundo at Dublin. In 1856 1 spoke of it in a new Preface I prefixed to the new Edition of my Church of the Fathers and in 1868 I reprinted the passage from my Dublin Lectures in a collection of passages made by a Roman Jesuit Father on the dogma, in an Italian translation. This is quite consistent, in my way of viewing it, in my being most energetic against the *definition*. Many things are true which are not points of faith, and I thought the definition of this doctrine *most inexpedient*. And, as

St Paul, though inspired, doubted whether his words might not do harm to his Corinthian converts, so do I now fear much lest the infallible voice of the Council may not do harm to the cause of the Church in Germany, England, and elsewhere. What I said in the private letter to my Bishop, to which Dr D. alludes, was that the definition *would unsettle men's minds*. This anticipation has been abundantly fulfilled. I said moreover expressly that it would be *no* difficulty to *me*, but that it was making the defence of Catholicism more *difficult*. As a proof that all this is the true view of my position, I have *never been called* on, as Gratry was, *publicly* to accept the doctrine – *because* I had never denied it. (v. 26; To Alfred Plummer, 19 July 1872)

You have inserted in your columns of yesterday some remarks made on me by Mr Capes, which, to use a studiously mild phrase, are not founded on fact. He assumes that I did not hold or profess the doctrine of the Pope's Infallibility till the time of the Vatican Council, whereas I have committed myself to it in print again and again, from 1845 to 1867. And, on the other hand, as it so happens – though I hold it as I ever have done – I have had no occasion to profess it, whether in print or otherwise, since that date. Any one who knows my writings will recollect that in so saying I state the simple fact. The surprise and distress I felt at the definition was no personal matter, but was founded on serious reasons of which I feel the force still. (v. 26; To the editor of the *Pall Mall Gazette*, 13 Sep. 1872)

Infallibility is not a *habit* in the Pope, or a state of mind – but, as the decree says, that infallibility which the Church has. The Church when in Council and proceeding by the strictest forms enunciates a definition in faith and morals, which is certainly true. The Church is infallible *then*, *when* she speaks ex cathedra – but the Bishops out of Council are fallible men. So the Pope is infallible *then*, *when* he speaks ex cathedra – but he has no habit of infallibility in his intellect, such that his *acts cannot but* proceed from it, *must* be infallible *because* he in infallible, *imply*, *involve*, an infallible judgment. . . . even on those grave questions the gift is negative. It is not that he has an inspiration of truth, but he is simply guarded from error, circumscribed by a divine superintendence from transgressing, extravagating beyond, the line of truth. And his definitions do not come of a positive divine guidance, but of human means, research, consulting theologians etc etc. It is . . . an aid eventual, in the event, and does not act till the event, not in the *process* . . . (v. 26; To Richard Frederick Littledale [?], 17 Sep. 1872)

[T]he subject matter of the Pope's infallibility is a truth, and truth in the province of religion and morals. The Pope is not infallible in his acts or his commands. Pope Honorius made a great mistake, when he advised a certain course of policy as regards a certain heterodox opinion. But, we should contend, he did *not* enunciate, and *could not formally* enunciate, a doctrine which was heterodox – not because he had a sort of inspiration by being Pope, but that a Providence is over the Church which would hinder a Pope (at the last moment) from teaching, propounding to be believed, an error. Revelation, in its very idea, is a revelation of truth – and it is a revelation not for the first century alone, but for all times. Who is its keeper and interpreter, or oracle, in centuries 2,3,4 as the Apostles were in the first? We do not want, nor do we recognise in St. Peter, an impeccable man, but a sure teacher of the truth. The Popes take his place. St. Peter erred in deed, and was reproved by St. Paul at Antioch – but when he spoke as the minister of heaven, he, as well as St. Paul (as in their Epistles) spoke truth and nothing but truth. We do not want more than this, viz. truth m but we do want as much. We can blame a Pope's actions, while we believe in his formal enunciations of Christian doctrine. (v. 26; To Arthur Arnold, 20 Sep. 1872)

[T]he *fact* of the definition increases the pope's power, but *the thing defined* is very moderate[.] (v. 26; To Miss Helen Gladstone, 22 Sep. 1872)

It is false that 'Father Newman,' then or at any time 'expressed the opinion that infallibility could only be said to reside in the voice of the entire clergy assembled in a Council,' or that it did not reside in the voice of the Pope. . . . It is false, that 'when the new dogma was promulgated, Fr Newman hesitated a long time, but finally resolved to give it a reluctant adhesion'; for his published works show, that he has held its truth for the last twenty years[.] (v. 26; To Thompson Cooper, 23 Nov. 1872)

I have distinctly insisted on the Pope's Infallibility in most of my books for the last 28 years . . . (v. 26; To Henry Tenlon, 23 March 1873)

As to the reports about myself which you mention, they are utterly unfounded. I never had even the temptation to disbelieve the infallibility of the Pope in matters of faith and doctrine – tho' I did not wish the doctrine to be made a dogma, *necessarily* to be believed by every Catholic. This was what the Catholic popular papers succeeded in getting defined. I believed it to be *true*, but not an article of Christian *faith*. *Now* I believe it as an article of faith. (v. 31; To James Crawford Bredin, 10 May 1886)

What Historical Evidence Suggests Belief in Papal Infallibility?

When it is said that 'no Father favours the infallibility of the Pope,' I should ask what do you mean by Father? are the Popes themselves Fathers? and what do you mean by infallibility? it is a word; – define it. As to my own opinion, I think it a very remarkable fact in Church history, that even from the first the Roman traditions about *all* matters have gone *beyond* those of the Easterns etc – and it is remarkable too that St Irenaeus, a representative of East and West and as early as A.D. 120-200, – the disciple of St Polycarp the disciple of St John, – says, 'If you wish to learn, go for the tradition to Rome, the Church of St Peter and St Paul.' Also that in matter of fact there were continual collisions between Rome and nearly every Church, and that

Rome was always in the right. . . . *Why* did the Pope always interfere and (if you will) dictate, except that he had a tradition of his infallibility? and why was he always right, except that he *was* infallible? (v. 24; To Mrs. Helbert, 10 Sep. 1869)

What you are called on to believe is the infallibility of the *Church*. If the Church, in the ensuing Council, said any thing about Papal Infallibility, it will be so strictly worded, with such safeguards, conditions, limitations, etc. as will add as little as is conceivable to what is *now* held – it will be so explained and hedged round as not to apply to the case of Honorius etc. It will not be, what Protestants fancy it will be, a declaration that 'whatever the Pope says is infallible.' It will not make acts like Honorius's infallible. (v. 24; To Mrs. Helbert, 28 Sep. 1869)

I am not quite sure, that the self-assertion of the Popes from the beginning, now for 1800 years, and the irreformability in *fact* of their decisions, (whatever appearances of fact may be adduced against it) is not a strong argument that the Pope is what he claims to be, the Prophet of God . . . did I receive it de fide, I should so do on this ground . . . (v. 25; To Frederick Rymer, 3 Aug. 1870)

For myself, I have ever thought the self-assertion, the ipse dixit, of Popes for 1800 years, a great argument for the fact of their infallibility, . . . (v. 25; To Emilie Perceval, 15 Aug. 1870)

I say for three hundred years the Church has acted on the doctrine – but the doctrine itself is far older than this – indeed from the very beginning of the Church, the Pope has so intervened and interposed in all parts of Christendom, so authoritatively, so magisterially, that it is very perplexing to suppose he had no divine gift of direction and teaching. (v. 25; To Anna Whitty, 31 Aug. 1870)

The whole body of theologians, Gallicans included, have always held, that what the Pope said ex cathedra, was true, *when* the Bishops had received it – what has been passed, is to the effect that what he determines ex cathedra is true *independently* of the reception by the Bishops – but nothing has been passed as to *what is meant* by 'ex cathedra' – and this falls back to the Bishops and the Church to determine quite as much as before. Really therefore nothing has been passed of consequence. Again, the decree is limited to 'faith and morals'-- whereas what the Ultra party wished to pass was 'political principles.' (v. 25; To Lady Simeon, 1 Nov. 1870)

[Y]ou cannot resist its [the Church's] witness about the Pope's infallibility in those things in which the Church is infallible, for this has been believed and acted upon by the great mass of Catholics for centuries. . . . Popes have virtually claimed infallibility from the first. (v. 25; To John Pym Yeatman, 10 July 1871)

Ever since I have been a Catholic, I have heard on all sides a profession of belief in the Pope's Infallibility. Before I was a Catholic, I was informed that the point had been decided, in the Jansenist controversy, as long ago as Innocent xi's Bull Unigenitus. My own reading before I was a Catholic strongly impressed me with the belief that as early as the 5th century St Leo acted as no Pope could have acted unless he was infallible. Long before that, in the 3rd century, Pope Dionysius claimed to act and was obeyed, in matters in which he could not have acted unless he had been generally considered infallible. Of course it is a difficult thing to determine when it is that he acted ex cathedra – and whether a particular subject is one in which, from its nature, he is infallible – but these difficulties in detail do not interfere with the abstract truth. (v. 26; To Lady Chatterton, 27 Feb. 1872)

You will say that Dollinger is an historian and has a right to go by facts. But more than an historian is necessary in this case – he is not (speaking under correction) a philosophical historian. . . . He does not throw himself into the state of things which he reads about – he does not enter into the position of Honorius, or of the Council 40 years afterwards. He ties you down like Shylock to the letter of the bond, instead of realizing what took place as a scene. How he can defend the 3rd General Council, and yet quarrel with the Vatican, I cannot make out – but perhaps by this time the very force of logic, to say nothing of philosophy, has obliged him to give up Councils altogether. . . . though I am sincerely afflicted that so great a man should be lost us, though I feel the scandal and the reproach which it is to us, and though I am indignant at the way in which he has been treated and am much distressed in his distress, still I think he has taken a wrong course, and has got the Catholic world against him – and whatever be the sins, the intrigues, the cruelties of individuals, Securus judicat orbis terrarum. (v. 26; To Alfred Plummer, 17 June 1872)

What are the Limits and Parameters of Papal Infallibility?

[Bellarmine's] thesis is 'the Pope cannot err in praeceptis morum, quae toti Ecclesiae praeseribuntur, and which are either necessary to salvation, or are intrinsically good or evil;' though he can err in other precepta morum. 1. Thus he says he never could commit the error of enjoining usury or forbidding restitution, for restitution is intrinsically good, and usury intrinsically evil. 2. Nor is it possible that he ever could commit the error or injoining circumcision or of forbidding baptism; for to be circumcised is to fall from Christ, and to be baptised is to be made partaker of His redemption[.] In other points of moral teaching he *may* err; e.g. as by injoining what is merely useless, or enforcing it with an excess of punishment, though still [[even]] in such a case, as being not one of salvation or intrinsic good or evil, it is the duty of the subject to obey. Then, in proving the first branch of his proposition, he says: All virtue is good, all vice is evil; if the Pope could commit the error of injoining vice or forbidding virtue, it would follow that the Church, in that it is bound to acquiesce in his judgment, would be bound, *which it never can be*, (Q.E.I) to believe that vice was good and virtue evil. The conclusion is, that, since an absurdity arises from the hypothesis of the Pope's contradicting the eternal moral law, therefore he never will contradict it, he will be divinely protected against contradicting it. The existence of an eternal, divine, sovereign immutable, imperative, Moral Law is ASSUMED, as the basis of the argument. (v. 20; To David Radford, 7 Feb. 1863)

It seems to me like madness for English Catholics to bind up the Infallible Church and the See of St. Peter with every act of every person who in the course of 1800 years has held eminent authority in it. Why do we not bind up the Church with what St. Peter himself did at Antioch as referred to in Galatians ii? or say that there was nothing human in the contention between St. Paul and St. Barnabas? . . . how Englishmen, who wish the conversion of England, can indissolubly connect it with Dogma, that a Pope cannot err as a private doctor or in particular points of conduct, is to my mind incomprehensible. . . . Where are we, if individuals or parties, according to their own feelings or views, can inflict on us additions to the Catholic Faith as once delivered? (v. 20; To William Robert Brownlow, 16 Oct. 1863)

I am confident that it [papal infallibility] must be so limited practically that it will leave things as they are. As to Ward's notions, they are preposterous . . . Then again as to the Syllabus [o Errors], it has no connexion with the Encyclical, except that of *date*. It does not come from the Pope. There was a great attempt to make it a formal ecclesiastical act, and in the Receuil you have. it with the censures annexed to each proposition, as it was originally intended – but the Bishops over the world interfered, and the censures were struck out – and it is not a direct act of the Pope's, but comes to us (the Bishops) from Cardinal Antonelli, with the mere coincidence of time, and as a fact, each condemnation having only the weight which it had in the original papal document (Allocution, Encyclical ere etc) in which each is to be found. If an Allocution is of no special weight, neither is the condemnation of a proposition which it contains. Of course nothing comes from the Pope without having weight, but there is a great difference between weight and infallibility. . . . But even if the Pope's Infallibility were defined, it is impossible that there would not be the most careful conditions determining what is ex cathedra – and it would add very little to the present received belief[.] But I don't think there will be any such decree, or about the temporal power. (v. 22; To Edward B. Pusey, 17 Nov. 1865)

I want then some better ground . . . before I receive the doctrine that what the Pope says, (that is, what the Church says, for no one says that the Pope is infallible except as being in himself the Church) is certain, when he is not professing to explain or declare the Apostolic depositum which has [come] down to him by tradition. (v. 22; To Henry Ignatius Dudley Ryder, 16 July 1866)

[T]he doctrine of Papal Infallibility must be fenced round and limited by *conditions*. (v. 24; To Peter le Page Renouf, 21 June 1868)

I think we must make a broad distinction between an initial or prima facie and ultimate, formal, and ex cathedra decision of ecclesiastical authority. As there are decisions of Councils which are not infallible – so there are decisions of Popes. I believe the Popes at first said strong things against Aristotle's philosophy. Pope Zozimus is said to have been taken in by the Pelagians. John the XXII professed views about the present state of the Saints which he himself retracted before his death, which his successor contradicted in a brief or bull issued on purpose, which the Council of Florence has made heretical. Pope Vigilius too is in some such scrape. (v. 26; To J. H. Willis Nevins, 16 June 1872)

Are Papal Encyclicals Infallible in Their Entirety?

I wish you would look at Ward's letter in the Register of this day. I am much tempted, almost as a matter of duty, to write to the Editor as follows:- 'Sir, A sentence in a letter inserted in your Paper of last Saturday (Saturday the 29th) runs thus:- "The recent Encyclical 'and Syllabus [of Errors] are, beyond question, the Church's infallible utterance." I beg leave to say that I do not subscribe to this proposition[.] (v. 22; To Henry Bittleston, 29 July 1865)

Should Popes Normally be Obeyed, Infallible or Not?

I say with Cardinal Bellarmine whether the Pope be infallible or not in any pronouncement, anyhow he is to be obeyed. No good can come from disobedience, his facts and his warnings may be all wrong; his deliberations may have been biassed – he may have been misled, imperiousness and craft, tyranny and cruelty, may be patent on the conduct of his advisers and instruments, but when he speaks formally and authoritatively he speaks as our Lord would have him speak, and all those imperfections and sins of individuals are overruled for that result which our Lord intends (just as the acts of the wicked and of enemies to the Church are overruled) and therefore the Pope's word stands, and a blessing goes with obedience to it, and no blessing with disobedience. (v. 23; To Lady Simeon, 10 Nov. 1867)

Did Pope Gregory the Great Deny Universal Papal Jurisdiction?

'St Gregory's alleged disclaimer of universal jurisdiction –' He does not disclaim it – but he disclaims being the *Bishop* of each diocese. Anyone who sees the working of the Catholic system, will feel how great the power of the Bishop is in *his place* – Never was a time when the Pope was so powerful in the Church than he is at present – yet I was quite astonished, when I became a Catholic, to find how powerful a Bishop is in his Diocese or

District – Now what Pope Gregory disclaims is, his taking on himself a Bishop's jurisdiction, <He says 'Si unus universalis est, restat ut vos Episcopi *non* sitis.'> ["If the one {the pope} is universal, it must be that you are not bishops."] or superseding the Episcopacy, which is a very different thing from saying that he has not himself a jurisdiction over them. The title 'Episcopus' par excellence is assumed by the Popes at least from the time of Innocent the 1st. i.e. at the end of the 4th century, two centuries before St Gregory. And St Gregory *did* claim universal jurisdiction, therefore he could not have meant that by 'Ecumenical Bishop –' He exercised jurisdiction in Africa, Greece, Gaul, Spain, Constantinople, and, I think, Alexandria. In one place he says 'De sede Constantinopolitana, quis dubitet eam Apostolicae Sedi esse subjectam?' ["That the Church in Constantinople is subject to the Apostolic See, no one can doubt."] Besides letters in the Council of Chalcedon, *before* St Gregory's time, call the Pope Universal Bishop. (v. 13; To Mrs. Martha Lockhart, 5 Nov. 1849)

Have Popes Properly Been Disagreed With?

St Cyprian did not quarrel with the Pope on a point of faith, but of discipline – and no one can deny that his language is violent – but he washed it all away in his glorious martyrdom. It is very common to speak boldly with the Pope – St Polycarp so spoke with St Anicetus, or St Irenaeus, I forget which. St Bernard with Eugenius iii – St Thomas of Canterbury with Alexander iii, as St Paul with St Peter – Human nature in southern climates flares up in a moment – and Popes have generally given way at the moment, as any superior should do. (v. 13; To A. J. Hamner, 21 Nov. 1849)

You need not believe any thing that the Pope says, except when he speaks ex cathedra. His chance sayings need not be better than another man's, nor his measures in detail. (v. 17; To Mrs. Catherine Froude, 20 May 1856)

[I]t was St Catharine who advised a Pope, and succeeded – but St Thomas of Canterbury and St Edmund tried and failed. (v. 21; To Emily Bowles, 31 March 1865)

[W]hen the Pope condescends not to command, but to reason, he puts the case as it were into our hands and makes us the ultimate judge, he taking the place of a witness of preponderating authority. (v. 23; To Lady Simeon, 10 Nov. 1867)

What Are we to Make of the "Bad Popes"?

As to the scandalous lives of some Popes, to which you refer, we not only allow but glory in, as showing the Divine Care of the Church, that, even in the case of those very men, the See of Peter spoke truth, not falsehood – As in Balaam, as in Eli, as in Caiaphas, as in Judas, God was glorified, so has He been glorified, in that respect in which the Pope is His appointed teacher, in Alexander VI and Leo Tenth. They have never spoken false doctrine. But as to the cases of Liberius, Honorius etc, they are doubtful. For myself I do not see that Honorius, any more than Liberius, spoke any heresy ex Cathedra. Others think he did. Therefore a definition of ex Cathedra is required. The definition given by Mr Renouf would be different from mine. You may be quite sure that if the Infallibility of the Pope was ever defined, this point also, what is ex Cathedra, would be cleared up. At present it is unsettled, because the Pope's Infallibility is unsettled. (v. 24; To Mrs. Helbert, 10 Sep. 1869)

I did not become a Catholic myself, as many have done, because of my belief in Papal infallibility. Doubtless, there is a great deal to deplore in the history of the Popes – but there is a bright side as well as a dark – and the bright side is, to say the least, as prominent as the dark. Protestant historians acknowledge it, and have expressed their admiration of the Popedom as an institution, and have been grateful for its beneficial operation and influence as sincerely as Catholics. . . . I detest many things historically connected with the Popes as much as you can; – but what I feel is this, that a Universal Church cannot, by the laws of human society, be held together without a head. (v. 25; To Anna Whitty, 9 Sep. 1870)

Did Pope Gregory XIII Give Assent to a Massacre?

You have lately, in your article on the Massacre of St Bartholomew's day, thrown down a challenge to us on a most serious subject. I have no claim to speak for my brethren; but I speak in default of better men. No Pope can make evil good. No Pope has any power over those eternal moral principles which God has imprinted on our hearts and consciences. If any Pope has, with his eyes open, approved of treachery or cruelty, let those defend that Pope, who can. If any Pope at any time has had his mind so occupied with the desirableness of the Church's triumph over her enemies, as to be dead to the treacherous and savage acts by which that triumph was achieved, let those who feel disposed say that in such conduct he acted up to his high office of maintaining justice and showing mercy. Craft and cruelty, and whatever is base and wicked have a sure *nemesi*s, and eventually strike the heads of those who are guilty of them. Whether, in matter of fact, Pope Gregory xiii had a share in the guilt of the St Bartholomew massacre, must be proved to me, before I believe it. It is commonly said in his defence, that he had an untrue, one-sided account of the matter presented to him, and acted on misinformation. This involves a question of fact, which historians must decide. But, even if they decide against the Pope, his infallibility is in no respect compromised. Infallibility is not impeccability. Even Caiphas prophesied; and Gregory xiii was not quite a Caiphas. (v. 26; To the editor of *The Times*, 9 Sep. 1872)

Can Popes Personally be Heretics?

As to the Pope being a heretic as a private person, while he is infallible ex cathedra, this is an idea quite intelligible. Balaam prophesied and preached the truth, yet, judging from his character, we can easily understand his throwing out, <as he did,> very wretched ideas to Balak in private. The old Prophet in Bethel told lies, yet at length was constrained by the power of God to declare judgment against the prophet from Judah. Caiaphas blasphemed our Lord, but, as the High Priest, prophesied. (v. 25; To John Pym Yeatman, 10 July 1871)

Does the Pope Honorius "Scandal" Disprove Papal Supremacy?

As to Honorius, I do not find any difficulty whatever in it – formidable as the case seems at first sight; . . . The Pope most imprudently encouraged a heresy by an unseasonable economy, using that principle of concession in *doctrine* which all Popes use in matters of *conduct*. Nor is there anything to show that his epistle was a dogmatic and public document – the contrary. The strong words of the 6th Council are to be interpreted by the language of St Maximus and others who go more into detail. To me it is wonderful, and a mark of divine superintendence, that a case which is so near being a real difficulty, is not one. Nor does it surprise me at all that in the long history of 1800 years, when the devil has ever striven to make the Oracle of Truth speak falsely, one or two apparent exceptions should occur. . . . As to your difficulty, do not wonder that among the thousand daily proofs of the Supremacy of the Pope, there should be some strong and specious facts the other way. Is the infallibility of the Pope more exposed to objections of fact than the inspiration of Scripture? Is Esther like an inspired book? [it never mentions God] how do you solve the difficulties of fulfilled prophecy? (v. 13; To A. J. Hamner, 21 Nov. 1849)

Honorius countenanced an heretical party. Here again he was like St Peter in Galat 2. He cannot be proved to have issued any dogmatic tome on the doctrine in dispute . . . (v. 14; To Francis Richard Wegg-Prosser, 25 Sep. 1851)

I certainly did not know how strong a case could be made out against Pope Honorius. But with all its power, I do not find it seriously interferes with my own view of Papal Infallibility . . . Fr Perrone does not contemplate the Pope's making any statement obligatory on our faith, on which the Bishops of the Universal Church had not *first* been bona fide consulted. If you prove on the one hand that Pope Honorius committed himself to a heresy, I can prove without difficulty on the other, that the Pope, in violation of Fr Perrone's condition, acted without consulting his natural advisers[.] (v. 24; To Peter le Page Renouf, 21 June 1868)

I welcomed the prospect of your Pamphlet, not only as expedient at a time when ecclesiastical history is studied less carefully than is its due, but especially because its publication is a virtual protest against that narrow spirit, so uncharitable to the souls of men, which turns theological conclusions into doctrines of obligation. (v. 24; To Peter le Page Renouf, 30 Nov. 1868)

As to the history of Vigilius and Honorius, it requires going into at length before it can be proved that the Pope's infallibility was compromised – for myself, taking the history by itself I should say that it told very strongly against the Pope's infallibility, though I don't think it actually disproves it, I have no hesitation in saying this, because I have never urged you to believe the Pope's Infallibility. I think that infallibility a point which *can* be defined by an Ecumenical Council – but till it *is* so defined, I only hold it as an opinion – I do not think that history actually proves that he is *fallible* ex cathedra, but I think there are facts which taken by themselves look like his fallibility. . . . The accusation against Honorius is that he wrote to the Eastern

Patriarchs two dogmatical epistles, which subsequent Popes and Councils declared to be heretical. Very well – then, if the Pope is declared in the approaching Council to be 'infallible ex cathedra,' *dogmatic epistles to the Eastern Patriarchs* will not be *enough* to be an ex cathedra act. See how tightly the cases of an ex cathedra decision will be restricted. (v. 24; To Mrs. Helbert, 28 Sep. 1869)

I wish you would tell me where you learn your *fact* that 'Honorius taught heresy ex cathedra.' It is your *inference* from certain historical facts – not a fact – and *my* inference is the other way. *I* say, from the facts of history, that he did *not* teach heresy ex cathedra. (v. 26; To J. H. Willis Nevins, 12 June 1872)

The question then is whether you can properly say that Honorius, in countenancing the Monophysite doctrine, spoke ex cathedra. Now here recollect that Popes do not decide on matters at the very beginning of a controversy, but at the end. It runs its course and then the Holy See speaks. The dogma of two Wills, was not decided till 40 years after Honorius's death – Monothelitism was no heresy in Honorius's time, any more than the double personality was a heresy before Nestorius. Ideas and words have to be defined, and they cannot be defined till controversy clears the matter. The great Council of Antioch in 364 [264] condemned the Homoousion, which the Nicene Council has made the test of orthodoxy. On the first blush of the matter a great deal might be said for Honorius's view, and recollect his great object was to heal a schism from which the Church suffers even now, which at the time was a great help to Mahometanism. That he was hasty, injudicious, intellectually hazy, one may grant. The question is whether he was intending to teach the Catholic Church – was he not rather experimentalizing? Is it not the part of a Lawyer or a Controversialist to argue from mere words or acts, and not to throw one's mind into the times, and to try to place ourselves in Honorius's place? I think Dollinger wants imagination, considerateness, charity. Poor Honorius died in peace. There was no popular general outcry against him, as in the case of John xxii

– Was there? I think not. This either shows his act was not a *public* one, or that it was so metaphysical a point, or grammatical even, that the delicate sense of Catholics was not shocked by it. Recollect St. Cyril holds the formula of the '*One* Incarnate nature of the Word.' We all explain him in an orthodox sense. . . . I am far from certain that in like manner we should not clear Honorius, though he boldly said beyond mistake 'one will', but for what happened after. Why don't we? let us see why. Honorius dies in peace. And his memory, I think, was safe *till* the 6th. General Council – a space of 40 years. Meanwhile the controversy went on; the Church gaining light, but its controversialists showing a great deal of angry zeal. The question became a party question. It was decided, and rightly, against Honorius, as in a former age it was decided against Cyril; but Honorius fell into hands not so kind as Cyril found. The forty years, which were necessary for a dogmatic decision, served to intensify the zeal of its promoters against those who had stood in its way. Honorius was pronounced a heretic. Recollect what that really means – not that he in his own person was heretical, but that he originated or promoted heresy. I know some or many theologians say otherwise – but I never can hold that e.g. Origen was a heretic, though he is so often called such. He is made a symbol of that heresy which was found after his day among his followers, and is anathematized as such – I think Honorius was a heretic in the sense in which Origen is. Here I am speaking of what in matter of fact is my own opinion – that Honorius in his own person was not a heretic – at the same time, if he was, that does not show that he has taught heresy ex cathedra – any more than Balaam or Caiaphas were excluded from being divine oracles because they were personally in pagan or Judaic error. (v. 26; To J. H. Willis Nevins, 16 June 1872)

Does Pope Liberius' Failure Disprove Papal Infallibility?

[I]t is most difficult to determine that he asserted ex cathedra any wrong doctrine. What he seems to have done, though the history is confused, is, by *not* positively confessing the Nicene Symbol, to *give a sanction* to the heretical party – as St Peter in Galat. 2. This is a sin, but not an ex cathedra error of faith. . . . Granting then that Liberius by his *acts* encouraged heresy, that as little implicates his ex cathedra decisions, as David's adultery and murder compromise his Psalms. (v. 14; To Francis Richard Wegg-Prosser, 25 Sep. 1851)

Popes have made great mistakes – and Popes have said and done heretical things – though they were not heretics, and did not say and do them *as* Popes. Pope Liberius, for instance, when he gave up St Athanasius, did it under constraint, when he wished to get back from exile, and was in the hands of the Arians. This was not an act of his *as Pope*, ex Cathedra, but as an individual, and an erring one. (v. 24; To Mrs. Helbert, 30 Aug. 1869)

What Was Newman's Personal Opinion of Blessed Pope Pius IX?

The Pope treated us as if we were the only people in the world he had to care for. He is a most wonderful Pope. (v. 17; To William Monsell, 11 Feb. 1856)

The Holy Father himself is a true friend to me and to us . . . (v. 18; To Edward Bellasis, 6 Nov. 1857)

If ever there was a Pontiff, who had a claim on our veneration by his virtues, on our affection by his personal beating, and on our devotion by his sufferings, whose nature it is to show kindness, and whose portion it is to reap disappointment, it is his present Holiness. If ever a Pope deserved to live in the hearts of his own subjects, and to inspire at home the homage which he commands abroad, it is Pius the Ninth. From the hour that he ascended the throne he has aimed at the welfare of his States, temporal as well as spiritual, and up to this day he has gained in return little else than calumny and ingratitude. How great is his trial! but it is the lot of Popes, as of other men, to receive in their generation the least thanks, where they deserve the most. (v. 19; To Viscount Feilding, 13 Feb. 1860)

[N]o one can have been more loyal to the Holy See than I am. I love the Pope personally into the bargain. (v. 20; To Emily Bowles, 19 May 1863)

I believe the Pope is my friend, as he ever has been; but he is besieged by people of all sorts who have ever acted an unfriendly part towards me. (v. 23; To Mark Pattison, 4 Jan. 1867)

Does 1 Clement Confirm Papal Supremacy in Apostolic Times?

[I]t is surely a remarkable fact, that the Bishop Of Rome *should* write a letter of exhortation to a distant Church, (just as an Apostle might, who had a universal jurisdiction, e.g. St Paul or St Jude) and more so when we find other marks in Antiquity all pointing in the same direction, viz. of the power of the Roman see and Church. They may not prove the full doctrine but they strikingly confirm it. (v. 22; To F. C. Burnand, 5 Nov. 1865)

Chapter Eleven

Theology of Salvation (Soteriology)

What is Grace?

'Grace' is in Scripture a word confined to Christianity – other dispensations contain a grant or at least a presence of God's *favor* and *aid*, but the peculiar acceptance and will and power, granted in the gospel, high above all gifts of other covenants, is Grace. Thus St John says 'The Law was given by Moses, but *grace* and truth came etc'. And St Paul 'where sin abounded *grace* did much more abound.' [Jn 1:17; Rom 5:20] I think then a state of grace is that state 'in which we stand by faith' by the mercy of God in Christ – and that it was not vouchsafed to the world till Christ came; and that all those words grace, life, righteousness, truth, light, etc. do, not indeed mean the same things, but all coincide in one and the same subject. I mean that there is one *certain* state, and that it, viewed on different sides of it, is in one aspect grace, in another truth, in another salvation etc. – just as you would say that God is One, and in one view of Him eternal, in another Almighty etc. etc. by which you do not mean to say that eternity is the same as omnipotence, but that the two coincide in one and the same subject. . . . the question turns on the *meaning* of the word, 'grace' – whether it stands for *any* divine help, or the help through the Spirit of Christ. Yet I do not think it is an indifferent question – first because *Scripture* seems to confine 'grace' to the Christian covenant – next because grace conveys the *two* ideas of acceptance *and* spiritual aid – whereas the deeds done by unjustified man, even through God's sacred aid, are not pleasing to God on account of original corruption, which is imparted to them till they come within the Covenant. (v. 8; To A. C. Tarbutt, 22 Jan. 1841)

How Powerful is Grace to Transform Men?

Now, independent of all other considerations, the great difference, in a practical light, between the object of Christianity and of heathen belief, is this—that glory, science, knowledge, and whatever other fine names we use, never healed a wounded heart, nor changed a sinful one; but the Divine Word is with power. The ideas which Christianity brings before us are in themselves full of influence, and they are attended with a supernatural gift over and above themselves, in order to meet the special exigencies of our nature. Knowledge is not "power," nor is glory "the first and only fair;" but "Grace," or the "Word," by whichever name we call it, has been from the first a quickening, renovating, organizing principle. It has new created the individual, and transferred and knit him into a social body, composed of members each similarly created. It has cleansed man of his moral diseases, raised him to hope and energy, given him to propagate a brotherhood among his fellows, and to found a family or rather a kingdom of saints all over the earth;—it introduced a new force into the world, and the impulse which it gave continues in its original vigour down to this day. Each one of us has lit his lamp from his neighbour, or received it from his fathers, and the lights thus transmitted are at this time as strong and as clear as if 1800 years had not passed since the kindling of the sacred flame. What has glory or knowledge been able to do like this? Can it raise the dead? can it create a polity? can it do more than testify man's need and typify God's remedy? . . . In morals, as in physics, the stream cannot rise higher than its source. Christianity raises men from earth, for it comes from heaven; but human morality creeps, struts, or frets upon the earth's level, without wings to rise. (v. 8: Letter to the *Times* by "Catholicus" in Response to Robert Peel ["Tamworth"], Feb. 1841)

Is Grace Required for Salvation?

[D]o you pray for 'effectual grace' –? Suppose I come to a high wall – cannot jump it – such are the moral obstacles which keep us from the Church. We see the Heavenly City before us, we go on and on along the road, till a wall simply crosses it. Human effort cannot clear it – there is no scaling, no vaulting over. Grace enables us to cross it – and that grace is called effectual grace. Our first grace is sufficient to enable us to pray for that second effectual grace – and God gives grace for grace. (v. 16; To Mrs. Catherine Froude, 2 March 1854)

What Does it Mean to Be in a "State of Grace"?

I suppose that it is quite possible to know and allowable to believe that we are reconciled to God and have not sin to be forgiven in the sense of its interfering with His presence. To have sin forgiven in this sense is only being in a state of grace – and though many persons may not have any vivid realisings that they are in a state of grace, this is not inconsistent with others having such realisings. Persons in a state have to pray concerning past sin in a very different way from those who are not in a state of grace – not that it may be forgiven unto justification, or in popular language 'forgiven,' but that it may continue forgiven, that we may not fall from a state of grace, that we may receive higher measures of justification, that the remaining consequences of sin, temporal or moral, may be forgiven etc etc. (v. 10; To Edward B. Pusey, 12 March 1845)

Is Grace Given in Different Measure to Different Men?

You know what an awful overcoming view Catholics take of the grace of God – as that which we cannot merit, which may be withheld without any injustice to us, which is not given to all in the same measure. (v. 13; To Henry Wilberforce, 1 Oct. 1849)

What is Apostasy, or Falling from Grace?

[A] person who falls from the state of salvation, falls from the state of grace, that state which 'the glory of the Lamb enlightens' [Rev 21:23] whether for peace, acceptance, holiness, love etc, etc. But in saying this, it is plain I do not intend to say anything so extreme as that a person who falls from a state of grace is therefore left without God's aids and providential leadings. How do men (adults) originally come for baptism? they are not yet justified or in a state of grace – they are heathen – but God whose mercies are over all His works draws them on to a state of grace by assistances which He gives apart from that state – thus whom He called them He also justified – that is, a state in which a man is helped is prior to that which is the state of grace. When a man falls from grace he relapses into some such state. . . . As to your case of the Prodigal Son, I quite agree with what you say. He who has once been God's Son, never can be such as he was before it. His privileges are not *forfeited* (except he commit the sin against the Holy Ghost about which we know nothing) but *suspended*. He falls out of grace, but not into the same state as he was in before he came into it. (v. 8; To A. C. Tarbutt, 22 Jan. 1841)

It is no absurdity to say that a man is in God's favour and in advanced holiness, yet may ultimately fall away; but it is (not 'horribly false,' but) a contradiction in terms to say that he is all this, yet at the time in utter damnation. (v. 14; To Henry Wilberforce, 11 March 1851)

Are we Saved by Verbal or Creedal Professions Only?

For to me words are no evidence by themselves – but works – and her error is that of multitudes in the so-called religious world . . . who think they know things because they can say them, and understand because they have heard them – or, account themselves Christians because they use Scripture phrases – or, to believe in Christ with the heart and to be changed in their moral nature because they assent fully to certain doctrines (not hard to admit as intellectual truths without any moral preparation) that we can do nothing of ourselves, have no merit, or are saved by faith; – or (again) imagine they have habits or a character when they have only feelings. (v. 2; To [brother] Francis William Newman, 1830)

This is why we see such multitudes in France and Italy giving up religion altogether. They have not impressed upon their hearts the life of our Lord and Saviour as given us in the Evangelists. They believe merely with the intellect, not with the heart. Argument may overset a mere assent of the reason, but not a faith founded in a personal love for the Object of Faith. They quarrel with their priests, and then they give up the Church. We can quarrel with men, we cannot quarrel with a book. It is very pleasant then to find a Frenchman, a good Catholic, reading and meditating on Scripture. I dare say there are many such, and they don't fall away. (v. 26; To Mrs. J. W. Bowden, 12 May 1872)

Speaking under necessary corrections which must be ever made, when we lay down an abstract proposition in a concrete and practical matter, I would make the following statement: 'No one will be punished hereafter merely for holding or not holding a given proposition.' A man must do, or have done, something more than this to incur punishment. (v. 26; To Isy Froude, 9 April 1873)

What is Faith and Where Does it Come From?

Surely faith is the gift of God, as it was in St Paul's day, and the divine election is as wonderful now as then. . . . the sons of God are born, not of the will of man, but of God. . . . the election is with God; we can but co-operate with him – and we must submit to His decision. (v. 13; To Catherine Froude, 14 July 1849)

No one ought to enter the Church without faith – no one can have faith for it by wishing or willing it, at the moment. Faith is a Gift of God; we can gain it by prayer, we cannot gain it at once; but we can gain it at last. I will quarrel with no one simply for not entering into the holiest and happiest of states on the spur of the instant – faith must be preceded by reason – but I will quarrel with him much, if he does not earnestly and continually ask of God the illumination which leads reason to faith. (v. 15; To Mrs. Catherine Froude, 23 Feb. 1853)

There is a natural love, and a supernatural; a natural exercise of the intellect, and a supernatural. Human faith is at least analogous to divine faith, tho' the former comes of pure intellectual exercises, and the latter from above. Human faith lies *in* the intellect as well as divine faith; but the former is created by previous acts of mere human reason, the latter is the creation of supernatural grace. (v. 20; To William G. Ward, 15 March 1862)

Faith is a gift of God, and a mere wish or a decision to join the Church is not necessarily faith. However, I would not say that you have not faith – but your faith is weak – and I speak of its being a gift of God to believe, to remind you, what it must be right to say, even tho' you do not need reminding, that you must pray for it. The Apostles said to our Lord 'Increase our faith.' [Lk 17:5] (v. 25; To Mrs. Wilson, 8 Jan. 1870)

I cannot believe merely because I ought to believe. I may wish both to act and to believe – though I can do neither – and, as I ask God for grace to enable me to act, so I ask Him for grace to enable me to believe. 'It is the gift of God – why does He not give it me?' Because you do not perseveringly come to Him for the gift, and do your part by putting aside all those untrue and unreal and superfluous arguings. (v. 25; To William Robert Brownlow, 29 April 1871)

Faith is a divine gift. It is gained by prayer. Prayer must be patient and persevering. (v. 31; To Alfred Henry Spurrier, 11 Dec. 1886)

What is the Gospel?

I do not object to bringing forward the atonement explicitly and prominently *in itself*, but under circumstances; i.e. where people are unfit to receive it. I think it should be taught all baptized children – that it is the life of all true christians – but that it is not the *means of conversion* (ordinarily speaking, or in the divine appointment) of those who are *not* religious. I think it ought not to be preached to infidels, immoral men, backsliders at first, but be *reserved* till they begin to feel the need of it. Consequently I object to the use of it so often made in our pulpits as *the one* doctrine to be addressed to *all*. It is but one *out* of others, and *not* addressed to all. There are various instruments of persuasion given in Scripture; the most familiar distinction is that of the Law and the Gospel. I consider that at this time the mass of our congregations, who have lapsed after Baptism require the Law rather than the Gospel. They require to be brought to a sense of sin, and I do not think that the preaching of the doctrine of the Atonement is intended to bring them to a sense of sin. I will add, first that in preaching the Law I do not mean of course to exclude the preaching of Divine *Love* and *Mercy* – but the insisting specially on the *Atonement*. Secondly the Atonement is not the only doctrine which under circumstances I would withhold – the Incarnation is another – The Apostles in the Acts are almost silent *both* about the Divinity of Christ *and* the Atonement. I only wish to follow their example. St Paul is said to preach the *faith of Christ* to Felix, when he but insists on righteousness, temperance, and judgment to come. Our Saviour Himself is said to *preach the Gospel*, yet even His death, and much more His Atonement, was a secret during His Ministry. (v. 9; To an Unknown Correspondent, 4 March 1843)

How Do we Prove that we Have a Genuine Faith?

[I]t is quite idle to pretend to faith and holiness, unless they show forth their inward principles by a pure, disinterested, upright line of conduct. (v. 1; To His Mother, 30 Aug. 1824)

What are the Fruits and Objects of Faith?

[T]here are two systems of doctrine, the Ancient which insists on the Objects and fruits of faith, and the modern which 'attempts instead to secure *directly and primarily* that "mind of the Spirit" which may savingly receive the truths and fulfil the obedience of the Gospel.' . . . Now I do not at all deny that the modern system does insist on the fruits and Objects of faith; . . . but I say it does not *directly* or *primarily*. If an awakened sinner asked an ancient believer what he must do to be saved, he would answer (I consider) look to the Word Incarnate, look to the Holy Trinity, look to the Sacraments God's instruments; and break off your sins, do good whereas you have done evil – But I conceive one of the modern school, without denying this would for the most part drop it and say instead, 'Your heart must be changed – till you have faith you have nothing – you must have a spiritual apprehension of Christ – you must utterly renounce yourself and your merits and throw yourself at the foot of the Cross etc' Now the question is not whether this is not *true*. I have said expressly 'That such a spiritual temper is indispensable, is agreed on all hands;' but whether it is *the way to make a man a Christian*. I would maintain, that if we take care of the Objects and works of faith, faith will almost take care of itself. This modern view says take care of the state of heart, and the Objects and works will almost take care of themselves. But I have been stating this modern view as judicious, pious, and moderate men put it forward abstractedly But the mass of men develop it, and then what is in itself (as I conceive) a mistake, becomes a mischief. One says '*Examine* yourselves whether you have this spiritual temper – Without it you are nothing though you abound in good

- 238 -

works and are orthodox in creed, you are but a moral man. – do you hate sin? do you love Christ? do you feel that. He is the pearl of great price?' etc etc Now such questions are either mere generalisms meaning nothing at all, or they lead to a direct contemplation of our feelings as *the* means, *the* evidence of justification. (v. 6; To Lord Lifford, 12 Sep. 1837)

What is "Fiducial Faith" or "Faith in Faith"?

[T]he so called Evangelical School makes a *certain inward experience*, a certain conscious state of feeling, the *evidence* of justification. . . . the ancient system insists on the Objects and fruits of faith as supplying the direct, natural, and necessary evidence of justification, and the modern on a certain state of inward feeling . . . (v. 6; To Lord Lifford, 12 Sep. 1837)

Will Faith be Tried and Tested?

Faith ought to be tried and tested, if it *be* faith. I don't like that faith, which, (as I have seen written to a new convert) is a 'precious tender plant,' to be sedulously guarded under a glass cover, or in a hot-house – an exotic – if so, our religion is a mere 'alien religion,' and 'Oriental faith and worship' – but it is a tough principle within us, bearing heavy weights and hard work, or it is worth very little. (v. 19; To Mrs. F. R. Ward, 8 May 1859)

Can we Obtain Absolute Assurance of Salvation?

[S]o sinful are we, it is very rare we can have an assurance we are in a saving state personally; when we consider our advantages and our little fruit etc. We are *preparing* for heaven, that is all. Our duty is *to look upon Christ*, as the Israelites bitten with serpents; to look out of ourselves, timidly, wistfully . . . to contemplate His perfections – etc *This is living and being saved* BY FAITH, which (depend upon it) I hold far more practically and fully than many of those who would say I denied 'justification by faith.' As to 2 Cor xiii, 'Examine yourselves etc' it is *negative*. We can and ought to clear ourselves of positive wickedness, e.g. 'debates, envyings, wraths, etc' xii, 20, 21 and we may be quite sure we are not 'in the faith' if we detect in us any habitual sins – yet after all this even St Paul says, 'I am not conscious of ought to myself; *yet am I not hereby justified*; but he that judgeth me is the Lord.' This is quite consistent with taking comfort from a clear conscience *in particulars*; just as one might appeal to God one had not robbed or murdered, not that one was in a spiritual or saving state. . . . If St Paul (Phil iii) had not 'attained', I suspect it does (as a general rule) in all cases take many years to attain a Christian mind . . . (v. 5; To Samuel Wilberforce, 4 Feb. 1835)

I do not say 'as certain as I am certain I shall perserve [sic] in the Catholic Church', for such perseverance comes, 'not of the will of the flesh, nor of the will of man,' [Jn 1:13] but of the electing mercy of Almighty God. But, though I cannot presume to anticipate the future, I can recall the past. I can affirm that by God's grace I have never for a moment doubted that the Roman Communion is the One Fold of Christ, ever since I entered it; and this experience of myself for 25 years leads me to trust that in me will never be fulfilled the woe pronounced on back-sliders. 'It had been better for them not to have known the way of righteousness, than after they had known it, to turn from the Holy Commandment delivered to them.' [2 Pet 2:21] (v. 25; To Edward Husband, 17 July 1870)

Can we Know Someone Else's Eternal Destiny?

I don't think it peculiar to myself, but really for myself it never occurs to me to fancy the final destiny of any living person. The result is so simply hid from us. In all the awful matters of the next world, I never have any temptation to go one single step beyond what is actually revealed, or logically follows on revelation – No one can say that the future state of individuals falls into this matter – and I can as little realize the future as see in the dark, except as faith enables me. It is not even a point of faith that Ananias and Sapphira were lost – indeed, one common opinion among Catholics is that they were not. I only know what is my duty – I only know theological truth, natural and revealed. (v. 17; To Mrs. Catherine Froude, 12 Dec. 1856)

What I have ever said is this – 'that Keble [his great friend who had just died] had from a youth a great drawing to Catholicism, and that Pusey had never had, as far as I can see, any such drawing.' People may have (if they please) their *own* sentiments, and *infer* from this, that Keble was not in good faith, and that I think so – but I repudiate and spit out the idea with great indignation – I never said or thought any such thing. I don't think I should dare to say of any one that he was not in good faith – or should presume to compare one man with another in the balance of responsibility. And whoever has so interpreted me, has coloured my words, with a meaning which I shrink from: If this is not the origin of the report, I can't tell what is. Any how, it is simply untrue. (v. 22; To Henry James Coleridge, 3 April 1866)

How Can we Discern Another Man's Spiritual State?

I know that the habit of religious conversation, the expression of opinions, fears, hopes, desires etc, and the ability to say prayers are by some accounted the signs of a true Christian. I cannot in a day or a year get at that hidden man of the heart in another which God alone sees constantly. My ground of sure hope as to another's spiritual state is the sight of a consistent *life* – and therefore there are very few people I can be *sure* of . . . (v. 2; To [brother] Francis William Newman, 1830)

How Shall we Approach the Doctrine of Predestination?

As far as I know there is nothing to say or to discuss on the subject of predestination. That there are great mysteries connected with it, is plain at first sight. 'It had been well' for Judas, 'not to have been born'; yet he was born. Here is a mystery from which one cannot escape, why Almighty Goodness should allow a soul to exist which He foresaw would be eternally lost. Again, when we see two persons, one going right, one wrong, the reason of this is quite beyond us – Calvinists attempt to solve it by imputing it to God's arbitrary will; but this is only throwing the difficulty a step back, for it is as mysterious that *He* should so will, as that *man* should will this way or that. Still it *is* a mystery, and we seem to have no data by which to determine it. Again the doctrine of eternal punishment itself is a great mystery. On the whole then I do not see that we have the means of discussing the subject, and I do not know who of our writers has done so profitably. We do not know what *design* is, when ascribed to Almighty God. It seems better to keep close to the words of Scripture and the Church and there to leave the matter. (v. 8; To H. W. Bellairs, 25 April 1842)

The chief authors of this re-action were the Jesuits – and it gave rise to two separate protesting movements-- one on the part of Baius – the other and more famous on the part of the Jansenists, who professed to take the part of St Augustine, and to enunciate his doctrine. *They were* certainly a kind of Calvinists – but, after a long struggle, were ejected from the Church. Whether St Augustine really sanctioned some things they said, is a contested point; doubtless he said strong things which no Catholic would say now; but they never have been said by the Church at any time. . . . Many great divines have taken St Augustine's view of predestination The Dominicans took a line very much like his. The Jesuits took the opposite side. Till lately no Saint was known to be with them – but now they can appeal to two – to St Francis de Sales, of whom a letter has been found on the subject, and St Alfonso Liguori. (v. 31; To A. H. H. Jesse, c. 1859)

How Important are Good Works According to Scripture?

The whole of Scripture speaks of holiness being indispensable, and a change of heart – the whole of Scripture speaks of our being judged by our works. (v. 5; To Samuel Wilberforce, 29 Jan. 1835)

Are we Saved by Works?

As to good works, no one is saved by good works without the atonement of Christ; and, without denying that great saints may do certain good works without sin in them (that is *through divine grace*) . . . (v. 21; To John F. Perrin, 9 Sep. 1864)

What is Merit?

[O]f no one, (excepting the Blessed Virgin) are we able to say that he has lived without the commission of sin, nor has any one, (even the Blessed Virgin,) any merit at all in any one of his acts, except by virtue of the covenanted promise of God in Christ, who has condescended to *give* merit to that which has no merit taken apart from that promise, just as the signature on a Bank note makes a poor bit of paper worth 5 [pounds]. (v. 21; To John F. Perrin, 9 Sep. 1864)

[H]uman charitableness, honesty, fortitude, patience, in the ease of heathen, may be assisted by actual grace, and bring the soul forward towards conversion, and have a congruous merit – but still they do not' cease to be acts of human nature. (v. 21; To J. Walker of Scarborough, 24 Oct. 1864)

What is Infused Justification?

[T]hat which justifies is a spiritual seed or element infused into us from above, and is neither faith, hope, love or contrition by itself, but all of these at once, or something of which these are distinct names. And as we should not say that we were pardoned by God's justice or taught by His power, though justice and power do but stand for the same subject as mercy and wisdom, so it is wrong to say that we are justified by contrition or perfected by faith, though contrition and faith are but aspects of that which is also love. (v. 10; To Thomas William Allies, 29 Dec. 1843)

[F]orgiveness of sins is the work of the Holy Ghost . . . It means that it is conveyed in the gift of grace – that justification and sanctification go together – that we are justified, not by external imputation, but by an inward gift. (v. 17; To Catherine Anne Bathurst, 27 Oct. 1856)

The whole application to individuals of the merit, of the Atonement is through the Holy Ghost. The medium is *grace*. The grace of Christ is through the Holy Ghost. . . . Grace is the medium by which sin is forgiven and the soul justified – the Holy Ghost is the Giver of Grace. (v. 17; To Catherine Anne Bathurst, 5 Nov. 1856)

What is the Relationship of Justification to the Sacraments?

Justification by faith *without* the Sacraments is the essence of sectarian and (modern) heretical doctrine. (v. 9; To an Unknown Correspondent, 4 March 1843)

Is Sanctification a Difficult, Lengthy Process?

No one must be surprised, particularly when first making an effort to live strictly, at discouragements, failures, and the apparent hopelessness of making progress. You must not mind these things – everybody experiences the like. You must not be impatient nor over-anxious – but go steadily on, feeling thankful that you have (please God) time before you. You cannot hasten the course of things – you cannot become what you would wish to be on a sudden. You can but do God's will, as far as may be,

according to your day, and leave the whole matter to Him. (v. 7;
To Miss Mary Holmes, 19 July 1840)

Does Sanctification or Holiness Admit of Degrees?

[S]anctity admits of degrees. You cannot talk of 'more one', you
can talk of 'more holy'. (v. 15; To Lord Charles Thynne, 24
March 1852)

How Close is Anglican Justification to St. Robert Bellarmine's?

I forgot to tell you, . . . how extremely useful I have found the
Bellarmine [*Disputationes*] you gave me. It has *written* my work
just published – and it has written my lectures on
Justification. . . . You really could not [have] given me a book
which I so needed, have so used, and found so useful . . . (v. 6; To
J. F. Christie, 14 June 1837)

How Should Evangelists Approach Dying Persons?

I would leave cases of alarmed sinners on the point of death to
the inscrutable mercies of God. Secret things belong unto Him.
Besides His rule, He has ten thousand ways unknown to us of
providing that not one single tear or cry of penitence should be
lost. If a man be dying and says 'What must I do etc', I am not
embarrassed by my Rule one whit; I bid him confidently look
unto Jesus, surrender himself to Him, 'to whom shall he go?' – I
cannot indeed promise him any assurance or point to any deed or
feeling of his which will bring him peace, but he may do what he
can – he may partake the Blessed Sacrament and leave all in His
hands who is more merciful than we can comprehend. In truth
there is much that is unknown. Infants are saved without a
formed character of holiness; God has other ways of saving. He
has many mansions in His house. (v. 5; To Samuel Wilberforce,
29 Jan. 1835)

What is Antinomianism, or "Cheap Grace"?

[I]t is matter of fact that Christians do labour in detail, do add to their faith virtue etc etc. – *how* they do it, is another matter – we know it is through the Spirit nevertheless, as a fact, *they do it* – and this age forgets they do it – and therefore it is necessary to bring out the fact in all its details before the world. In truth men *do* think that a saving state is one, where the mind merely looks to Christ – a virtual antinomianism. Lately a person I know asked a friend who professed peculiar opinions '*How* he should act different from what he now did, supposing he were not a spiritual believer, as he professed to be.' He confessed, *in no respect* – his outward actions would be the same – *still* his motives (he said) feelings, thoughts would be different – now he looked up to Christ, sanctified his life by faith etc etc. Therefore, I maintain, it is necessary to bring out the details of the Christian life, *as matters of fact*, before the world. Men will confess they are sinful in the abstract. Spoken to in the abstract they do not know whether they are spiritual or not. . . . good work[s] . . . are the fruits of a spiritual faith . . . (v. 5; To Samuel Wilberforce, 4 Feb. 1835)

Is Preaching a Primary Instrument of Saving Faith?

Certainly in my judgment Preaching is not the means of conversion – but a subsidiary, as rousing, convincing, interesting, and altogether preparing the way; a work especially necessary now, when Christians need the exhibition of (what is called) the Law, as much perhaps as when St James wrote his (uninfluential) Epistle. The Church with the Sacraments etc, and the life of good men seem to me the great persuasives of the Gospel, as being visible witnesses and substitutes for Him who is Persuasion itself. Yet surely He in His day had so little success, that even the Church His representative, much more a mere preacher, may well acquiesce in failure. (v. 5; To James Stephen, 27 Feb. 1835)

What is the Goal of Preaching?

I would say the *general object* of preaching is to enlighten the mind as to its real state – to dig round about the Truth – to make men feel they are sinners and lost – to make them understand their need of pardon and sanctification – and the difficulty of the latter, to hinder them for mistaking words for ideas, and going on in a *formal* way, (which I cannot but think *does* follow that style of preaching, called simple and elementary, which the Evangelicals adopt, as if to speak of Christ's righteousness, or blood, or our spiritual renovation, conveyed in the very form of words any true sense to the mind, much less the depth of meaning and extent of truths which alone adequately answer to those phrases, as if men might not go on year by year, as proficient in algebra, using terms and working out conclusions truly yet blindly) . . . (v. 5; To James Stephen, 16 March 1835)

What Will Judgment Day be Like?

First I consider that Scripture expressly tells us that the secrets of all hearts will be openly disclosed at the last day, 1 Cor iv, 5. and that this is implied in the full force of the words 'the Day shall declare every man's work.' 1 Cor iii. 13. . . . Next I make *my own deduction* from this doctrine – viz if disclosed, *to whom* if not to the individual himself? and again, if disclosed to him, it will be a most fearful and trying disclosure. . . . I have said that I consider that the view of ourselves at the last day will be terrifying; but that to those who on earth have duly believed in our Lord, it will be without harm as being supported by His strength; however, that to others it will be a spiritual agony and second death. (v. 7; To Charles Crawley, 15 April 1840)

What is Original Sin?

Catholics hold that Original sin is mainly an external evil, Protestants an internal. According to us, it is not propagated in the way of cause and effect, but by an act of the will of God, exerted and carried out on each child, as it is conceived. I repeat, this is not *de fide*, but it is what I conceive theologians teach. (v. 19; To Arthur Osborne Alleyne, 15 June 1860)

Our doctrine of original sin is *not* that of Protestants. We do *not* hold *infection* of *nature* – but we place original sin in the *absence* of *super*natural grace. (v. 19; To William Wilberforce, 9 Dec. 1860)

[I]t is the Catholic, though not the Protestant, doctrine that Adam till the fall was *not in a state of nature*, but *above* nature from a definite gratuitous gift of grace; and that one school of theologians teaches not only (as all Catholics hold) that original sin *consists* in the removal of this grace, but moreover that that removal has involved no deterioration at all of his original nature. (v. 21; To George William Cox, 4 Feb. 1865)

By original sin is meant the state of degradation and disadvantage in which the whole world lies in consequence of the fall of Adam. This state is reversed in baptism, when the grace of God is first given to the soul. Then by that grace the soul is brought into the family of God, as Adam belonged to it in the beginning. (v. 22; To Lady Chatterton, 2 Oct. 1865)

We hold that 'original sin' is in its first idea a deprivation – a deprivation of that garment of grace which made the soul pleasing to God. The soul has been stripped of it – and the consequence of this loss is, that it cannot govern itself. That stripping may be likened to a surgical operation which leaves the patient weak and suffering, and exposed to illnesses, as to fever. Each one of us is brought into being by God in this state; but there is nothing unjust in this dispensation on God's part, for He gives to each of us such grace as is abundantly sufficient for our need. (v. 26; To H. A. Woodgate, 23 Feb. 1872)

What are the Consequences of Sin?

Sinning has two out of many consequences – it throws us out of God's favor, and it incurs a punishment. These are not identical. God often punishes those whom He loves, and then we call the punishment chastisement. (v. 7; To Miss Mary Holmes, 19 July 1840)

Does Sin (or Rebellion) Have Degrees of Willfulness?

Those who *wilfully* sin against the authority of the Church, are guilty; but who of men can tell whether *this* or *that* man has sinned wilfully? we leave this to God. (v. 8; To Miss Formby?, 6 April 1841)

Can we Sin in Ignorance?

[N]o one can commit sin without knowing it; and ignorance is possible of all points of moral duty except the most elementary. (v. 26; To an Unknown Correspondent, 5 Sep. 1873)

What are the Conditions for Mortal Sin?

No one can commit mortal sin without 'advertentia' and 'consensus'; that is without his intellect and his will being parties to the act. (v. 26; To an Unknown Correspondent, 5 Sep. 1873)

What is Invincible Ignorance in Relation to Final Salvation?

[P]ersons who died in Protestantism are saved on the conditions, first of their being in invincible ignorance, i.e. ignorance which they could not help – secondly if they make an act of contrition on their deathbeds or rather their dying moments, so as never to fall into mortal sin after it. Now considering the anxious thought these two conditions give rise to, it seems to me you have ground enough to urge any, the most holy (to human eye) of Protestants, to be converted. The *nearer* they are the Church, (which is the case you put,) the greater danger is there, that they are *not* in invincible ignorance; and, though when a good Protestant is dead, you may often fairly argue, 'he *was* in invincible ignorance, for he died a Protestant,' still surely this does not interfere with your duty to consider, while he is alive, whether he really is or is not in ignorance, or whether he is not bound to examine the question more exactly, *whether he puts it aside*. And then again, it is true that numbers of Catholics, dying without the Sacraments, nay all Catholics, depend at the last either on their not being in mortal sin, or on an act of contrition to restore their souls to grace; but who with any feeling of charity to his neighbour, would like to leave him thus to himself? and even if to a Catholic, and the holiest, you bring the last Sacraments, and would sin if you did not, will you not much more bring the Sacraments to a Protestant, who has not *lived* on them (in former receptions of them), and if saved, is saved by the grace which had its wellspring, and origin in Baptism only? (v. 13; To A. J. Hamner, 16 Jan. 1850)

I certainly do not consider, speaking under correction, that in order to be in invincible ignorance one must be out of sight and hearing of Catholicism; and that to be near Catholics is incompatible with such an ignorance. Habit, formation of mind, prejudice, reliance and faith in others, may be as real walls of separation as mountains. Members of one and the same household may be more distant from each other in the intercommunion and mutual apprehension of ideas, than they would be made by the interposition of an ocean. Your dear Mother may have been in perfect good faith. And, if we once get so far as to feel the possibility of this, then we may take comfort to ourselves and believe, that all those tokens of sincerity and devotion which we see in our Protestant friends, are not mere appearances and pretences, but real evidence that their ignorance was *not* vincible, and their separation from the Church not voluntary. I cannot get myself to believe that the many dear friends and relatives I have lost are without the hope of salvation; I do not know what obliges me to think so; I do not see why I should adopt the contrary views of this Catholic or that who is narrowminded in his view of doctrine, and has not the experience of fact, of the lives of Protestants, as I have. Till then I am called by the voice of the Church to think otherwise, I shall think hopefully, where others who have no means of judging, rashly despair. (v. 20; To Sophia Ryder, 4 Sep. 1862)

I know perfectly well, and rejoice in knowing, that invincible ignorance is a possible state, and no one can be condemned for doing that which he did not know was wrong, . . . (v. 21; To Helen Douglas Forbes, 4 Oct. 1864)

God alone can tell who has thus rebelled, and who has not, – who is invincibly ignorant and who is not. In this respect I differ from Manning, because he attempts to define the classes, who are, and who are not. (v. 21; To Edward B. Pusey, 25 Nov. 1864)

I believe great numbers are in invincible ignorance, therefore are not answerable for not doing what they have never known they ought to do. They are saved in their ignorance, but their ignorance does not avail those whom God calls by His grace. But when the question is asked *who* are those who are called, and *when* are they bound to act upon it, of course caution is necessary in dealing with individuals. (v. 24; To Gilbert Simmons, 28 June 1868)

You know that no fault attaches to your dear parents for not being Catholics – no one is in fault who does not wilfully reject the truth . . . (v. 26; To Lady Chatterton, 24 March 1873)

You also ask, whether you have gone too far in what you say of invincible ignorance; I think not, supposing what you say be coupled with the proviso that we can as little decide absolutely that a man is in invincible ignorance, as that he is not. No one has a right to be sure that he is in invincible ignorance. I think I have heard Keble say, 'Well, all I can say is, that, if the Roman Communion is the One True Church, I do not know it, I do not know it.' (v. 26; To Edward B. Pusey, 27 April 1873)

Chapter Twelve

Jesus Christ (Christology)

Can we be Certain of the Divinity (Godhood) of Jesus?

Can a man be as sure to himself of the fact that Christ once was on earth and was God, as I that my friend is alive and is a second self to me? Catholics say that a man can; that, by the operation of grace and by natural experiences, he can apprehend the Object of faith, as men in general apprehend objects of sight. And many of them bear witness with St Polycarp that such is their own case. (v. 24; To G. A. Cox, 17 Jan. 1868)

How Central is "Christ Crucified" in Christianity?

[T]he doctrine of Christ crucified is the only spring of real virtue and piety, and the only foundation of peace and comfort. (v. 1; To His Mother, 28 July 1824)

Was the Incarnation Strictly Necessary?

Certainly I wish to take the Scotist view on that point. It seems to me more philosophical (if one has a right so to talk) to throw the difficulty on creation – as if creation is *the* great mystery – and if the Supreme condescended to create, to partake in creation was involved. But as I understand the Scotist view it simply is, that He would have been incarnate, even had man not sinned – but when man sinned it was *for* our redemption; in *matter of fact* the end was to make satisfaction, . . . (v. 13; To Frederick W. Faber, 9 Dec. 1849)

How Are Christ's Two Natures Explained?

We believe our Lord is *One* Person: there is One Lord, One Christ, One Emmanuel. And, since He has two natures, divine and human, He is at Once without beginning and with beginning Son of God and Son of Mary; He cannot, never could suffer, yet He did suffer on the Cross. Moreover, on account of that ineffable oneness of Person, we may say of Him, God is man, and man is God: God was born of Mary, and the Son of man is in heaven (John iii, 13) – God purchased us with His own blood (Acts xx, 28) and a man shall judge the world (Acts xvii, 31). Hence, from the same absolute oneness of Person, we may (reverently) speak of God's Mother, God's flesh, God's face, God's hands. Hence too, when we worship the Eternal Word Incarnate, we cannot *help* by one and the same act worshipping His human nature, as being one with Him, not separate; else, we should not be worshipping Him at all; for we must worship Him *as He is*, and His human nature is united to Him after the manner of an attribute, and, as, in worshipping His infinite Wisdom and Goodness, we worship Him, so in like manner, as to all that is His, we cannot divide Him into two, or worship Him at all, without at the same time worshipping His manhood and all that appertains to His manhood, because His manhood is inseparably one with His Person. Therefore, when we say that we worship that manhood, we really meant that we worship His Divine Person *through* His manhood – in order to plead with Him His gracious incarnation. (v. 26; To Mrs. Henry Wilberforce, 21 Oct. 1873)

How Shall we View the Atonement or Propitiation of Christ?

There is nothing against reason (i.e. as I feel) in the doctrine that one person should suffer in the place of another for that other's offence, when both he and the person offended against are willing, as he may be for various reasons. Such a proceeding I should not say was rigorously a satisfaction to justice, but it might be called a satisfaction in a true form, in a case where one man went bail for another, even when the (vicarious) payment was one of personal suffering. This being my own feeling, I have taken the words of the Fathers, as they come without any particular interest of my own in weighing their significancy. Now I fully grant that the Greek Fathers, of whom I have read more than of the Latin, look at our Lord's death more as a matter of grace to us than as the vicarious penalty of our sin; but I have never fancied that, because they held this view more explicitly, they did not hold the other view implicitly also. So too they consider original sin as a loss of grace rather than as a positive state of natural weakness; yet I have never felt this to be inconsistent with the Tridentine words about Adam's fall, . . . I am prepared to believe, however, that in the Western Church the notion of vicarious atonement was brought out distinctly. (v. 21; To the Author of "Propitiatory Sacrifice and the Sacrifice of Christ", 7 August 1864)

As to the Atonement, . . . Since I was a boy I have always known it as 'reconciliation between God and man through the sufferings of Christ.' But *how* those sufferings effected reconciliation, and *why* they were necessary, this certainly I did not know then, nor do I know now, and never shall know in this world. (v. 23; To an Unknown Correspondent, 4 Feb. 1867)

Was Jesus Omniscient (All-Knowing)?

I think suspense and the anxiety connected with it one of the greatest of mental troubles. . . . it is one of the sufferings of human nature which our Blessed Lord could not have – ignorance being one of those four penalties of Adam's sin which He did not share. Of course knowledge has its own incommunicable sufferings but still ignorance has its own too, and these we must bear by ourselves without his experimental sympathy. (v. 18; To Lady Henry Kerr, 8 Dec. 1857)

Was Jesus Subjected to Concupiscence?

Our Lord then as little took on Him the wound of ignorance, as He did of concupiscence . . . (v. 15: To William Dodsworth, 21 March 1852)

Can God Suffer?

But how could an Eternal Almighty Person, how could God the Son suffer? what, that is, for the question which you propose does it matter whether we speak of God the Son suffering, or the Divinity suffering? Much: – the divinity has not a human nature, but God the Son has. The Divinity is nothing but the Divinity; but God the Son is also man. When then it is said that God (the Son) suffered, it is meant that God the Son suffered *in the flesh* or in his humanity; whereas the Divinity has no flesh to suffer in, and therefore cannot suffer, and cannot be said to suffer at all. When then it is said 'God suffered on the Cross,' it is meant He suffered in that which could suffer, that which he had made one with Himself, or taken into His personality, viz in his human nature. When I say 'I weep,' 'I bleed', I do not mean to say exactly that my Person weeps or bleeds, but that something belonging to me, to my Person, my eyes or my arm weeps or bleeds. Now then to answer your questions – You say 'The Divine Person or Nature was God; the Divine Person or Nature did not suffer. Ergo – God [did] not suffer.' Here one of your premisses must be distinguished into two propositions, one of which is true, and the other false. That 'the Divine Nature did not suffer' is true; that a 'Divine Person' did not suffer is false – for that Divine Person who is called the Son did suffer, but not in His Divinity, but in His human nature. Now the contrast here between the Divine Person and His human nature is intelligible enough –; what is *not* intelligible [is] the contrast between the Divine Person and His Divinity. This is a mystery – *the* mystery, in which all the difficulty of the question lies. You quote a passage of mine, and you ask 'Do you mean to say that God, the Divine

Person, was with the soul and body [[of the man Christ]] during the passion, but did not and could not suffer [[with them]]? or do you mean that it was this soul which was taken and clothed with flesh of the Blessed Virgin that alone suffered while God remained impassible in heaven?' Now this is my answer, God, i.e. the Person of the Son, God the Son, was one with His humanity much more intimately than our soul is one with our body. I mean then to say that in the passage in question that God the Son, who, *as* God, could not suffer, did suffer really in that humanity which He assumed; as I am said to turn pale, when, properly speaking, it is not I, but a part of me, my face which turns pale – I so understand the passage from the Catechism of the Council of Trent which you quote [ch. 5, 2]. It says that the human nature suffered, the divine nature did not suffer. Certainly, but since the Person of the Word had made that human nature His own, He suffered in that human nature, without any suffering of His Divine Nature. (v. 19; To E. A. Wilson, 4 June 1860)

Chapter Thirteen

God the Father (Theology Proper)

Is God Self-Existent and Self-Sufficient?

Could God create a second God? No – why? because that there can be no God but one is implied in the very idea of God. But Why? why not dualism? why at least not a quasi dualism? why a strict unity? if then unity is implied [,] dualism is negatived [,] in the idea of God prior to His will, why may not a certain moral character? God wills that moral character as He wills His existence, and could as little destroy it as He could annihilate Himself or could restrict his infinity. Could the Father annihilate the Son? is He less God because He cannot? (v. 21; To James MacIvor, 23 May 1865)

How Much Does God Love Us?

The Prodigal left the state of grace when he left his father's house – The father's going out after him when a great way off means no more than, what I have said above, that God's love extends *beyond* the Home of His Saints and the Church of His Elect – He went out to recover, as originally Christ came to 'seek and save those who were lost' [Lk 19:10] – to 'seek' them in order to bring them into a state of grace to 'save' them. So the householder, as we have read this morning, went out to hire labourers and bring them into his Vineyard [Mt 20:1-16]. (v. 8; To A. C. Tarbutt, 22 Jan. 1841)

. . . His infinite mercy who loves you as entirely and wholly as if there were no other souls on earth to love or take care of. (v. 15; To Catherine Anne Bathurst, 8 Nov. 1853)

No one but the Creator Himself reads our hearts and is able to decide on our responsibilities. None loves the soul so well as He , – none wishes for its salvation as He wishes for it. To Him we must leave our nearest and dearest, with a full confidence that not one of those pleas, which we are able to urge for them, but are understood much better by Him. (v. 19; To Mrs. J. W. Bowden, 30 Sep. 1860)

[T]here is One above who reads your heart as no one on earth can read it, who will supply all its needs, and can and will do more for those, whose future is so anxious to you, than could have been done for them, had every thing happened as you wish. So do not be cast down, but put your trust in God, and be sure that every thing happens in the best way for those who love Him. (v. 20; To Mrs. Edward Bellasis, 21 May 1863)

Put yourself then, my dear Child, into the hands of your loving Father and Redeemer, who knows and loves you better than you know or love yourself. He has appointed every action of your life. He created you, sustains you, and has marked down the very way and hour when He will take you to Himself. He knows all your thoughts, and feels for you in all your sadness more than any creature can feel, and accepts and makes note of your prayers even before you make them. He will never fail you – and He will give you what is best for you. And though He tries you, and seems to withdraw Himself from you, and afflicts you, still trust in Him, for at length you will see how good and gracious He is, and how well he will provide for you. (v. 22; To Marianne Frances Bowden, 5 June 1866)

He never fails those who place themselves in His hands. I have lived a long life and can witness to His faithfulness. He is a true friend, and the more you can trust Him, the more you will gain from Him. (v. 31; To Charles Smyth Morris [?], 4 Jan. 1885)

How Shall we Regard God's "Superintendence"?

In the last extremity (to judge from appearances) something always turns up, some unexpected chance, some seemingly casual coincidence shows at once the power and superintendence of our heavenly Father and leads us to put our whole trust in Him. . . . I am certain that, whatever trial He may see good or ordain, He will support you by His grace and ready help. (v. 1; To [Aunt] Elizabeth Newman, 28 April 1822)

We are all in God's Hands, and He orders us about, each in his own way; happy for us, only, if we can realise this, and submit as children to a dear Father, whatever He may please to do with us. . . . God is great and good. (v. 13; To John Edward Bowden, 21 Sep. 1849)

How Should we Conceive of God's Will?

You have not yet subdued your feelings or your will to the Will of God – you think of yourself more than of Him. You do not enough consider that you are a creature of His, and thus while on the one hand under His care, on the other at His disposal. Here is hope and fear at once – here is an awful thought – You are under His mighty hand – humble yourself under it. You are His creature; rejoice that He has hold of you, submit where He fixes you. (v. 8; To Miss Mary Holmes, 15 Aug. 1841)

What is God's Providence?

We are in the hands of One who knows what is best for each of us, who has appointed our birth, our state and country, our desires, and our purposes, and whatever He does towards us, is only a reason for our loving and trusting Him more, and therefore we must give Him glory, . . . (v. 17; To Sister Agnes Philip Moore, 10 July [?] 1856)

Is Discerning God's Providence Difficult?

Do not think that I wish to speak lightly, or even sceptically, of the existence of a divine and miraculous system of Providence among us even now – but I think it a kind of evidence as to which one is very likely indeed to deceive oneself – and that if any evidence required time and delay before it was received, it was this. (v. 8; To Miss Mary Holmes, 7 Nov. 1841)

Are Images of God the Father Permissible?

[W]e allow a representation of the Eternal Father, because Scripture supplies us with it in Dan. vii. 9. 10. Ez. i. 26. 27 viii, 2 . . . (v. 16: To Mrs. Catherine Froude, 17 March 1854)

Chapter Fourteen

The Holy Spirit (Pneumatology) and Trinitarianism

How Can we Conceptualize the Mystery of the Holy Trinity?

The truth is the essence of the doctrine <mystery> seems to me to be that God who is necessarily Personal, is and is revealed . . . as begetting, begotten, and proceeding – i.e, is Three Persons; – so that it is truer to say that God is Three than that Three are God. (v. 8; To Thomas Mozley, 14 March 1842)

That the Father is God, is in form an intelligible proposition; and so also, that the Word is God; and again, that the Holy Ghost is God. Again, it is sufficiently clear what we mean when we say that there is only one God: but take all four propositions together, and you have the Mystery. It lies in the impossibility of any human intelligence being able to perceive how propositions can be all true, which seem to it destructive of each other, that is, as self- destructive as the above mathematical dictum that a line is always approaching what it never reaches. Theologians cannot comprehend these relations more than we can; but they can give *names* to them. They cannot understand the distinction between God and the Word, or between Father and Son, more than the dullest clodhopper; but they can distinguish them from each other in scientific language. The name which they have given, – given under a supernatural guidance, – is just as unintelligible as the truth itself is incomprehensible. We gain nothing by it in the way of explanation, but it is a *recognition* on their part that there *is* a mystery – that is the first gain; next, it is a declaration in *what* point or points the mystery lies; and thirdly, it does for the mystery what the symbol x does for an unknown quantity, – it enables the mind to use it freely, to recognise it whenever it comes up again in the course of investigation, and to speak of it and discuss it with others. The term which we introduce as regards the doctrine of the Holy Trinity is the word *Person*. It expresses, it does not explain, the point of mystery. We know nothing more than before; but we have located the mystery, and may shut up the subject. (v. 19; "Questions and Answers," *The Rambler*, May 1859)

Is Faith in the Holy Trinity Necessary for Salvation?

As baptism is necessary for salvation as a mean, so is faith in the Holy Trinity as a condition. So that there cannot be any escape from culpable unbelief in those who refuse to accept the doctrine. I don't see how there is any 'non-natural' explanation in this; nor does it oblige us to pronounce absolutely on the future state of any one, for we cannot tell what takes place on a death bed. (v. 26; To Edward B. Pusey, 27 April 1873)

How Does the Indwelling Holy Spirit Work in Us?

If I must express broadly my view of spiritual influences on the heart and will etc. I should say, that they were vouchsafed *according to the constitution of man's nature* – i.e. so as not to change it *from* its ordinary workings, but to make use of these. The Holy Spirit addresses us thro' our reason, affections, conscience, passions, natural-affections, tastes, associations etc but (generally and usually) only thro' them; He does not come immediately to change us, but through these. Again whatever happens to the mind naturally, that may happen in grace – as the natural mind generally changes slowly, so does the mind of the spirit; as sudden conversions happen in nature (e.g. the spend-thrift suddenly becoming a miser,) so they may in grace. . . . the ethics or metaphysico-ethics of the way of the Spirit is so little understood among us that I have enlarged upon the system of reason, conscience, etc etc. in my Sermons.
   . . . Now I conceive as far as sanctification goes, the work

of the Spirit is, as I have described it overleaf; He acts t*hrough the properties etc of the mind*; nor do I know what authority we have for speaking of Him as the ultimate Agent, and not our own free will (to speak more strongly than I like.) In this sense salvation depends on ourselves, on our own willing or not, i.e. prompted, enlightened, aided, carried on, perfected by the influences of grace. . . . I conceive it to be the great gift of grace, marvellous beyond words, exceeding in bounty, and freely given to those whom God has chosen in Christ and brings to baptism. It is the indwelling of the Holy Spirit in the soul as in a Temple – the Spirit of adoption. In the first place it has (so to say) a physical, or (as we term it) a mystical influence on the soul, uniting it to Christ – it distinguishes the Christian from all unregenerate men, and it is of course attended by larger measures of sanctification . . . (v. 5; To Samuel Wilberforce, 29 Jan. 1835)

In these later times it is usual to say that the Third Person of the Blessed Trinity resides in the soul by means of His *grace* – but it is still a theological opinion maintained by great divines (and I suspect the old opinion,) that His Presence in the soul is not merely His grace but *Himself.* (v. 24; To W. J. O'Neill Daunt, 17 Sep. 1868)

How Does the Holy Spirit Interact with Christians?

[T]he Ancient Church seems to have believed as follows – that the Holy Ghost, who is the present Lord and animating Principle (Power) of the Church, communicates Himself variously to its members; – first in Baptism, in another way in Confirmation, in another way in the Holy Eucharist. His first gift or communication is forgiveness, justification, acceptance – and this is the distinguishing gift of Baptism. He is the Spirit of Justification. vid I Cor vi. 11. 2 Cor iii. 6-9. This gift He gives complete and whole, and such as is never repeated in this life; – but He also gives the beginnings of other gifts, which are *more fully* given afterwards, viz His sanctifying influences; and since these are those which are more commonly, even in Scripture, called the Spirit, it follows that in *one* sense the Spirit is not given, or hardly given in Baptism. (v. 6; To [sister] Jemima Mozley, 4 June 1837)

Is the Unitarian Rejection of Trinitarianism Based on Scripture?

The Trinitarian admits all that the Unitarian affirms, from the Old Testament etc. ((that Christ is man)); the Unitarian does not admit what the Trinitarian affirms from St John etc (that Christ is God.) Thus the Trinitarian takes the *whole* of Scripture, as it stands, whereas the Unitarian makes the doctrine of one part the rule of interpreting, and the reason for not literally interpreting, the other part; which is unfair unless what are obvious senses of this and that portion respectively be inconsistent with each other. Thus the Unitarian does not argue from Scripture, but from the assumption that 'He who is literally and wholly man, cannot be literally and wholly God.' This may be right or wrong, but it is not an argument from Scripture. (v. 7; To [brother] Francis W. Newman, 22 Oct. 1840)

What is Circumincession *or* Perichoresis?

What one Person of the Everblessed Trinity does, all do – their act is *one*; but in Scripture different operations are assigned to each, which we receive without understanding. Thus the Eternal is called Creator emphatically – and the Holy Ghost Preserver – though we believe in the 'Creator Spirit,' etc. Our Lord acts towards us *thro'* the Holy Ghost. (v. 17; To Catherine Anne Bathurst, 5 Nov. 1856)

What is "Divine Nature" or "Divinity"?

It is usual with theologians to distinguish between Divine Nature or Divinity and God. Each of the Three Persons is equivalent with the idea expressed by the word 'God' – but not with the 'divine nature' or divinity for Person and Nature are contrasted singly. The divinity did not take flesh but the Divinity in the Person of the Son or God the Son. How the Divinity is in the Three Persons, or in other words how the Father and Son are each God, and the same God, and yet the Son could take flesh without the Father taking flesh, how they have a common divinity, yet there is but one God, we do not know[.] But if so it is (as the Catholic creed teaches) that 'Divinity' is not equivalent to one of the divine Persons, then we cannot conclude because God the Son became man that therefore the Divinity became man; though how the Divinity simpliciter did not become incarnate and suffer whereas God the Son did, is as much beyond our knowledge, as how the Divinity simpliciter is not God the Son. It is a point of faith then, that God the Son, took on him human nature; but that the Divinity, simply considered, did not. Hence we cannot say that the Divinity died on the Cross, but we can say that God the Son, died on the Cross. This distinction in meaning and idea between 'Divinity' and 'God' has always obtained as a matter of Catholic faith, However, though the ideas have ever been distinct, the words have sometimes been confused. 'God' has sometimes, been used for 'divinity.' Hence some early writers have said that God did not suffer on the Cross and others that He did; but they used the word 'God' in different senses. Those who denied it meant that the divine nature itself could not suffer – those who affirmed it meant that the Son of God, the Divine Person, suffered. (v. 19; To E. A. Wilson, 4 June 1860)

Chapter Fifteen

The Blessed Virgin Mary (Mariology)

Does Mary Intercede for us in a Special Way?

[I]f the Intercessions of the Saints have influence with Christ, surely it is not any extreme position to suppose that the greater Saints have greater influence – or that St Mary, as being our Lord's Mother, is a greater Saint. (v. 10; To an Unknown Correspondent, 12 Jan. 1844)

As to my Lectures, they have cost me, no one knows how much thought and anxiety – and again and again I stopped, utterly unable to get on with my subject, and nothing but the intercession of the Blessed Virgin kept me up to my work. (v. 15; To Charles Newsham, 15 June 1852)

[T]he power of God is able to do all things, and He takes pleasure in doing His most wonderful works at the intercession of the humble-hearted Mother of God, whom the world despises, . . . (v. 20; To Miss Maria Rosina Giberne, 28 Aug. 1861)

'What is there between Me and thee?' – and 'my Hour is not yet come.' . . . Levi, the Priestly tribe, had said to his father and mother, 'I know you not –' vid (I think) last chapter but one of Deuteronomy. Our Lord said Himself, in His teaching, 'He who leaves not father and mother etc' 'He who loves father or mother more than Me etc' Accordingly, when He came forward as a teacher and a priest, when His ministry was beginning, He too gave up His home, gave up His mother. He separated Himself from her – She sought Him on one occasion, but He said 'Who is My Mother' etc etc He did not recognise her till the Sacrifice was made and He hung on the cross. Then He said 'Behold my mother etc.' The hour of recognising His mother, therefore, did not come till His Sacrifice was finished (St Augustine, I think, says this) or, as left to myself I should have been led to say, till His ascension, or her assumption. However, this is a secondary point. The main point is, that at the time when she asked Him for a miracle, His time of exaltation, her time of influence, the time of the New Dispensation, when she was to be exalted as 'advocata nostra,' had not come – On the contrary, it was a time when Son and Mother were to be separate, and there was to be *nothing* 'between them.' Therefore, while He grants her intercession before the time, he records that it was an exception. (v. 20; To W. J. O'Neill Daunt, 21 Oct. 1862)

May our dear Lord who has so wonderfully brought you to this, and His Blessed Mother who has brought it about, guide you on safely through all trials till you see them in heaven. (v. 21; To Miss Maria Rosina Giberne, 29 Jan. 1864)

The Blessed Virgin is the great pattern of prayers, especially intercessory. . . . If she is the Intercessor, and the effectual intercessor, she is so as regards earth, as regards Purgatory, as regards the whole created Universe. But more than this general view, I believe to be a matter of devotion. (v. 21; To Edward B. Pusey, 3 Feb. 1865)

Should we Invoke, or Ask for the Intercession of Mary?

And so far from the teaching of the Church concerning the Blessed Virgin being a burden, it seems to me the greatest of privileges and honours to be admitted into the very family of God. So we think on earth, when great people ask us into their most intimate circle. This it is, and nothing short of it, to be allowed to hold intercourse with Mary and Joseph; and, so far from its hindering our communion with out Lord, and our faith in Him, it is all that we should have had without it, and so much more over and above. As He comes near us in His Sacrament of love, so does He bring us near to Him by giving us an introduction (as I may say) to His Mother. In speaking to her, we are honouring Him; as He likes to be petitioned by His chosen ones, so does He especially love the petitions which she offers Him; and in asking her to intercede for us, we are pleasing both her and Him. Every society has its own ways; it is not wonderful then, that the Catholic Church has its own way of praying, its own ceremonies, and the like. These are strange and perhaps at first unwelcome to those who come to them from elsewhere, just as foreign manners are unpleasant to those who never travelled. We all like home best, because we understand the ways of home. Abraham doubtless found his life in Canaan not so pleasant to him, as his native Mesopotamia. We ever must sacrifice something, to gain great blessings. If the Catholic Church is from God, to belong to her is a make-up for many losses. We must beg of God to change our tastes and habits, and to make us love for His sake what by nature we do not love. (v. 22; To Lady Chatterton, 29 March 1866)

Which Heresies Denied that Mary was the Mother of God?

[T]he whole kit of Gnostics, Manichees, Apollinarians and Eutychians denied that our Lord took flesh *of* His Mother – even when they granted that He was born of her, they would not allow He was made from her. . . . Manichees and Eutychians either assigned to him a phantastical or a heavenly body. . . . The Gnostics are most known perhaps for . . . teaching [that] the Mother of God was a mere channel through which the Heavenly Body passed, . . . (v. 15; To J. M. Capes, 28 Dec. 1853)

What Does it Mean to Call Mary the "New Eve"?

Of course the comparison between Eve and Mary is in all the Fathers 'mystical throughout,' not literal. Our Lord is Adam mystically – and Mary is Eve. Unless there is a likeness, there would be no mystical relation. The Lamb of *God*, the King of Israel, the Elias that was to come, the New Jeru salem are all mystical; but we interpret the new by the old. We say that our Lord was a sacrifice, because he was mystically a Lamb – and Mary sinless because she was mystically Eve. (v. 22; To Robert Charles Jenkins, 26 Feb. 1866)

What is the Doctrine of the Immaculate Conception of Mary?

You wished, I believe, to know what the doctrine of the Immaculate Conception is :- it is this, that the Blessed Virgin is exempt from original sin. . . . In some rare cases, as in St John Baptist's, this grace has been given before birth; so that St John was *not* born in original sin. But, since his soul existed before our Lady's visit to his Mother, up to that time *had* been in original sin; therefore *he was* conceived in original sin, or his conception was *not* immaculate. By conception is meant the creation of the soul, when at once it is united to the body, and becomes a human being or person. In the first instant then of St John's existing, or on his conception, he was at once, (as being of the lineage of Adam,) brought into the state of degradation to which Adam had reduced himself and his offspring, But, when divine grace was given him at the time of the Visitation, he was taken out, ipso facto, of that fallen state. Had grace been given to him, not merely three months before his birth, but from the first moment of his existence as a human being, then it would have been right to say of him, that he was conceived without original sin, or that he had an immaculate conception. Now this we believe to have been actually the case as regards the Blessed Virgin. At the very time that her soul was created, grace was given to her, so that she never was without grace, never under the power of sin, even original, never otherwise than immaculate. (v. 22; To Lady Chatterton, 2 Oct. 1865)

As to your question how our Lady can be immaculately conceived, *yet* it can be true that she sinned in Adam, you will find it explained in my Pamphlet. She sinned in Adam, but, *before* she actually came to be, the sin was taken off her. Thus a rebel's children and posterity may be disinherited. They all suffer in him by anticipation, but before the great-grandchild is born the forfeiture may be reversed, and *he* may actually come into the property from his birth. (v. 24; To Mrs. Helbert, 28 Sep. 1869)

How was Mary's Immaculate Conception Proclaimed in 1854?

It is remarkable that the Bull does not define the doctrine, but defines that it is *revealed*, and *therefore* of faith. (v. 16; To J. D. Dalgairns, 22 Jan. 1855)

Why Do Catholics Adhere to Mary's Immaculate Conception?

[I]t *does* surprise me that you find a difficulty in the Immaculate Conception – and, as you say that 'it presents such obstacles to *Anglicans*,' I am led to assure you that I for one felt it no obstacle – on the contrary it seems to me the most natural and necessary of doctrines – and I cannot enter into the minds of those who feel it difficult. . . . In a Sermon published in 1835, ten years before I became a Catholic, I say, 'What, think you, was the sanctity and. grace of that human nature of which God formed His sinless Son; knowing, as we do, "that what is born of the flesh is flesh," and that "none can bring a *clean thing out of an unclean*?" I was accused of holding the doctrine of the Immaculate Conception, for it was clear that I connected 'grace' with the Blessed Virgin's *humanity* – as if grace and nature in her case never had been separated. All I could say in answer was, that there was nothing against the doctrine in the 39 Articles. St John Baptist was without original sin three months before his birth – what is then strange or unchristian in the doctrine that our Lady was free from it for nine months that is, from her conception? The grace of God in that case was given to her six months earlier than to the Baptist. Is there anything monstrous in this? If I am asked for proof of the doctrine being held in the early Church, I answer that it seems included in the general belief that the Blessed Virgin was without sin – and, while not much is said about her at all, when she is spoken of, she is spoken of in this aspect. I need not do more than remind you of the well known passage of St Augustine, in which he says that, when Mary is named, he does not wish to make any mention of sin, as if the two names were antagonistic – but what to me is, and ever has been, most striking, is the series of passages from the earliest Fathers in which Mary is contrasted to Eve, as typical contrasts. St Justin (A.D 160) St Irenaeus (A.D. 170) Tertullian (A.D 200) all enlarge on this contrast – and later Fathers hand down the Tradition. The very point indeed in which the contrast is made, is that of *obedience* – but, when St Irenaeus says, 'mankind is surrendered to death by a *Virgin*, and is saved by a *Virgin*,' he surely implies that as Eve was without sin, so was Mary. Why indeed is it difficult to suppose that Mary had at least the privilege of Eve? – and Eve had an immaculate conception and birth. . . . I think I am right in saying, that the only great historical difficulty of the doctrine is the opposition, if it may be so called, of St Bernard and St Thomas – yet to my mind it is clearly shown that they did not mean by the doctrine what the Church now means . . . the two saints in question were opposing what no one now thinks of maintaining . . . (v. 19; To Arthur Osborne Alleyne, 30 May 1860)

Why is the Immaculate Conception Implausible to Protestants?

The difficulty which Protestants feel in receiving the doctrine lies in this, that they consider it a substantive self dependent doctrine more than we do. There are doctrines so intimately one with other doctrines, that they are rather their parts or aspects, than distinct from them; so that to prove the one is to prove the other. On the contrary there are doctrines so distinct from each other, that each requires its own proper proof, and to prove the one is no step at all towards proving the other E.g. the doctrine of our Lord's divinity, and that of the Holy Ghost's, are independent of each other. *This* does not imply *that*; to prove the one is not to prove the other. Again: our Lord's birth from Mary is one doctrine, and her sanctity is another. The one indeed tends to imply the other, but still they are independent, and must each be proved by itself, if their truth is to be ascertained by argument at all. In these two cases, to say that the second doctrine is an extension of the first, and that it is sufficient to prove the first in order to the reception of the second, few men would allow. On the other hand, if I say, 'God is Almighty, and is Allwise;' or 'the Son of God, is eternal, and He is incomprehensible,' or 'the Holy Ghost is in the unity of the Father and the Son, and He is God,' I put together pairs of propositions, which form parts of one idea respectively, and which are such, that to prove the one is virtually to prove the other. . . . In this then lies the difference of view, taken by Catholics and Protestants respectively, of the doctrine of the Immaculate Conception; that Catholics do not view it as a substantive and independent doctrine, so much as one of a family of doctrines which are intimately united together, whereas Protestants consider it as separate from every other, and as requiring a proof of its own as fully as if it were the only thing that we knew of the Blessed Virgin. Catholics think it not much more of an addition to what they otherwise hold of her, than it would be to say, 'The Son of God is God, *therefore He is immensus*,' whereas Protestants think it as little connected with what Catholics themselves otherwise hold of the Blessed Virgin, as the Doctrine of our Lord's divinity is with that of the divinity of the Holy Ghost.

Next, *why* do Protestants thus differ from Catholics in their mode of viewing the doctrine of the Immaculate Conception? I think it arises from the different view which the two religions take of that doctrine, out of which the Immaculate Conception arises, viz the doctrine of original sin. Protestants consider original sin to be an *infection* of nature, so that man's nature now is not what it was before the fall. Accordingly, to be conceived without original sin is to have a *nature* different from that of other men. Hence, according to them, it is blasphemy to say that our Lord was born of the nature of fallen Adam; and it is blasphemy according to their view of that nature. . . . Now I do not deny that Catholics consider that the natural powers of man are enfeebled by the fall; but they do not admit any infection of nature. They consider (or, they are free to consider) that the Blessed Virgin, that our Lord Himself, though both of them were without Original Sin, still both of them had the nature of fallen Adam. For Original Sin, according to them, consists in the deprivation of the grace of God, which was a gift external and superadded to Adam's nature. The presence of divine grace is the justifying principle, which makes the soul acceptable to Almighty God; moreover, there are degrees of justification, as there are degrees of grace. Not all the grace conceivable would, in the view of a Protestant, destroy Original Sin; it ever remains an infection, even though it be not imputed; but to a Catholic, on the contrary, the entrance of grace into the soul, as a presence, ipso facto destroys Original Sin. In the view of a Protestant it is no recommendation of the doctrine of our Lady's Immaculate Conception to urge that St John the Baptist was within six months of such a conception himself; but to a Catholic, who believes that the entrance of grace at the moment of conception is an ipso facto reversal of Original Sin, it acts as a probable argument in favour of her having been saved from Original Sin, that the Baptist, who was below her in dignity, was sanctified three months before his birth.

This difference of view is the cause of what has seemed so strange to you. As a Protestant would think a disputant captious and unfair, who asked for a distinct proof from Scripture, that 'the godhead and manhood were joined in one Person, *never to be divided*,' so a Catholic cannot comprehend why Protestants make so much difficulty and noise about the doctrine which to them is so natural, so intelligible, as the Immaculate Conception. Any passage of the Fathers, which speaks, vaguely but largely, of the grace given to Mary, tells, in his judgment, for the doctrine; for that privilege is but the fulness of grace. On the contrary, to a Protestant it does not go one hair's breadth toward proving it, for not all the grace conceivable can overcome, as he thinks, a fault of nature. In like manner, any passage of the Fathers, as that of St Augustine, which generally separates her off from sin, suggests to the Catholic the doctrine that she was without original Sin; whereas on the Protestant it has no such effect whatever, because Original Sin, in his view, is not a state different from Adam's, but a nature different from Adam's. And further, to the Catholic, (at least before he plunges into past controversy,) it is as little surprising that the Church should define this point and declare it to be *de fide*, as that the Athanasian Creed should call the Holy Ghost God, though the Nicene does not: to the Protestant on the other hand, it is 'an unwarranted and audacious addition to the articles of faith' etc etc. (v. 19; To Arthur Osborne Alleyne, 15 June 1860)

What is the Historical Evidence for the Immaculate Conception?

[A]s to the *antiquity* of the doctrine. In the first ages original sin was not. formally spoken of in contrast to actual. In the fourth century, Pelagius denied it, and was refuted and denounced by St Augustine. Not *till* the time of St Augustine could the question be mooted precisely whether our Lady was without original sin or not. Up to his time, and after his time, it was usual to say or to imply that Mary had *nothing to do* with sin, in vague terms. The earliest Fathers, St Justin, St Irenaeus etc. contrast her with Eve, while they contrast our Lord with Adam. In doing this – 1. they, sometimes imply, sometimes insist upon, the point that Eve sinned when tried, and Mary did not sin when tried; and 2. they say that, by not sinning, Mary had a real part in the work of redemption, in a way in which no other creature had a share. This does not go so far as actually to pronounce that she had the grace of God from the first moment of her existence, and never was under the power of original sin, but by comparing her with Eve, who *was* created of course without original sin, and by giving her so high an office, it implies it. Next, shortly after St Augustine, the 3rd General Council was held against Nestorius, and declared

Mary to be the Mother of God. From this time the language of the Fathers is very strong, though vague, about her immaculateness. In the time of Mahomet the precise doctrine seems to have been taught in the East, for I think he mentions it in the Koran. In the middle ages, when everything was subjected to rigid examination of a reasoning character, the question was raised whether the doctrine was consistent with the Blessed Virgin's having a human father and mother – and serious objections were felt to it on this score. Men defined the words 'Immaculate Conception' differently from what I have done above, and in consequence denied it. St Bernard and St Thomas, in this way, were opposed to it, and the Dominicans. A long controversy ensued and a hot one – it lasted many centuries. At length, in our time, it has been defined *in that sense* in which I have explained the words above – a sense, which St Bernard, St Thomas, and the Dominicans did *not* deny. The same controversy about the sense of a word had occurred in the instance of the first General Council at Nicaea. The Nicene Creed uses the word 'Consubstantial' to protect the doctrine of our Lord's divinity against Arius, which the great Council of Antioch some 70 years before had repudiated as a symbol of heresy. In like manner great Saints have repudiated the *words* 'Immaculate Conception,' from taking them in a different sense from that which the Church has accepted and sanctioned. (v. 22; To Lady Chatterton, 2 Oct. 1865)

As to the Immaculate Conception, I consider its tradition, (Quod semper) from the first, is contained in the doctrine *'Mary* is the *Second Eve.'* (v. 24; To Edward B. Pusey, 4 July 1869)

Why Did the Immaculate Conception Take So Long to Develop?

You will ask perhaps, 'Why then was there so much controversy about the doctrine or about its definition?' . . . I do not see any difficulty in the matter. From the beginning of the Church even good and holy men have got involved in controversies of words. .

. . The *devotion* to her has gradually and slowly extended through the Church; the *doctrine* about her being always the same from the first. But the *gradual* growth of the devotion was a cause why that doctrine, in spite of its having been from the first, should have been but slowly recognised, slowly defined. . . . 'The new devotion was first heard of in the ninth century.' Suppose I say, 'The new doctrine of our Lord's immensity, contradicted by all the Ante-nicene Fathers, was first heard of in the creed of St Athanasius?' or 'The Filioque, protested against by the Orthodox Church to this day, was first heard of in the 7th Century?' Whatever principle is adduced to explain the latter statement will avail for the first. . . . The Holy Ghost's eternity is involved in His divinity; the Blessed Virgin's immaculateness in her conception is involved in the general declarations of the Fathers about her sinlessness. If all Catholics have not seen this at once, we must recollect that there were at first mistakes among pious and holy men about the attributes of the Holy Spirit. . . . I fully grant that there is not that formal documentary evidence for the doctrine in question which there is for some other doctrines, but I maintain also that, from its character, it does not require it. (v. 19; To Arthur Osborne Alleyne, 15 June 1860)

Is the Immaculate Conception Rationally Difficult to Accept?

I never meant to say that I never knew of any one who required *information* on the doctrine of the Immaculate Conception – but that I never heard of any one who had 'difficulties' in receiving it when he understood what it was, who had not other real difficulties too. Did you tell me, after 'asking counsel of me' that your difficulties continued as they were? I assure you such a state of mind as inquires and is at length satisfied did not enter into my thoughts when I wrote, nor, as I think, is implied in my language. (v. 21; To J. T. Rodmell, 20 June 1864)

How Could Mary Have a "Savior" if She Was Immaculate?

'In Adam all die;' yet no man was yet in existence, when Adam fell. They *died* before they *lived*. As the whole race could die, at God's will, before they existed, so one of that whole race could (at the same will) not only die before she was in being, but be made alive again also. And this last remark suggests to us, how it is that she is to be considered as *really* redeemed by her Son, *though* in fact she had no sin to be forgiven. . . . Yes: she is indisputably among those whom our Lord suffered for and saved; she not only fell in Adam, but she rose in Christ, before she began to be. . . . In truth, Catholics consider her as the signal and chiefest instance of the power and fulness of redeeming grace; for her Son merited for her that initial grace which was the prevention of Original Sin. (v. 19; To Arthur Osborne Alleyne, 15 June 1860)

Does Mary's Immaculate Conception Have a Physical Element?

As to the Immaculate Conception, I am perfectly convinced Protestants don't know what our doctrine is. Dear Robert [Wilberforce] did not, when he wrote his book on the Incarnation as I pointed out to him. There is nothing physical at all in it. The doctrine is simply this – 'As St John Baptist's soul was sanctified by the Holy Ghost three months before his birth, so the Blessed Virgin's soul was sanctified, as many months as it had existed before her birth, i.e. from its very first creation.' Physical questions do not come in at all *in the doctrine* – they come in only when, in controversy, we have to *reconcile* our doctrine with the text, 'In sin has my mother conceived me – ' *then* we are accustomed to say, 'The Psalmist speaks of the conception of the body – but our doctrine speaks, *not* of the body, but of the time when the soul is created, or begins to exist.' . . . Now we say, that the Blessed Virgin had from the first moment of creation the *presence or gift* of grace – AS ADAM HAD – and we only say that *she* was restored (for the sake of the Atonement which was to come) to *Adam's* state, and never was in any other state. (v. 19; To William Wilberforce, 9 Dec. 1860)

Was Mary's Assumption Very Widely Believed Before 1950?

[E]ven our Lady's Assumption is not de fide. Yet what political tenet can compare to it to [in] extent and duration of reception? (v. 20; To William Robert Brownlow, 16 Oct. 1863)

The Assumption of our Lady is more pointedly and in express words held by all Catholics, and has been for a thousand years, than the proposition 'The Holy Ghost is God' was held by the Catholic world in St Basil's time. . . . If the Assumption of our Blessed Lady were now defined at the Vatican Council, I should say that plainly it, as the Immaculate Conception, is contained in the dogma 'Mary the Second Eve –' . . . as to the Assumption, if Mary is like Eve but greater, then, as Eve would not have seen death or corruption, so, while Mary underwent death because she was a child of fallen Adam and sinned in Adam, she did not see corruption because she had more than the prerogatives of Eve. (v. 24; To Mrs. Helbert, 10 Sep. 1869)

Is Mary Our Spiritual Mother?

Put yourself ever fully and utterly into Mary's hands, and she will nurse you and bring you forward. She will watch over you as a mother over a sick child. (v. 14; To Miss Mary Holmes, 31 July 1850)

I trust and know that God and His Mother will be with you wherever you are. (v. 14; To Miss Mary Holmes, 25 Jan. 1851)

[O]ur Lady will carry you through May . . . (v. 14; To Frederick W. Faber, 3 May 1851)

[O]ffer yourselves, my dear children, to your great and tender Mother in heaven, the Blessed Mother of God, who will not refuse to have you, and to watch over you, and to give you all that gentle and true guidance which you need so much, . . . (v. 21; To Henry Bowden's Children [who had just lost their mother], 28 June 1864)

Should we Venerate Mary?

All praises to the Madonna and your and our Saints. (v. 15; To Sister Mary Imelda Poole, 22 June 1852)

Did Mary Have an Extraordinary Intellect?

Catholics believe that the Blessed Virgin, though *she grew* in all graces, yet had a consciousness and an active intellect from the moment of her conception, She partook in her degree of that perfection which was the attribute of her Son. (v. 13; To Henry Wilberforce, 1 Jan. 1849; footnote: "This is the opinion of certain theologians; St Francis of Sales, Suarez and others")

Did Mary Die?

I suppose I am right in saying that *death*, in the cases of our Lord and B M V [Blessed Virgin Mary], was the *penalty* of their *nature*, tho' they personally were sinless . . . (v. 17; To John Stanislas Flanagan, 11 July 1856; the Church also allows the opinion that she did *not* die]

Is Mary a Mediatrix and Channel of God's Graces?

. . . what is taught us by the primitive Fathers, as St Justin and St Irenaeus, that, as Eve had a share in our fall, so Mary had a share in our redemption. (v. 22; To Edward Berdoe, 2 Oct. 1865)

Our received doctrine is, after St Justin and St Irenaeus, as we interpret them, that as Eve had a secondary part in the fall, so had Blessed Mary in the redemption. And interpreting them still, it is our belief, that, whereas all the Saints intercede for us, through the merits and in the grace of Christ, she . . . is *the* Intercessor or Helper <(Advocata, St Irenaeus)> – that this is her distinct part in the economy of human salvation – so that, knowing the Will of our Lord most intimately, she prays *according* to His will, or thus is the ordained means or channel by which that will is carried out. Therefore 'everything goes through the hands of Mary –' and this is a great reason for our asking her prayers. But there is all the difference in the world between saying that 'without her intercession no one is saved –' and 'without her invocation no one is saved –' . . . (v. 22; To John Keble, 8 Oct. 1865)

It is quite true we think salvation is gained thro' the Blessed Virgin's *intercession* – but not necessarily by her *invocation* . . . (v. 22; To J. R. Bloxam, 19 Oct. 1865)

Our Lady has nothing of her own, that is, nothing, which is not the gift of God to her. When then we ask her for any grace, we are in fact asking her to pray to God for it for us. (v. 24; To Miss Ellen Fox, 25 Feb. 1868)

Do the Marian Devotions of Some Catholics Go Too Far?

I never can deny my belief that the Blessed Virgin prays efficaciously for the Church, and for individual souls in and out of it. Nor can I deny that to be devout to her is a duty *following* on this doctrine – but I never will say, . . . that no one is saved who is not devout to her, . . . (v. 22; To John Keble, 8 Oct. 1865)

Chapter Sixteen

Angels and the Communion of Saints

What is the Communion of Saints?

Faith, viewed in its history through past ages, presents us with the fulfilment of one great idea in particular – that, namely, of an aristocracy of exalted spirits, drawn together out of all countries, ranks, and ages, raised above the condition of humanity, specimens of the capabilities of our race, incentives to rivalry and patterns for imitation. (v. 8: Letter to the *Times* by "Catholicus" in Response to Robert Peel ["Tamworth"], Feb. 1841)

Man is formed for society, for sympathy. God is his happiness, but as the sun's light comes to us reflected & refracted, so God's saints are the means under which His glory comes to us. (v. 10; Reflections from an Advent Retreat at Littlemore, 21 Dec. 1843)

We believe in a family of God, of which the Saints are the heavenly members and we the earthly – yet one family embracing earth and heaven. We believe we have access to the heavenly members, and are at liberty to converse with them – and that we can ask them for benefits and they can gain them for us. We believe at the same time that they are so different from us, and so much above us, that our *natural* feelings towards them would be awe, fear, and dismay, such as we should have on seeing a ghost, or as Daniel's when he fell down and quaked at the vision of the Angel – these feelings being changed into loving admiration and familiar devotion, by our belief in the Communion of Saints. Moreover, we believe them present with us as truly as our fellow-men are present. (v. 22; To Edward Berdoe, 2 Oct. 1865)

Don't fear that our dear Lord and His Blessed Mother, and your patron Saints, and your guardian Angel will not aid you. (v. 23; To Marianne Bowden, 5 Feb. 1867)

Are Departed Saints Aware of Earthly Events?

Moses, when he saw, as far as flesh can see, the face of God, had revealed to him what was going on at the foot of the mount. Much more then can the Blessed Virgin and the Saints, who actually enjoy the beatific vision, receive from the Omnipresent, Omniscient God, such information about things on earth, as He thinks fit to communicate. The remarkable circumstance in the case of Moses, is, that the Almighty informs him of the sin of his people *in order that he might intercede for them* – which is just the object for which Catholics say the prayers of the faithful are revealed by Him to the saints. . . . *how* in *this* world and in *nature* are things made known to us? by the medium of light, of sounds, of electricity – these agents connect spaces millions upon millions of miles distant from each other. The whole of the super-natural system implies a parallel correspondence of part with part, though we do not know the Medium. Angels who see the face of our Father are yet our guardians . . . (v. 15; To Mrs. Catherine Froude, 8 March 1853)

Should we Venerate the Saints?

All praises to the Madonna and your and our Saints. (v. 15; To Sister Mary Imelda Poole, 22 June 1852)

Before a person is a judge, whether our devotions to the Blessed Virgin and the Saints are idolatrous or not, he must place himself in the position towards them in which, as a matter of faith, we hold ourselves to be. . . . Now consider the honours paid to monarchs on earth – men kneel to them, bow to their empty throne, pay them the most profound homage, use almost the

- 286 -

language of slaves in addressing them, and dare not approach them without a ceremonial. Much more reverently ought the Saints to be treated by us, in proportion as heaven is higher than earth – yet I do not think we observe that proportion – our language towards our Lady and the Saints is not so much above that which is used towards great personages on earth, as immortal blessedness is above temporal power. Or take the words used to express human love – they are almost idolatrous – in some cases they are so – i.e. in the *spiri*t in which they are uttered – yet I should be very unwilling to allow that the general body of lovers were idolators. Why is it that we are so little jealous of human love, yet suddenly so shocked if we find Catholics transported by affection towards the Saints? Any unconcerned person will feel inclined sometimes to laugh at the terms of endearment used by parties who are attached to each other, and will easily be led to say that they are in very bad taste – such exhibitions are sometimes made when private letters turn up in courts of law, yet no sensible person will doubt on the one hand their reality as confessions of feeling, on the other their exemption from any fair imputation of being idolatrous. I have not yet touched upon the incommunicable relation of the Blessed Virgin to our Lord, as His Mother . . . (v. 22; To Edward Berdoe, 2 Oct. 1865)

I cannot help having as great a devotion to St Chrysostom as to any saint in the Calendar. On his day I came to Birmingham to begin the Mission 18 years ago. It was very kind of you to say Mass for me under his intercession. I have said above 'I cannot help,' because in most cases, from circumstances, one chooses one's Saints as Patrons – but St Chrysostom comes upon one whether one will or no, and by his sweetness and naturalness compels one's devotion. (v. 23; To James Laird Patterson, 30 Jan. 1867)

Is Veneration Infinitely Different from Adoration of God?

God is to be worship[ed] with an honor of His own, infinitely distinct from any honor we give His creatures, even Mary, the first of them, . . . (v. 16; To Mrs. Catherine Froude, 2 Jan. 1855)

Should we Venerate the Angels?

I think the Archangel St Gabriel the most beautiful of the Angels (excepting my own Guardian Angel) as Mary is the Fairest among women, . . . for that glorious Messenger of the Highest. I have, as far as I have any right to have it, a special devotion. (v. 17; To Sister Mary Gabriel du Boulay, 6 May 1856)

Does Everyone Have a Guardian Angel?

It is our common belief that every soul has its guardian Angel, but, if so, is it possible that a good Angel should not whisper high truths to poor little heathen infants? or at least is it not allowable to think so? (v. 26; To Edward Bellasis, Jr., 6 April 1872)

How Eminent is Rome as a Place of Saints and Martyrs?

[A]s being the place of martyrdom and burial of some of the most favoured instruments of God, it has an interest and a solemn charm which no other place can possess except Jerusalem. Before the remains of the Saints the grandeur of pagan Rome crumbles as utterly as have its material structures, . . . (v. 3; To John Frederic Christie, 6 April 1833)

[I]ts memory will ever be soothing to me – Jerusalem alone could impart a more exalted comfort and calm than that of being among the tombs and the Churches of the first Christian Saints. . . . the dust of the Apostles lies there, and the present clergy are their descendants. (v. 3; To Samuel Rickards, 14 April 1833)

Was Prayer for the Dead an Apostolic Practice?

As it was, the early Fathers *found* the custom [of liturgy facing east] in their Churches, and proceeded to *account* for it in different ways. In like manner they *found* the custom of praying for the dead in Christ and proceeded to noeticize reasons – such as the fire of judgement etc. (v. 5; To Simeon Lloyd Pope, 30 June 1836)

Was Prayer for the Dead Well-Attested in the Early Church?

As to the evidence, I consider there is evidence enough that the Church prayed for the dead in Christ, but not evidence that they knew *why* – for they give various reasons. Tertullian . . . gives as a reason that the departed may have part in the first Resurrection – but other petitions offered referred to their having rest and peace now, and a merciful trial at the last day. . . . As to the *date* of the evidence, I would only suggest this – that as far as I know, there is as good evidence for this usage as for the genuineness and authenticity of many books of the New Testament . . . (v. 6; To George Stanley Faber, 16 May 1838)

Is Prayer for the Dead a Biblical Teaching?

You seem to ask me whether I am an advocate for prayers for the dead in Christ . . . Now Prayer for the Dead in Christ is an ordinance; and Catholic Tradition may as suitably sanction it as it sanctions the change of the day of rest from the seventh to the first, or teaches us that washing one another's feet is not literally binding on us. For myself I do not believe it *is* commended in Scripture, being included in such general expressions as 'for all the Saints – ' Eph vi. 18. (v. 6; To George Stanley Faber, 11 April 1838)

It is just a case in which I seem to feel the privilege it is, to be able to remember him before God. This seems so natural, where one can do nothing else, that I do not see anything could interfere with it but a prohibition in Scripture, which I nowhere see. (v. 8; To [sister] Jemima Mozley, 9 April 1841)

[W]hat does St Paul mean when he says of Onesiphorus 'The Lord grant him to find mercy of the Lord in that day?' [1 Tim 4:19] did his prayer go for nothing? To say that he prayed that Onesiphorus might so conduct himself on earth as to receive mercy at the Judgment seems a refinement; not to say that from the run of the passage O. seems to be dead when St P. wrote. (v. 10; To Anthony John Hanmer, 16 March 1844)

What is the Anglican Teaching on the Communion of Saints?

[I]n our daily service we say, 'O ye spirits and souls of the righteous, O Ananias, Azarias, and Misael, bless ye the Lord,' which would seem to show that there are invocations which are not 'Romish.' (v. 7; To Henry Moore, 21 May 1840)

As to the doctrine of God's receiving our prayers by the intervention of the Saints, I am not aware that our Church has given an opinion about it. It speaks against 'the Romish doctrine of invocation –' and it does not in the Prayer Book *recognize* the doctrine of Saints' Intercession – but it seems to me to leave it open. (v. 7; To Miss Mary Holmes, 10 June 1840)

I do not know that our Church any where speaks against the *intercession* of Saints. (v. 10; To an Unknown Correspondent, 12 Jan. 1844)

I do not think it wrong to address the Saints – I think our Church considers it inexpedient. (v. 10; To Anthony John Hanmer, 16 March 1844)

Is Invocation of the Saints Unbiblical?

There is nothing *in Scripture* against invocation of Saints. The practice is right or wrong according as the church allows it or not – but where it is a Church ordinance, still it may be abused. (v. 9; To an Unknown Correspondent, 4 March 1843)

Do the Saints Pray (Intercede) for Us?

[C]an I doubt that the Blessed Virgin and all Saints are praying for and with the Church? (v. 8; To Miss Mary Holmes, 6 Sep. 1841)

That you should all have written to me on St Catharine's Day, is a proof to me that she, that glorious Saint is not altogether without some kind of good feeling for me, though I have done nothing to deserve it. (v. 17; To Sister Mary Imelda Poole, 6 May 1856)

The intercession of the Blessed Virgin and the saints does not differ from ours for each other, except that it is more perfect than ours, and comes from those whose holy lives have given them a covenanted claim on God's special notice and indulgence. (v. 21; To John F. Perrin, 9 Sep. 1864)

The worst is over to your dear Mother, and now she either is in heaven or will be shortly. How much she will now be able to do for you, which with all her fervour she could not do here! (v. 24: To Mother Mary Imelda Poole, 12 May 1868)

Are All Images in Worship Idolatrous?

As to the Second Commandment, with reference to Sermon 15, I have been accustomed to think that in the words 'Thou shalt not make to thyself' the force of the sentence lies in 'to thyself.' The sin was not in bowing down to a created emblem of the Creator, but to a self-devised emblem. In Exod. xxxiii, 10, the people fall

down before the cloudy pillar as the token of the unseen God. They were told in like manner to look upon the Brazen Serpent in order that they might live. On the other hand that the fault lay in the 'making *to themselves'* emblems is implied in Amos v, 26 (so also Acts vii, 43) where vid St Jerome's comment. . . . Jeroboam sacrificed 'unto the calves which he had made' – 'in the month which he had devised of his own heart –' The same emphasis occurs in Judges xviii. I should say then, if asked, that the sin denounced in the second commandment is unauthorized worship.
. . . Scripture prohibitions are not simple prohibitions but secundum quid. ['according to the manner in which they act on a human agent'] (v. 10; To John Keble, 26 Feb. 1844)

Do Catholics 'pray to images'? I suppose there are great numbers, (say Neapolitans,) who, in one sense, do 'pray to images', not 'in the persuasion that they have the power of granting their requests,' (which, if they did, they would be idolaters,) but still with a sort of confusion between the Object and its representation. Of these multitudes there are good speciments and bad. In England Catholics pray *before* images, not *to* them. I wonder whether as many as a dozen pray *to* them, but *they* will be the best Catholics, not ordinary ones. The truth is, that sort of affectionate fervour which leads one to confuse an object with its representative, is skin-deep in the South and argues nothing for a worshipper's faith, hope and charity, whereas in a Northern race like ours, with whom ardent devotional feeling is not common, it may be the mark of great spirituality. As to the nature of the feeling itself, and its absolute incongruity with any intellectual intention of addressing the image as an image, I think it is not difficult for any one with an ordinary human heart to understand it. Do We not love the pictures which we may have of friends departed? Will not a husband wear in his bosom and kiss the miniature of his wife? Cannot you fancy a man addressing himself to it, as if it were the reality? (v. 20; To William Robert Brownlow, 25 Oct. 1863)

Do Miraculous Relics Exist?

Direct your attention, as you will, to the curious phenomenon, that miracles of blood seem so frequent in the Neapolitan territory. At the end of August St John B's [Baptist's] blood liquifies and another Saint's (which we saw) in Naples – St Nicholas's at Bari, I think. At the Gesu I saw blood liquify on a table of the holy Jesuit da Ponte. St Pantaleon's is in a Church over Amalfi. I wish you had time to go there. It liquifies when a relic of the Holy Cross is brought near it, . . . (v. 13; To T. W. Allies, 12 July 1849)

Did I tell you that St. Philip had done three *grazie*, or semi-miracles for us? if they are not to be called whole miracles; i.e. his relics have raised up from death or almost death, two young women and one child – three instances too might be added. Indeed he can do anything for us. (v. 13; To Mary Holmes, 29 Jan. 1850)

Chapter Seventeen

Purgatory

Are There Experiences in This Life Analogous to Purgatory?

To those who are conscious that they long to love God and to be perfectly holy, every dispensation of Providence, which the dull world is accustomed to regard as unfortunate, gives rise to the most fervent gratitude; and they exult in undergoing trials and passing through the flames of calamity, for they trust and expect to come forth purified and refined, with the dross of human corruption purged away. (v. 1; To [Aunt] Elizabeth Newman, 7 Nov. 1821)

Is Purgatory a Third Possible State After Death?

You have been very much tried, but it is a great blessing to know the meaning of trial. All trial, I suppose, is purgatorial of sin after baptism – and in this general sense of the word I suppose it is impossible to doubt that the intermediate state is purgatorial. (v. 9; To Miss Maria Rosina Giberne, 28 Feb. 1843)

Is Purgatory a Biblical Doctrine?

I will not prove (e.g.) purgatory from Scripture to please the Protestant. Not that I don't think purgatory is in Scripture, but I will not do anything to seem to grant to the Protestant that Scripture is the *whole* Rule of Faith. (v. 14; To Francis Richard Wegg-Prosser, 24 Sep. 1851)

Is Everyone in Purgatory Saved?

[T]he infliction of punishment in Purgatory is in place of those 'temporal punishments which had not been inflicted on earth.' 'There is nothing of atonement in it,' in the sense in which you use the word; i.e. of reconciling man to his Maker. The death of our Lord is the only reconciliation, and no one suffers purgatory except those who have been *already* reconciled in this world, before they go there. No unholy, unjustified soul can go to Purgatory. (v. 21; To John F. Perrin, 9 Sep. 1864)

What we cannot accept (any more than the mass of Protestants, and of divines of the ancient church) is one of your incidental statements, that man's probation for his eternal destiny, as well as also his purification, continues after this life. . . . there are innumerable degrees of grace and sanctity among the saved, and . . . those who go to purgatory, however many, die one and all with the presence of God's grace, and the earnest of eternal life, however invisible to man, already in their hearts . . . (v. 25; To Edward Hayes Plumptre, 26 July 1871)

Do Souls in Purgatory Suffer More than we Do?

The souls in purgatory are without sin, and are visited by Angels, yet, though they have higher privileges, they have more pains, than we here – and that in spite of their having no bodies to be the seat of the suffering[.] (v. 20; To Miss Mary Holmes, 17 Oct. 1861)

Is There Fire in Purgatory?

[T]he Poena sensus is held by Latin tradition to be fire – but it is not a Catholic dogma – nor is it clear that the fire, in the Latin tradition, is more than metaphorical. (v. 23; To Edward B. Pusey, 19 June 1867)

Chapter Eighteen

Penance and Asceticism

Are Penance and Absolution Necessary?

The promises of forgiveness of sin have as full an application after baptism as before, but not in the same free, instantaneous way. They are regained gradually, with fear and trembling – by repentance, prayer, deprecation, penance, patience. (v. 9; To an Unknown Correspondent, 4 March 1843)

As our Lord breathed on the Apostles and said Receive etc., When He gave them power to forgive sins – so the forgiveness still is transmitted to the 'penitent thro' the priest by the 'breath' of the Holy Ghost. (v. 17; To Catherine Anne Bathurst, 5 Nov. 1856)

What is an Indulgence?

Certainly an indulgence is a remission of penance – but we go upon the principle 'Sin is ever punished in this world or the next –' and again 'The later the punishment, the heavier.' Purgatory then is the substitute or equivalent for present penance – and therefore to pardon is indirectly to remit the pains of purgatory. Suppose I was told by the Board of Guardians, of whom I bought my 5 acres, 'you shall either pay 9000 [pounds] down – or pay that sum with accumulations at compound interest 20 years hence.' A friend who gave me the price at *once*, would indirectly save me (if I had not means of paying now) of the necessity of paying twice and more than twice the money 20 years hence. I am only explaining, not arguing[.] (v. 21; To Edward B. Pusey, 31 Dec. 1864)

I cannot see the difficulty of believing that for the merits of Christ and the Saints Almighty God listens to our prayers for the dead. The doctrine of *preachers*, viz. about the uncertainty of the availableness of Indulgences will, I think, be found to be the same. The only remaining question, I see, relates to the Pope's power of *opening* the treasures of the Church – which are two-fold (over and above the merits of Christ) the intercession of the Saints and the gemitus columbae, i.e. the prayers of the Church Militant. Now, if the Pope be the head of the Church on earth, and is so acknowledged in Heaven, (and what he binds on earth etc) there seems nothing difficult in the doctrine that the King of Saints should have given him the power of using His and their merits for good or important purposes on earth, not infallibiliter, but according to His will. (v. 21; To Edward B. Pusey, 4 Jan. 1865)

Is Self-Denial for the Cause of Christ a Good Thing?

When they find that they have no means of following out those feelings and desires, which they know to be Catholic and Scriptural, and doubt begins to steal on their minds whether that can be the true Church, which forbids them to act upon them . . . Say then that men for whatever reason, as being penitents if you will, wish to live a life of self restraint or austerity, and our Bishops turn upon them and say 'Pack o'nonsense – don't be formal, methodistical, papistical, ultra, etc etc.' the consequence is plain – they go where they *can* practise what they feel they have a call to practise. (v. 9; To Charles Henry John Anderson, 4 August 1842)

Is Suffering Spiritually Beneficial?

Pain is a duty – we get to heaven by suffering. (v. 14; To William Gowan Todd, 20 Aug. 1850)

[L]et me bear witness, not only as a matter of faith, which we all receive, but as a point, which the experience of life has ever been impressing on me, more and more deeply, from my early youth down to this day, that unusual inflictions, coming on religious persons, are proofs that they are objects, more than others, of the love of God. Those whom He singularly and specially loves, He pursues with His blows, sometimes on one and the same wound, till perhaps they are tempted to cry out for mercy. He loves you in proportion to the trials He sends you. (v. 16; To Lady Georgiana Fullerton, 4 June 1855)

[T]he many kindnesses I have received from you and Lord Arundel make me earnestly desire to express to you how much I feel the succession of trials which a good Providence has brought upon you. However; such a visitation (as you know so well,) is the greatest mark of His love: – or rather, who would have any encouragement to hope that his name was written in heaven, if he passed through this life without affliction! Be sure, you are dearer to God and His Angels than ever you were, now that you are suffering so much, and, unwelcome as suffering is, so willingly. (v. 16; To the Countess of Arundel, 29 July 1855)

I do not think it unkind, if I say, that if there be one gift I would ask of St Philip for my Congregation, now and in time to come, [it] is that (while serving God zealously of course,) it should be unthought of and despised. I do not ask for *persecution*, I do not ask for *evil fame*; for I do not see that St Philip has suggested these trials to me; but I ask for our being overlooked, passed by, and not known to be true children of our Father, till men come close to us. I ask this, not only from love of St Philip, but from the experience which God has given me; for I know well, that, as to myself, all through life, when I have been despised most, I have succeeded most; and I feel confident that to ask for scorn, contempt, slight, and the like treatment for my Congregation, is to ask for a *great* success, for *real* work, for fruits, which are not unveiled here, in order that they may be reserved in all their freshness and bloom and perfection for manifestation at the marriage feast above. (v. 17; To Ambrose St. John, 9 Nov. 1855)

All pain is good, for it comes from a loving Father. (v. 17; To Lady Henry Kerr, 5 Dec. 1855)

I suppose it is the rule of God's Providence towards us, that, the better we bear trial, the more He gives us to bear. (v. 20; To the Duchess of Norfolk, 26 July 1862)

For ourselves here, of course the School is a perpetual anxiety, though we have been abundantly blessed in our endeavours – but it is a hair shirt, and nothing short of it – and one which you can never put off. . . . the never-ceasing sense of responsibility, the chances of the day and hour, the prospect of accidents, the caprice of parents, the imperative need of unflagging vigilance. May we be able to offer it up to God worthily, and gain merit from it. (v. 20; To Robert Ornsby, 27 Dec. 1863)

I doubt not you will be supported through your suffering, and learn to love God more and more, the more He afflicts you. (v. 21; To Henry Bowden, 28 June 1864)

Should All Clergymen be Celibate?

You mistake me, if you think I consider clergymen, as such, should not marry, I only think there should be among the clergy enough unmarried, to give a character of strength to the whole – and that therefore, every one should ask himself whether he is called to the celibate. (v. 3; To Henry Wilberforce, 26 Feb. 1832)

If you do not feel some such good reason for quitting the celibate, let me tell you the times require you to stop in it – vid 1 Cor vii. For years I have made up my *mind* to remain in single blessedness – but whether my *heart* be equally made up, time alone can tell. (v. 3; To Simeon Lloyd Pope, 9 April 1832)

Is Celibacy a "Higher" Calling?

It is quite absurd to suppose that you are not *at liberty* both to marry and to go into the Church – indeed I think that country parsons ought, as a general rule, to be married – and I am sure the generality of men ought, whether parsons or not. The celibate is a high state of life, to which the multitude of men cannot aspire – I do not say, that they who adopt it are necessarily better than others, . . . (v. 3; To George Ryder, 22 July 1832)

Chapter Nineteen

The Holy Eucharist

Is the Holy Eucharist Necessary for Salvation?

[I]t is a situation of indefinite peril for a Christian to be excluded from those means of grace (that especially which we believe to be 'generally necessary to salvation,') which are to our souls what food is to our bodies. God, indeed, might support our souls by miracle, as He did the bodily life of the Israelites by manna in the wilderness; but the Lord's Supper is His ordinary means; and as we have slender reason to expect miracles now, under any circumstances, still less have we in behalf of sinners whom the Church rejects. (v. 4; To the Editor of *The Record*, 31 Oct. 1833)

How Do we Know that Biblical Eucharistic Language is Literal?

You asked me . . . whether 'This is my Body –' may not be like 'I am the Vine?' In other words *how* are we to discriminate between figurative expressions and those which are not such? If I say 'Caesar was the conqueror of Pompey' – it is literal – but 'Caesar was a lion' is figurative – consider the two propositions carefully and you will see *this* difference, viz that the one which is literal admits of being what is called 'converted,' but the figurative proposition does not. I can say, not only 'Caesar is conqueror,' but also 'a certain conqueror is Caesar' – but though I can say 'Caesar is a lion' I cannot say a certain lion, or this or that lion, is Caesar. In like manner 'Christ is a vine,' but this or that vine is *not* Christ; whereas He says, not only 'I am the true Bread,' but 'This Bread is I' i.e. 'my Body':– not only 'My Blood is drink,' but also 'This (drink) is my Blood.' (v. 21; To Miss Maria Rosina Giberne, 24 Aug. 1864)

What is Transubstantiation?

As to the word 'accidents' it has high authority, but is a scholastic, not a dogmatic word – 'Substance' however is dogmatic, and the simple question is, what it means. The Church gives her own sense to words; and this very word 'substance' which occurs in the Nicene Creed, did not take its place there without fearful controversies and divisions, from the unwillingness of numbers to give up their own sense of the word and to accept the ecclesiastical. Now as to the Holy Eucharist, the word 'substance' denotes nothing which enters into the idea of *effect*, nothing which appeals to the senses. Intoxication is an effect – poisoning is an effect – they are the effect of a *force* – but force is distinct from substance. What we see, taste, hear etc etc. is no part of the substance of a thing. . . . Catholics hold, that, though the bread, that is, the *substance* of bread is not present, yet all those effects upon our senses and upon our bodies, which would follow, were it present, *do* follow though it is not present – viz colour, size, taste, solidity, power of nourishing (for Saints have lived upon the Sacred Host) power of poisoning etc etc. – The change which takes place in Transubstantiation has nothing to do with these effects, – it relates to that *which we know nothing about*, and *can* know nothing about – that substance which is something altogether hidden from us. It is nothing to the purpose then, that, as you say, the species of wine after consecration can intoxicate. (v. 22; To J. O. Wood, 24 Oct. 1865)

What Did Newman Believe About the Real Presence in 1834?

E.g. it seems so very irreverent and profane a thing to say that our Savior's own body is carnally present on the Altar. That He is in some mysterious incomprehensible way present I fully believe; but I do not know what way – and since the way is not told us in Scripture or the ancient Fathers I dare pronounce nothing. Much less dare I be so irreverent as to determine that His flesh and blood are there as they were on Calvary. Surely He who came into the apartment the doors being shut, has ways of being there innumerable, such as we know not – We believe that now He has a 'spiritual body' – and a spiritual body may be present, the bread and wine still remaining. Therefore it seems safe and according to Scripture to say He is present *in* the bread and wine – but unnecessary and irreverent to insist on our saying that the bread and wine are *changed* into that same flesh and blood which were on the Cross. (v. 4; To Mrs. William Wilberforce, 17 Nov. 1834)

Does the Grace Received from the Holy Eucharist Vary?

The Catholic doctrine is, therefore, that the Bread being changed into the Body of Christ, the wicked, in communicating, receive the Body; but that the Divine Presence does not in *them* exercise that vivifying power, the res Sacramenti, which is the *end* of the Sacrament. Moreover, Catholics hold that, the more perfect are the dispositions with which the Body of Xt [Christ] is received, the greater is the grace which It dispenses to the soul; – and that, all the time It is present; so that the longer time the Presence continues, the greater treasure of grace is poured out upon the recipient. (v. 13; To William Maskell, 31 March 1850)

Is Eucharistic Adoration Spiritually Beneficial?

[W]hat exercise of devotion is there, which equals that of going before the Blessed Sacrament, before our Lord Jesus really present, though unseen? To kneel before Him, to put oneself into His hands, to ask His grace, and to rejoice in the hope of seeing Him in heaven! In the Catholic Church alone is the great gift to be found. You may go through the length and breadth of England, and see beautiful prospects enough, such as you speak of, the work of the God of nature, but there is no benediction from earth or sky which fails upon us like that which comes to us from the Blessed Sacrament, which is Himself. (v. 22; To Lady Chatterton, 29 March 1866)

For years past my only consolation personally has been in our Lord's Presence in the Tabernacle. (v. 25; To Lady Simeon, 18 Nov. 1870)

[W]hen we worship His Body and Blood in the Holy Eucharist, we worship His Person *through* His Body and Blood, in order to plead His sufferings in our behalf, which are the symbol and means of our reconciliation. (v. 26; To Mrs. Henry Wilberforce, 21 Oct. 1873)

What is the Reasoning Behind Communion in One Kind?

[F]rom the first there has been very great variation in the mode and circumstances of administration of the Holy Eucharist. Our Lord seems to have administered it in the form of *bread only*, to the two disciples at Emmaus (Luke xxiv) so again St. Paul Acts xx. 11. The disciples are spoken of as breaking *bread* from house to house Act ii. 46. In the time of St. Cyprian (A.D. 250) children were communicated in the species of *wine* only. The monks in the desert (as the private christians also in the time of Tertullian A.D. 220) were permitted to take the Blessed Sacrament home with them, to keep it, and administer it to themselves, under the form of *bread*. In the fourth century we have evidence that communion in bread only was the usage, or at least permitted, in Asia Minor, Africa, Egypt and Milan. After this date we apparently meet with a like usage in Spain. When Anglicans object to us that we keep the Chalice from communicants, we may ask them why they keep both the species of bread and wine from *infants*. St. Augustine considers infant communion to be of Apostolic origin. It was continued in the West down to the 12th century – it *continues* among the Russians, Greeks and Syrians down to this day. We at best act under authority, the authority of the Church, but Anglicans act, in their withholding the communion from infants without any authority whatever, we under the authority of the Popes and Councils at the middle ages. Why have they followed the Church of Rome in forbidding *infant* communion, yet protest against her for forbidding the Chalice to the laity? The truth is *'whole Christ'* is received under *either* species, and it is sometimes said that this was one reason for the present usage among us, viz. because there were heretics who *denied* this, as indeed Protestants really do now. As to the second question, the Scriptural authority, I have given some texts above, to which may be added 'Whosoever shall eat this bread OR drink this cup etc. I. Cor. xx. [should be xi] 27 verse, also Acts. xxxii. [should be xxvii] 35 (The Protestant version mistranslated)[.] (v. 23; To Alexander MacDonald, 20 Jan. 1867)

One of the reasons for withholding the Precious Blood from the laity, was the notion which obtained, I believe, in some places, that the Blood and the Body of our Lord were separated – so that they worshipped the Body as one object of worship, and the Blood as another, instead of worshipping the One Person of Christ, who is present in Divinity and soul as well as in Body and Blood in the Sacrament. (v. 26; To Robert Charles Jenkins, 29 Sep. 1873)

Does Validity of the Eucharist Depend on the Priest's Holiness?

We are sure, as in the case of the administration of the sacraments, that the holiness of actors in them is not a necessary condition of God's working by means of them. (v. 25; To Mrs. F. R. Ward, 9 July 1870)

[T]he Holy Sacrifice gains benefits for us 'ex opere operato', whatever the personal worth of the celebrant[.] (v. 31; To Geraldine Penrose Fitzgerald, 5 Dec. 1885)

What Does it Mean to Say That the Mass is a Sacrifice?

We all hold the consecrated elements are a sacrifice *so far* as the purpose of partaking them goes – a sacrifice brought (so to say) from the one cross, and renewed in the form of a feast . . . Even supposing it is not expressly ordered in Scripture, was there any thing unnatural in the Church making the elements before consecration the plea and memorial of Christ's atonement . . .? (v. 4; To Henry Wilberforce, 10 March 1834)

[W]e bring back (as it were) the solemn event completed on Mount Calvary, and 'show forth,' reiterate, and continue on 'the Lord's death' till He come. (v. 5; To James Stephen, 16 March 1835)

I believe the Church Catholic has considered the Eucharist Holy ever not only a sacramental representation, and also a real and proper sacrifice of bread and wine, but a sacramental presence of Christ Crucified – the shadow, as it were, of the Cross on Calvary being continued on to the end of the world; – or, again, the worshippers being carried back as if to the very foot of the Cross. In Hebrews 10, it is said typical sacrifices are at an end. This is not a typical sacrifice. As a Sacrament is not a mere type, but an outward form of Christ's exalted, so the Sacrifice is not a type, has nothing substantive, but is the offstreaming of that which it represents. (v. 6; To Miss Holdsworth, 6 Feb. 1838)

The Eucharist is a proper Sacrifice made by the Priest, as Christ's *representative* but only as such. (v. 9; To an Unknown Correspondent, 4 March 1843)

[A]n Altar implies a sacrifice. (v. 10; To Simeon Lloyd Pope, 20 March 1845)

Why Do Catholics Offer Masses for the Dead?

When then we allow Mass to be indirectly offered for Protestants departed, it is because we would not for the world say, because, in particular cases which we know, we hope and believe, that they have departed in love and contrition; not as if ruling and defining that they have done so. Moreover supposing they *are* in

Purgatory, yet its pains will be shortened and lessened in an indefinitely great measure to those who die *in* the Church – from the communion of the merits of the Saints. The *whole* body of the Church exhausts together the temporal punishment, which belongs to it. Mortal sin does *not* belong to the Church, but such sin as is possible in members of the Church, as such, they exhaust together. A Catholic is one of a company, and has a benefit when he dies, which those who do not belong to it have not. (v. 13; To A. J. Hamner, 16 Jan. 1850)

Was the Last Supper a Passover Meal?

Was then the last Supper, the Paschal supper or not? St Matthew etc speak of it as 'eating the Pasch.' There are many interpretations and reconciliations. One simply is, that our Lord *anticipated* the real Pasch – which is to me incomprehensible, since the three Evangelists speak of it as the Paschal feast, and St John carries our Lord on from the Supper continuously to his betrayal and passion. Another account is that the Jews got wrong in their usage, from the time of their captivity, and that our Lord (who was just about to destroy the *whole* system) restored the proper day, on that occasion. What is, I think, generally received, and quite natural is this – viz that the Jewish day began in the evening, therefore the Paschal Feast was on Thursday evening. However, to the Romans, whose day began at midnight, as ours, the *Friday* would be called the 'feast day'. St John then, writing after Jewish times, speaks as if Thursday evening was *before* the Feast, whereas it was the beginning of it. (v. 25; To Emily Bowles, 10 April 1871)

Chapter Twenty

Devotions, Liturgy, and Worship

What is the Relation of Faith and Emotions?

Then as to your coldness which you complain of, I am sorry I can give no *recipe* here either. I can only say that I have much to lament in that way myself; that I am continually very cold and unimpressed, and very painful it is; but what can be done? Would we could so command our minds as to make them feel as they ought – but it is their very disease that they are not suitably affected according to the intrinsic value of the objects presented to them – that they are excited by objects of this world, not with the realities of death and judgment, and the mercies of the Gospel. Meanwhile it is our plain *duty* to speak – to explain and to pray even while we find ourselves cold – and, please God, while we thus do what *is* a plain duty, perchance He may visit us and impress us with the realities of what we are speaking of. (v. 4; To R. F. Wilson, 15 June 1834)

How Shall we Prevent Formal Prayers from Becoming Trite?

It is indeed a pious and delightful practice to give the close of each day to God; but let the student appoint a much earlier period of the evening for his more fixed devotions, including, as of course they ought, prayer, meditation, self-examination, and the reading of the holy Scriptures. This edifying process, if delayed till the powers are exhausted by study will generally be cold and spiritless: nor is it very reverent to set apart for heavenly things, a time in which the mind is languid and worn out with the labours of the day. . . . I allude to the ordinary attendance at chapel, . . . The frequency of attendance, the repetition of the same service, excellent as it is, the indifference and coldness which too generally prevail on all sides, the lingering thoughts of worldly subjects from which the collegian has just separated, all conspire, unless the greatest care be taken, to render his prayer formal and heartless. Let him earnestly pray and strive against the first approaches of indifference and formality; for bitterly will he have cause to mourn if he once allow the words of devotion to become so trite that he repeats them without feeling their force. For the mischief does not stop at this point; it soon extends from the daily to the Sunday service. . . . It is with pain I proceed to observe, that the deadness-of soul which steals on the collegian in his public worship, even extends to the most awful of the Christian mysteries, the communion of the body and blood of Christ; especially when, in addition to his own deficiency of spiritual appetite, he sees around him countenances embarrassed from conscious unfitness, or cold from unconcern, or settled into a more awful expression of pride and carelessness. (v. 1; To the Editor of the *Christian Observer*, 22 Sep. 1822)

Are Shorter Form Prayers Preferable to Longer Ones?

Another characteristic of the Breviary Services is the shortness of the prayers they contain. Dear Froude used to say that 'long prayers' were peculiar and came in at the Reformation. Verses and Responses, Sentences, and Collects are much easier to attend to. This is one great excellence of the Psalms – as being not *continual addresses* to Almighty God, (which require a great effort and stretch of mind) but meditations on His attributes etc. mutual exhortations, interspersed with some more like prayers. . . . Tastes and feelings so differ, that I never would *prescribe* for another – but if asked what *I* should wish Services formed upon, I should unhesitating say the model of the Breviary . . . I like their ["the Latins'] mode of reading, i.e. not long passages of chapters – but short and broken portions with responses – attention is thus kept up . . . (v. 6; To Henry Wilberforce, 25 March 1837)

What Makes The Lord's Prayer so Unique and Special?

The Lord's prayer can be more or less entered into by all, (tho perfectly by none) and this arises in great measure from the simplicity of its language. – Poetical language is the expression of the mind *at its highest flight*, – or under some *particular* feeling; it is *personal* – or (viewing it as religious) it expresses excited religious feeling, which comes and goes. (v. 2; To John Keble, 30 Aug. 1831)

How Relatively Important are Sermons for the Clergyman?

As to Town-preacherships, they seem to me dangerous to the holder, as corrupting the minister into the orator. The *realities* of our profession are in parochial and such-like engagements – the sickbed, the school-room, the accidental intercourse of the week – but a pulpit makes one *un*real, rhetorical – conceited – it hardens the heart, while it effeminates it. . . . One out of many dilemmas in which a London-preacher finds himself, is the following – let *him withstand* the popular love of novelty and desire of excitement, he must preach (what will be called) *dully* and if so, he will *empty his chapel* – let him try to keep his congregation together, he will be pampering their bad tempers and habits. (v. 2; To Simeon Lloyd Pope, 21 June 1831)

How Does Kneeling Help Us to Receive Christian Truths?

. . . the idea which had actually been the rule of the Primitive Church, of teaching the more Sacred Truths ordinarily by rites and ceremonies. No mode of teaching can be imagined so public, constant, impressive, permanent, and at the same time reverential than that which makes the forms of devotion the memorial and declaration of doctrine – reverential because the very posture of the mind in worship is necessarily such. In this way Christians receive the Gospel literally on their knees, and in a temper altogether different from that critical and argumentative spirit which sitting and listening engender. (v. 5; To James Stephen, 16 March 1835)

In What Sense Can a Crucifix be Worshiped?

St Thomas expressly tells us that the *adoration* we pay the Crocifisso is the *highest*, latria – viz because we contemplate *in it* the Prototype. (v. 14; To William Monsell, 1 May 1851)

The word 'Il Crocifisso' . . . means to an Italian 'the crucified One' primarily, directly, and naturally – but 'Crucifix' to an Englishman means primarily the wooden image. Hence, you have the'greatest difficulty in translating Italian devotions, for the Crocifisso is 'He,' and you find 'He' loves you, and can do you all mercies and bestow on you all blessings.. Still, were an Italian asked 'Do you think that wooden image hears you or can think about you?' he-would answer 'How can you think me such a fool?' However ardent then his devotion to it, he *really* only holds it to be a symbol or sacramental of his Lord and Saviour and he prays not *to* it, but *before* it, which is the *sober, formal* language of *theology*. (v. 16; To Mrs. Catherine Froude, 17 March 1854)

How Much Does Scripture Teach About Public Worship?

[H]ow little is in Scripture for Public Worship – Accordingly Milton gave it up. (v. 6; To H. A. Woodgate, 23 Feb. 1838)

How Should we Regard Purported Miracles?

As to the alleged miracles in the Tyrol, I think I should wish to follow the example of St Ignatius . . . I would not deny, but I would suspend my judgment. . . . often suggestions which are made upon our minds are so ambiguous as not to declare their origin – they may be from above – or from beneath. It is rash to decide at once. (v. 9; To Miss Mary Holmes, 8 March 1843)

I certainly *do* think that the ecclesiastical miracles *are* as credible (in this sense) as the scripture miracles – nay, more so, because they come after scripture, and scripture breaks (as it were) the ice. The miracles of scripture begin a new law; they innovate on an established order. There is less to surprise in a second miracle than in a first. . . . Ecclesiastical miracles are *probable* because scripture miracles are *true*. . . . I really cannot conceive a thoughtful person denying that the history of the ark at the deluge is as difficult to reason as a saint floating on his cloak. . . . Moreover, I believe with a like certainty every one of the scripture miracles, not only that apostles and prophets 'in their lifetime have *before now* raised the dead to life,' etc., but that Elias did this, and St. Peter did that, and just as related, and so all through the whole catalogue of their miracles. . . . Protestants are most inconsistent and onesided in *refusing to go into the evidence* for ecclesiastical miracles, which, on the first blush of the matter, are not stranger than those miracles of scripture which they happily profess to admit. (v. 14; To Samuel Hinds, Bishop of Norwich, 11 Oct. 1851)

[T]he miraculous gift has never left the church since the time of the apostles, though displaying itself under different circumstances, and that certain reputed miracles are real instances of its exhibition. The former of these two points I hold in common with all Catholics; the latter on my own private judgment, which I impose on no one. (v. 14; To Samuel Hinds, Bishop of Norwich, 19 Oct. 1851)

What is the Great Attribute of Catholic Devotional Literature?

The great benefit I feel in Roman books of devotion is their great and business-like practicalness, if I may so speak. They do for one what one wants, as being the writings of persons who *knew* the wants of people. (v. 9; To Miss Mary Holmes, 8 March 1843)

What is the Evidence of a Particular Personal Calling?

And now as to your vocation, . . . I should say that one of the most necessary tests of you being able to judge whether you had a calling or not (I am not speaking of tests of a calling, but of power of judging) is your finding yourself remain long and equally in one state of mind. (v. 10; To Miss Mary Holmes, 16 April 1844)

What is the Relation of Doctrine to Devotional Practices?

There is a marked contrast in Catholicity between the views presented to us by doctrine and devotion respectively. Doctrines never change, devotions vary with each individual. Catholics allow each other, accordingly, the greatest licence, and are, if I may so speak, utter *liberals*, as regards devotions, whereas they are most sensitive about doctrine. That Mary is the Mother of God is a point of faith – that Mary is to be honored and exalted in this or that way is a point of devotion. The latter is the consequence indeed of the former, but a consequence which follows with various intensity, in various degrees and in various modes, in various minds. We know from the first that St Joseph was our Lord's foster father and the guardian of Mary – we know nothing more now than was known by St Irenaeus and St Cyprian – yet till two or three centuries ago the devotion to St Joseph was almost unknown in the Church; now it is one of the dearest devotions, and closely connected with the affections and enshrined in the hearts, of myriads. It is not to the purpose here to inquire the philosophy of this – but so it is, we live in devotions to which our next door neighbours are dead; we do not find fault with them, nor they with us. . . . As far as I can make out from history and from documents St Chrysostom had not the devotion to Mary, which St Buonaventura had or St Alfonso – but they agreed together most simply and absolutely that she was the Mother of God. (v. 16; To Mrs. Catherine Froude, 2 Jan. 1855)

Do Catholics Have a Wide Freedom of Devotional Practice?

While private judgment is forbidden to Catholics in matters of divine revelation, it is fully accorded to them in matters of devotion. Worship is a free-will service. It is our response to God's voice. He speaks, and what He speaks is dogma – it cannot be altered – it never was ours – it comes to us, not from us – it is objective – but worship is essentially subjective – it is what *we* give to God – and (under rational limits) we have power over our own acts. Therefore the Church is very loth to interfere with it. Catholics may choose *their own* saints to be devout to. They may honor this one, they may pass over that. They have their own 'special devotions.' And as they choose the object or the matter to which they are specially devout, so (under the same rational limits) they choose the manner. (v. 20; To Lady Chatterton, 16 June 1863)

As to the Devotions to Saints, including those to our Lady, the only objection which is plausible, is, that certain forms etc. are allowed and not condemned. Few are injoined. We are quite at liberty to dispense with those which are used in Italy or elsewhere. (v. 20; To William Robert Brownlow, 16 Oct. 1863)

What is the Rationale Behind Devotion to Jesus' Sacred Heart?

I am far from denying there are 'perils' in the devotion of the Sacred Heart, where men are not well taught – but so there were even in the doctrine of the Holy Eucharist. . . . as our people are always taught that it is the Person alone of Emmanuel that they worship, and both His Divine Substance and His human nature in all its parts as (for instance) His heart *in* that Person, I don't see how there is more peril in worshipping Him in His Heart than in His Body and Blood. His Divine Person is in His human nature, and His human nature in His Divine Person. (v. 26; To Robert Charles Jenkins, 29 Sep. 1873)

When we worship the Sacred Heart, we worship the *Person* of our Lord and Saviour, and His Sacred humanity, and therefore His Sacred Heart is *included* in His Person. His Sacred Heart is *He*. We worship *Him* through His Human Heart. (v. 26; To Mrs. Henry Wilberforce, 21 Oct. 1873)

And, if we worship His Divine Heart, still it is the Second Person of the Holy Trinity that we worship, *through* that Heart which is one with Him, and which is the Symbol of that over-flowing compassion towards us which is human while it is divine. (v. 26; To Mrs. Henry Wilberforce, 21 Oct. 1873)

Chapter Twenty-One

The Sacrament of Baptism

What is the Relation of Baptism to the Church?

I conceive that a state of union with the Church *is* a state of justification; . . . Moreover, that the Church, into which Baptism grafts us as an instrument, is not merely the *visible* Church is to me evident from the Baptismal Service speaking of incorporation into God's '*Holy* Church,' which the mere visible Church is not . . . (v. 6; To George Stanley Faber, 11 April 1838)

Does Baptism Regenerate?

Now one article of the Creed is that there is 'one baptism for the *remission* of sins –' . . . Clergymen then who deny baptismal regeneration . . . would seem to contradict the faith once delivered to the Saints. (v. 7; To Miss Mary Holmes, 10 June 1840)

No other *appointed* means but Baptism is *revealed in Scripture* for regeneration. (v. 9; To an Unknown Correspondent, 4 March 1843)

The Catholic doctrine is that all souls, which are baptized, are regenerate – even though they be baptized by heretics; and that they do not fall from that state of grace, except by mortal sin. (v. 13; To Mrs. Wootten, 30 March 1850)

How is Baptism Related to the Holy Spirit and Justification?

The indwelling Spirit enters through Baptism, and henceforth faith is both lively and the instrument of justification. Baptism is the original instrument and issues in the entrance of the Spirit – *in* which, not as by a second process, consists our justification. (v. 6; To George Stanley Faber, 16 May 1838)

What is Conditional Baptism?

There is *grave* irregularity in the Baptisms of Anglican clergymen – even of the high Church party. I speak from my own knowledge. Therefore out of love to you, the Priest who baptizes you will pour water on you with the words '*If* thou art not already baptized, I baptize thee etc'. I don't see how you can scruple at that. On the contrary, I am sure, as time went on, you would be very unhappy, if you had *not* received this simple precaution. (v. 24; To Miss Ellen Fox, 25 Feb. 1868)

Is There Such a Thing as "Baptism of Desire?"

As to the question of danger to your soul from delaying, you know that the belief in the early Church concerning catechumens who died without Baptism was, that on death they were for their intention-sake, received into that grace which they were seeking. Can you suppose that, if you are really seeking, God will cut short life that you may not find? either He will not cut it short, or He will grant the grace while shortening it. (v. 8; To Miss Mary Holmes, 8 Aug. 1841)

I believe implicit desire of the Sacrament is sufficient in unbaptized heathen for Salvation. (v. 26; To Catherine Froude, 5 July 1872)

Chapter Twenty-Two

Sacraments and Sacramentals

How Do we Define a "Sacrament"?

They are the embodied forms of the Spirit of Christ. (v. 5; To Samuel Wilberforce, 10 March 1835)

. . . the presence of Christ in the Church for doctrine and grace – a continual revelation of the Incarnation. (v. 5; To James Stephen, 16 March 1835. Newman was perhaps referring to the Eucharist alone)

Sacrament, (Lat. Sacramentum etc) is the received name for the seven special sacred rites of the Catholic Church; viz Baptism, etc. . . . In the original sense of the word Sacramentum, it signified the military oath etc etc . . . or any oath – and hence the oath or vow on being initiated into the Sacred Rites of Religion – and hence those secret and sacred Rites themselves. Sacraments are distinguished from all other rites, as being both signs and means of grace, instituted by our Lord Himself, whether immediately or through His Apostles. By their being *means* of grace, is meant that they are instruments, through or together with which supernatural grace is given to the recipient; and by their being *signs*, that the visible rite is symbolical (or analogous) of the particular kind or virtue of the grace given. . . . a sacrament consists of two parts, a sign and a thing signified. Hence St Augustine defines it ..... and the Council of Trent... The outward sign may be considered more distinctly under the division into matter and Form; the matter being the ordinary element or natural substance (as water in Baptism) which is used for a religious or supernatural purpose, and the form being the ministerial words which appropriate it to that religious purpose, and thereby separate it from other matter of the same kind, as water used for washing the face etc. . . . Hence the matter and form are all that are intrinsically required for the constitution or confection [of] a Sacrament, it produces its effect, that is, it confers grace ex opere operato, i.e. by its own vis (without depending) on the recipient. (v. 18; To Henry Bittleston, 29 June 1857)

What are the Attributes and Benefits of Sacraments?

Catholics consider that in each sacrament there is 1. what is properly called the Sacrament, i.e. quod significat, et non significatur – the *matter and form* – 2. quod significatur et non significat, or the res sacramenti, or virtus sacramenti, viz *grace*. 3. quod et significat et significatur, and is both res and sacramentum. The third is in three sacraments the *character*, which comes in a certain sense between, (e.g.) water and baptismal grace. (I do not mean in the order of causation). – In Matrimony it is the marriage bond, which is *signified* by the mutual consent of the parties, and *signifies* the union of Christ with his Church and the soul with God. In Extreme Unction it is bodily health. Now in the Eucharist this third, both Sacramentum and res, is the Body of Christ, signified by the sacramental Species, signifying the grace of the Sacrament, the nutritive grace. (v. 13; To William Maskell, 31 March 1850)

The grace given in a sacrament is two fold – first habitual grace, by which the soul is sanctified and united with God and lives, and secondly the grace just alluded to or the sacramental grace <grace of the sacrament>, which is that which is denoted under the outward sign. This sacramental grace implies a certain analogy between the requirements of body and soul. Thus Baptism gives life, Confirmation etc. (v. 18; To Henry Bittleston, 29 June 1857)

What is Sacramental Disposition?

[M]ore or less grace is given, or more effectually given according to the disposition of the recipient, . . . he can suspend its effect altogether, e.g. . . . he may make it invalid, by the absence of a . . . <passive> intention. (v. 18; To Henry Bittleston, 29 June 1857)

What is the Relationship of Preaching to Sacraments?

The Puritans etc. . . . looked upon Sacraments chiefly *as* Sermons, and thought their grace lay in their kindling impressions in the mind. Hence they generally started with a long preachment. . . . In the primitive way, the worshipper did not think of himself – he came *to* God – God's House and Altar were the Sermon which addressed him and roused him. His Sacraments were the *objects* of his regard. Words were unnecessary. (v. 6; To [sister] Jemima Mozley, 4 June 1837)

What is the Sacrament of Confirmation?

[T]hose who have been regenerated and pardoned, are to be 'strengthened' by the Holy Ghost, and to have imparted to them the Seven gifts of grace which were poured upon Christ; again that they are to be 'defended', made to 'continue' and 'increase'; lastly that they are to be placed under the protection of God's 'fatherly hand' and to be led forward in obedience. Here we have an 'interpretation' quite sufficient of the word 'Confirmation;' viz as a deep fixing, establishing, rooting in of that grace which was first given in Baptism. . . . confirmation seals in their fulness, winds up and consigns, completes the entire round of those sanctifying gifts which are begun, which are given inchoately. in Baptism. . . . If it be asked, what is the *peculiar* grace of Confirmation, I answer it seems as the Greek name implies to be a Perfecting, or man-making. We in it become men in Christ Jesus. The baptismal grace is principally directed towards the abolition of existing guilt, e.g. original sin – the child is comparatively speaking incapable of actual. The grace of Confirmation is directed to arm the Christian against his three great enemies, which, when entering into his field of trial, he at once meets. (v. 6; To [sister] Jemima Mozley, 4 June 1837)

Confirmation cannot be repeated – it is a sort of appendix or ratification of Baptism – and to repeat it would be what the Church calls a sacrilege. Doubtless grace is conferred by laying on of the Bishop's hands. (v. 7; To Miss Mary Holmes, 16 August 1840)

Is Confession a Helpful and Biblical Practice?

As to your more serious question about confession, I feel sure that we should be all in a much better state, were it practised – but I see very great obstacles to reviving it. I think it should always be *sacramental* – performed in Church and face to face. And it requires so strong a *received faith* to do this. I mean, it should be a *received* truth that confession is necessary. . . . It must not be an individual opinion of private judgment, but a belief of a Church, to secure us with any tolerable certainty, from wavering of mind, and confession turning out a misery instead of a comfort. . . . I am sure that we are not a real genuine Church, a Church all glorious within, till we return to this primitive and Scriptural practice. (v. 7; To Miss Maria Rosina Giberne, 22 Dec. 1840)

Gladstone . . . seems to think it had better be begun, not to Priests, but to any one, by way of accustoming people to the *thing itself*. Yet so very awful a thing, as it is to many persons, requires that support from sacred and sacramental sanctions which a Priestly ordinance alone can give. Confession cannot well be disjoined from absolution. (v. 10; To Edward B. Pusey, 11 July 1844)

As to confession, when it cannot be made, from circumstances, true contrition, with a desire for the opportunity of making confession is sufficient for reconciling the soul to God. And no confession or sacerdotal absolution avails at all without true repentance and contrition. (v. 21; To John F. Perrin, 9 Sep. 1864)

Can a Person Possibly be Saved Without the Sacraments?

Contrition with the desire of the Sacrament of Penance is sufficient for salvation, when the Sacrament cannot be procured. This is, I think, of FAITH. (v. 17; To Mrs. Catherine Froude, 30 Nov. 1856)

Is the Sign of the Cross Permissible?

There is nothing in Scripture about using the Cross in Baptism – so that, if your way of viewing the matter were correct, one might say 'No one can use the Cross, without thinking such a usage pleasing to God – but *that* is a doctrine – and it is not in Scripture that the use of the Cross is pleasing to God – therefore it is unlawful – for no doctrine is lawful which is not in Scripture.' I on the other hand should urge that it is a Catholic usage, accidentally involving doctrine. (v. 6; To George Stanley Faber, 16 May 1838)

How Can we Know that We Have a Vocation to the Priesthood?

Almighty God calls the soul in various ways and seasons. It is very seldom that one can know at *once* that one is called. I think that time is generally necessary. This requires patience, and patience is very difficult. I do not see that you can know in three days that you have a vocation to the *priesthood*. But till you know, your father has a call on you. If you were quite sure, you must follow God. Again if papa says 'I urge nothing' – then you may at once follow that path which, even if it did not turn out in the event to be your vocation, would, while you were in it, be of great use to you, and which may turn out in the event to *be* your vocation – but if papa said definitely 'I Wish you to remain at home,' or 'I wish you to go Oxford,' I donor think that you have that certainty about your vocation, to warrant you to go against his wishes. All this has reference to the *Priesthood*. (v. 21; To Robert Edmund Froude, 24 July 1864)

How Important is it to Follow Our Vocation?

[I]f one may lose one's soul by *not* following a religious vocation when one *has* it, one may incur the same loss also by *embracing* a religious life *without* a vocation. (v. 21; To Robert Edmund Froude, 28 July 1864)

Can People be Mistaken About Their Supposed Vocation?

Another danger is this, lest a postulant and novice, being young, with warm affections and religious earnestness, should have all the signs of vocation and take the vows, and then after a while fall into a state of tepidity, which may indeed only be a fault of natural weakness and a re-action of mind which is to be resisted as a temptation, but on the other hand may quite as easily be the result of that spiritual constitution which God has given him, and such, that, if it had shown itself in him *while* he was a novice, might have made clear that, without any fault of his, he had *no* vocation for a religious state at all. Certainly, I think I see men who have made serious mistakes in becoming religious suddenly. Of course there are always two ways of explaining the failure – it may be said 'he *fell* from his vocation' – or – 'he *never had* a vocation' As this applies to an ecclesiastical vocation as well as to a religious, I will instance it in the case of Mr Conelly, . . . He separated from his wife; she became a religious . . ., he a Priest. Then he found he had mistaken his vocation – wished to get back his wife – left the Church and is now an Irvingite. (v. 21; To Robert Edmund Froude, 3 Aug. 1864)

Chapter Twenty-Three

Heaven and Hell / Satan and Demons

What is the Beatific Vision in Heaven?

[N]one are in heaven who do not see the face of God, according to the words of Pope Eugenius [bull Laetentur Caeli, 6 July 1439] . . . It seems to me then that being in heaven, seeing the Divine Essence, and being blessed, are convertible terms; and that these terms are equivalent also to the word 'salvation' . . . equivalent also to 'eternal life;' according to our Lord's own definition . . . (v. 22; To an Unknown Correspondent, end of 1866?)

What is the Blessedness of Heaven?

[T]he blessedness of heaven does not consist strictly in its never ending, but in the sight and fruition of Almighty God, and the certainty and absolute security and peace which that fruition involves. (v. 26; To an Unknown Correspondent, 5 Sep. 1873)

Is Hell Eternal?

In all these matters I speak under correction of divines, and the infallible decision of Holy Church, but for myself I discern clearly but one thing, viz that the state of the lost is never reversed, that they never will see the face of God, or enter heaven, that they never will be annihilated, yet never be in company with the Saints. These are awful *negatives* – but they are negatives which are inflicted by lost souls on themselves – for it would be but an increase of misery for an unholy soul to be brought into heaven, and it remains unholy by its own act. No positive infliction of pain is necessary for the fulness of the second death. Sinners are self condemned, self punished. (v. 23; To an Unknown Correspondent, 3 July 1867)

Does Eternal Punishment in Hell Make Any Sense?

As to what you say about eternal punishment, it is to me, as to most men, the great crux in the Christian system as contemplated by the human mind . . . Reason is able to approve of much – is it to approve of all? Another consideration is our utter ignorance of what is meant by eternity – it is not infinite time. Time implies a process – it involves the connection and action of one portion upon another – if eternity be an eternal *now*, eternal punishment is the fact that a person *is* in suffering; – he suffers today and tomorrow and so on for ever – but not in a *continuation* – all is complete in every time – there is no memory, no anticipation, no growth of intensity from succession. I will not say I am right in so considering it, for I have not consulted divines, (and certainly popular views, sermons etc are against me, for in them the growth of pain from succession is expressly insisted on) but if I *be* right, then the question is merely, should a soul suffer, should sin be punished, which few will deny. (v. 13; To J. M. Capes, 2 Dec. 1849)

In denying that 'eternity was without duration,' you seem to me denying, not an assumption of mine, as you view it, but the common voice of all nations . . . And by saying that what *did* relieve you was the mystery of God's ante-eternity, you seem taking up yourself my very argument – for the mysteriousness of it shows that we don't know *what* eternity *is* – and if our notion is so defective as to make us think the divine a parte ante beyond Divine Omnipotence, that same defect may be the cause of eternal pain seeming to contradict the Divine Allmercifulness. (v. 13; To J. M. Capes, 27 Jan. 1850)

What is it Like to Experience Eternal Punishment?

As to that awful doctrine, I observe 1. That it is a negative one, viz., that the lost will never go to heaven, that there will be no restitution. What eternity in itself involves positively, in its idea, we have no notion whatever. 2. Succession of thought, the sense of a succession of time, is not logically involved in the idea of eternity. In the legend of the Monk and the bird we find centuries of pleasure seeming to be no longer than a few minutes; so may it be with centuries of pain. 3. Taking punishment to mean pain, there is an infinite number of punishments in degree. There is nothing to show that, in a multitude of cases, the only punishment will be the poena damni, that is, the loss of heaven. 4. There is nothing to make it necessary to believe that one and the same individual will for ever have one and the same degree of punishment. 5. Theologians of weight have advocated, and have been allowed to advocate, a gradual mitigation of punishment in the lost. 6. And many ancient Missals contain a Mass for the alleviation of their pains. It is difficult to speak on this subject, for the Church has said little – and one has little guide beyond one's own private judgment. The great truth is that death ends our probation, and settles our state for ever; but there is no passing over the great gulf; that our only happiness is to be with God, and that those who are not with God are without Him. (v. 26; To J. H. Willis Nevins, 4 June 1872)

Is Satanic Oppression a Continuing Reality?

[F]rom the time of Moses and Saul down to the middle ages and thence to a recent date, we have, independent of these manifestations, historical evidence of the fact that men can have dealings with the devil. And again, in proportion as we accept the testimony of the Martyrologies and Saints' Lives, we see that the evil spirit is allowed to tempt even holy persons in the guise of an Angel of light. (v. 20; To David Melville, 6 Sep. 1861)

Chapter Twenty-Four

Education

How is Christianity Related to Education?

Christianity, and nothing short of it, must be made the element and principle of all education. Where it has been laid as the first stone, and acknowledged as the governing spirit, it will take up into itself, assimilate, and give a character to literature and science. Where Revealed Truth has given the aim and direction to Knowledge, Knowledge of all kinds will minister to Revealed Truth. The evidences of Religion, natural theology, metaphysics, —or, again, poetry, history, and the classics,—or physics and mathematics, may all be grafted into the mind of a Christian, and give and take by the grafting. . . . Far from recognizing this principle, the teachers of the Knowledge School would educate from Natural Theology up to Christianity, and would amend the heart through literature and philosophy. (v. 8: Letter to the *Times* by "Catholicus" in Response to Robert Peel ["Tamworth"], Feb. 1841)

Will not the same fanaticism which resolves to have all the primary schools throughout the country in its hands, agitate for some means of exerting a control and introducing a teaching of its own into all the higher schools, some twenty years hence? Religion is in process of exclusion from the education of high and low, and what will be the issue of this tyranny? (v. 26; To J. Walker of Scarborough, 5 Jan. 1873)

What is the Purpose of a University?

The direct object of a University *as such*, is to teach *all* knowledge. The subject matter of *faith* comes into the idea of 'all knowledge.' Therefore a University *must*, cannot help, as such, teaching the faith and nothing else. Therefore it does *directly*, . . . teach and inculcate Catholic expression, feeling, fact etc etc. and leavens all instruction with Catholicism. So much for a University in its *idea*. But a *Catholic* University professes Catholicism in the sense of honoring it, keeping feast days, having sermons etc. But this it does, not by virtue of its being a University, but because it is a *Catholic* University. . . . Therefore, looking at the whole, we may say in a broad way, that the office of a Catholic University is to teach *faith*, and of Colleges to protect *morals*. (v. 15; To J. D. Dalgairns, 23 July 1852)

What is the Philosophy of History?

My notion of the Philosophy of History is the science of which historical facts are the basis, or the laws on which it pleases Almighty Providence to conduct the political and social world. . . . (v. 16; To T. W. Allies, 3 Sep. 1854)

Does Much Education Tend to Counter Christian Discipleship?

[A]s the rich man, or the man in authority, has his serious difficulties in going to heaven, so also has the learned. . . . the more a man is educated, whether in theology or secular science, the holier he needs to be, if he would be saved. . . . devotion and self rule are worth all the intellectual cultivation in the world. . . . in the case of most men, literature and science and the habits they create, so far from ensuring those highest gifts, indispose the mind towards their acquisition. (v. 19; To William G. Ward, 8 Nov. 1860)

Chapter Twenty-Five

Atheism, Agnosticism, Liberalism, and Secularism

What is Philosophical and Theological Liberalism?

The tendency of the age is towards *liberalism* – i.e. a thinking established notions worth nothing – in this system of opinions a disregard of religion is included No religion will stand if deprived of its forms. (v. 2; To Simeon Lloyd Pope, 15 Aug. 1830)

Liberalism is the *development* of Rationalism. It views faith as a mere *natural* gift, the like and the consequence of reason and the moral sense; and by reason and the moral sense he estimates it and measures its objects. A man soon comes to be satisfied with other men, though they ignore faith and its objects, provided they recognise reason and the moral sense. This is Liberalism. (v. 31; To Richard A. Armstrong, 23 March 1887)

How Should we Regard Theological Liberalism?

I am tempted to put it to you whether the persons you meet generally . . . believe in Christianity in any true meaning of the word. No, they are liberals, and in saying this, I conceive I am saying almost as bad of them as can be said of any man. . . . Shall we not have men placed in the higher stations of the Church who are anything but real Churchmen? . . . I would rather have the Church severed from its temporalities and scattered to the four winds than such a desecration of holy things. (v. 2; To John William Bowden, 13 March 1831)

What a miserable state the Country is in! the ministry now show themselves to be, what they have always been, tho' charitable persons denied it, deeply infected with the cold-hearted indifferent spirit of liberalism; mere Gallios. May I be kept from having any thing to do with those who are 'neither hot nor cold –' It is only a great blessing we have not fallen under such men before. To neglect personal religion (with some other ministers) is bad enough – but, to become a public instrument in overthrowing the truth, not even to have the *fear* of God before their eyes, is wretched indeed. (v. 3; To [Aunt] Elizabeth Newman, 24 Aug. 1832)

[W]e must aim at the 'rising generation' – One cannot expect to get over those whose minds are formed by long habit. But young men feel a disposition (bad enough) to rise against the system they have been brought up in, and I trust the true one being suggested will keep them from taking up with liberalism etc., etc. (v. 5; To John William Bowden, 10 April 1835)

[L]iberalism viewed as a *system*, . . . *is* a definite doctrine, and perhaps may be fairly called a heresy; however we word its main and elementary tenet. (v. 7; To Edward B. Pusey, 20 Feb. 1839)

I never read a word of [Unitarian William Ellery] Channing – and am surprised (disgusted) to find much I have prophesied about liberalism etc anticipated in him. (v. 7; To Thomas Mozley, 29 Dec. 1840)

Are you aware that the more serious thinkers among us, as far as they dare form an opinion, are used to regard the spirit of Liberalism as the characteristic of destined Antichrist? . . . The spirit of lawlessness came in at the Reformation – and Liberalism is its offspring. O that you would keep quite clear of it. (v. 8; To Ambrose L. Phillipps, 12 Sep. 1841)

The Church of England must certainly be very seriously affected, should the Protestant party succeed in throwing out their antagonists. I suppose, there will be a dreadful move towards liberalism. (v. 10; To Simeon Lloyd Pope, 20 March 1845)

Have you heard of the most dreadful autobiography of Blanco White which has been published? It must have an effect, I think, if read, in frightening people back from liberalism, though some persons it will unsettle utterly. I am told this is what is happening in Oxford, where liberalism is sadly on the increase. Poor B W. gives up the personal immortality of the soul, and the idea of a God who has power over nature. As to our Blessed Lord, he does not believe the Gospels – and hardly thinks anything is known about Him. (v. 10; To Mrs. Elizabeth Bowden, 8 May 1845)

I cannot *conceive* how the Holy See can suffer the University [of Dublin] to perish, considering it represents the principal of unmixed Education against the Queen's Colleges etc etc. It is practically giving up Ireland to Liberalism. (v. 19; To John Stanislas Flanagan, 14 Feb. 1859)

[T]he soul of any one for whom Christ died is precious, and is worth keeping from liberalism. (v. 21; To Edward B. Pusey, 25 Nov. 1864)

I wonder whether the wounds I have received will do me any good with the people in London who go about saying I am a liberal. As they have said this up to now, in spite of my Apologia, I suppose the testimony of the Saturday [Review] in my favour may go for nothing . . . (v. 22; To J. Walker of Scarborough, 2 July 1865; referring to the article, "Dr. Newman and Liberalism": 24 June 1865)

I am struck from your letter with the difference of senses in which the word 'Liberalism' is used. You consider it designates a course of action, I a set of principles. You would call Gladstone a liberal, I an Anti-Liberal. You might call me a liberal, because I do not deny that under existing circumstance the abolition of tests is the advisable course; I should call myself an Anti-Liberal, because, in harmony with the Pope's syllabus, I should say that the best thing of all is to have a Unity of religion in a country and that so *real* that its Ascendancy is but the expression of the universal mind. (v. 24; To Richard Frederick Clarke, 20 Dec. 1868)

Is Political Liberalism Hostile to Catholicism?

Catholics find it difficult to realize the extreme contempt which the advanced Liberal party feels of our holy religion, and therefore the intolerable irritation they feel, when a religion which they despise as obsolete and a piece of lumber and a cumbrance, presumes to be so offensive as to show itself in open day and to take part in public matters, and to affect an illumination and to aim at a knowledge which it cannot really have. I have a brother [Francis] connected with the London University. I am on the best terms with him and have frequent communications with him – and he wishes to be as kind, as in heart he is affectionate – but the abhorrence, the scorn, and the indignation, and, when even he wishes to be most civil, the niggardly condescending courtesy he shows to my religion, must be witnessed to be understood. (v. 19; To Henry Weedal, 25 Jan. 1859)

Are There Jewish Analogies to Christian Theological Liberals?

It is the peculiar commendation pronounced upon Zacharias and his wife, that 'they were both righteous before God, walking in all the commandments and ordinances of the Lord blameless.' This was 1500 years after the Mosaic law had been given. Now let us consider how much might have been speciously said in that day, by those who wished to ease themselves of its yoke. True, its precepts were clear and explicit; but then how circumstances had changed since the time of Moses! It might have been plausibly argued, that the miraculous Providence had long come to an end; that the affairs of the Jewish nation went on as those of any other state; that Judas Maccabeus had conquered by his own sword and his own right hand; that Herod the King was in alliance with the Romans; that prophecy had ceased; Solomon's temple destroyed; the ark lost; the Shechinah withdrawn; that the Jews were now almost 'as the heathen, as the families of the countries.' This would have been the notion of a liberal Jew; and, if he fell in with one of the stricter sort, as Zacharias, is it not certain, he would have regarded him with jealousy and disdain, thought him narrow-minded, fanciful, heated with a vision of past years, and unable to adapt himself to changed circumstances, and spoken of him as 'one of those extraordinary men who attempt to revive what is dead, and graft primitive practices on a later age?' Yet in spite of all this worldly philosophy, 'Zacharias was righteous before God, walking in all His commandments and ordinances.' (v. 4; To the Editor of *The Record*, 7 Nov. 1833)

What is the Result of Resisting Theological Liberalism?

I must consent to be in an apparent minority . . . Doubtless I have made up my mind, as every one must, who tries to stand against the torrent, to be misunderstood and called names . . . when I think a person a heretic, *I* shall never call him religious. A spiritually minded heretic may exist in the 'Protestant' world, but not in the Church. (v. 4; To Samuel Rickards, 30 July 1834)

Where Does Accommodation to the "Spirit of the Age" Lead?

[O]ne must go by one's own judgment – and I may account that to be indulgence to the evil principles of the age which another may consider a necessary and prudent accommodation. Again I am persuaded that often, when one accommodates the age, one hurts posterity. What is the reason that this or that man's works are brought to countenance errors now extinct, except that he has yielded to the superstitions or fancies of his own time? . . . Again the Church and its Minister are by very profession *protests* against the peculiar errors of every age, as it comes – so that one must not be surprised to find a great *agreement* in various sorts of objectors against this or that point one advances, which is not therefore proved to be wrong. (v. 4; To Samuel Wilberforce, 10 Nov. 1834)

Is Atheism Fundamentally Bigoted Against Christianity?

I wish it to be distinctly understood that I consider the rejection of Christianity to arise from a fault of the *heart*, not of the *intellect*; that unbelief arises, not from mere error of reasoning, but either from pride or from sensuality. It is important that at starting I should premise this, lest I should appear inconsistent, and to assert *both* that the Christian evidences are most convincing, and yet that they are not likely to convince those who reject them. A dislike of the *contents* of Scripture is at the bottom of unbelief; and since those contents must be rejected by fair means or foul, it is plain that *in order to [do] this* the evidences must in some sort be attacked. But this is quite *an afterthought*; and, thus unbelievers (as I observed in my last letter) reverse the legitimate process of reasoning, and act in a manner which would be scouted as unfair were they examining Newton's Principia or Lavoisier's Chemistry. Hence the most powerful arguments for Christianity do not *convince*, only *silence*; for there is at the bottom that secret antipathy for the doctrines of Christianity, which is quite out of the reach of argument. I do not then assert that the Christian evidences are *overpowering*, but that they are *unanswerable*; nor do I expect so much to show Christianity *true*, as to prove it *rational*; nor to prove infidelity *false*, so much as *irrational*. (v. 1; To [brother] Charles Robert Newman, 24 March 1825)

Do Skeptics Assume Certain Premises Hostile to Christianity?

But you will say you have arrived at certain hitherto undiscovered principles, which at once solve the whole matter in dispute; which justify you in despising all who have as yet treated it, and supersede the necessity of diligent and cool investigation. Yet how monstrous is it to attempt overturning a system by a-priori objections to its doctrines; while the great body of external evidence on which it is founded remains untouched – as if a man should endeavour to refute Newton, not by showing some flaw in his reasoning, but by expatiating on the antecedent absurdity, the ridiculousness of supposing the earth to go round the sun. Remember too the external evidences are built upon the obvious and general canons by which we judge of the truth or falsehood of every thing we hear; not on rules peculiar to religion, or modelled by it: here at least we do not argue 'on Christian principles.' The internal evidence depends a great deal on moral feeling; so that if we did not agree, we might accuse each other of prejudice or pride: the external is founded on purely logical principles. – You may indeed say that you can overturn that also; still you have not done so . . . (v. 1; To [brother] Charles Robert Newman, 3 March 1825)

I have pointed out what I consider the error in the inquiry you have been prosecuting, viz that you *did* decide against Christianity FIRST from its doctrines and THEN *with this prejudice against it on your mind* proceeded to examine the . . . evidence of which in consequence you were no fair judge. I have stated what I consider a *fact*; that your doubts of the truth of Christianity *originated* in a dislike of its doctrines. I wished therefore to draw near and put my finger on the seat of the disease . . . (v. 1; To [brother] Charles Robert Newman, 26 July [?] 1825)

It seems to me you take the true and normal way of meeting the infidelity of the age, by referring to our Lord's Person and

Character as exhibited in the Gospels. Philip said to Nathanael 'Come and see' – that is just what the present free thinkers will not allow men to do. They perplex and bewilder them with previous questions, to hinder them falling under the legitimate rhetoric of His divine Life, of His sacred words and acts. They say 'there is no truth because there are so many opinions,' or 'how do you know that the Gospels are authentic?' 'how do you account for Papias not mentioning the fourth Gospel?' – or 'how can you believe that punishment is eternal?' or 'why is there not stronger proof of the Resurrection?' With this multitude of questions in detail they block the way between the soul and its Saviour, and will not let it 'come and see.' We act otherwise in matters of this world – a judge says 'I am not satisfied with affidavits – I want to see the witnesses face to face –' In the Novel, the Duke of Argyll thought nothing better than to introduce Jenny Deans to her Majesty, and let her speak for herself – Such was the effect of our Lord's presence that his hearers said 'Never man spake as He spake –, but this is just what we should not be allowed to do at all, if these new lights had their way. All one can say is, that, miserable as it is, it is so unnatural, that I should think it cannot have success for any long time, but common-sense will re-assert its sway over men's minds. (v. 26; To David Brown, 11 Jan. 1873)

Will Atheism Satisfy the Deepest Longings of the Soul?

I sorrowfully prophesy waverings of opinion, wanderings, uncertainty, continual change. Or if you appear at all consistent, the only maxim in which you will be so (however you may attempt to disguise it from yourself by spreading it out into a system) is, that Christianity is wrong. Almost every other principle will be fluctuating and transitory. – But even admitting you arrive at some certainty in your principles, peace at least you will never have. In spite of the allsufficiency of knowledge, you will find it a cold and bleak state of things to be left carelessly and as it were unkindly by the God who made you, uncertain why you are placed here, and what is to become of you after death. Truth indeed is to be preferred to comfort; I only warn you not to expect more than you will find. Your greatest peace will be the calm of hopelessness . . . (v. 1; To [brother] Charles Robert Newman, 3 March 1825)

How Should we Approach a Media Hostile to Christianity?

I do not deny the power of the periodical Press, or the duty of making use of it when one can, – and very much obliged of course I must be to such friends as attempt to check its violence against ourselves personally, – but after all I do not hope or fear from it much. The hope of the Church does not lie with Newspapers readers. It lies with thoughtful men, and young men – whether lay or clerical. These are the men who must have weight, and these are the men whom Newspapers do not, for the most part, affect. And they will in their sphere and place spread the truth against the Newspapers; and in the long run be believed against them, as being not anonymous declaimers but men known and valued in their neighbourhoods. In everything of the kind there must be misrepresentation at first – and it is a work of time to set it right. Men *will not* be set right at once – they refuse to be – but they right themselves by a natural course. . . . You must not interpret me to mean that it is not desirable to influence the Periodical Press (as you seem to have been so successful in doing) when we *can* – but that we need not be surprised or frightened at seeing prejudice. (v. 7; To A. Belamy, 25 Jan. 1839)

Chapter Twenty-Six

Ecumenism

Can a Person Have Faith Without Having Heard the Gospel?

I answer plainly, *Yes*. Rahab had not received the Gospel. (v. 5; To Samuel Wilberforce, 4 Feb. 1835)

I know there is such a thing as *implicit* faith. (v. 7; To Miss Maria Rosina Giberne, 23 Nov. 1840)

Can Non-Catholics Receive Grace?

All this does not involve a denial of grace being given to those who are external to the Church. All we say is this, that grace is given them in *order* to bring them into it . . . (v. 14; To Mrs. Lucy Agnes Phillips, 5 June 1851)

Can Non-Catholics Possibly be Saved?

As to your anxiety about her religion, I think you may simply dismiss it from your mind. Of course it is indescribably better in every way, in this life, and on the death bed, and between death and judgment, and after that in eternity, to have been in Catholic communion, but it cannot be said that she is old enough or has seen or thought enough to have *rejected* grace offered her – and, while you do all you can to make her a Catholic, up to the point of teasing or unsettling her, which would only be so much harm, you must leave her to that God who loves her more than you can love her, and as to whom you can only say that, while He loves her, He has shown greater mercies to her sister and brothers. It still may be His purpose to convert her, but you may have a cheerful hope about her even though she died a Protestant. (v. 21; To Catherine Froude, 7 Feb. 1864)

Can a Good Man in Another Religion Espouse Christianity?

Looking at the whole world then as under religious training with varying light, I consider that every good man under a worse religious system will (as a general rule) joyfully accept the news of a more perfect system, and after examination pass on into it, with more or less conviction of its truth according to the evidence it offers . . . till he is proselytized into the perfect system, Christianity. – Hence the fact of a person being an unbeliever under the light of the Gospel truth, is to my mind a general evidence of a defect in his moral character . . . (v. 2; To [brother] Charles Robert Newman, 19 Aug. 1830)

Can God Use Mistaken or Heretical Men for His Purposes?

Providence continually brings good out of evil. I conceive Mahometanism is a great advance from idolatry. Where a Mahometan conqueror has converted idolators, he has been so far God's instrument. And if this be true of a false religion, how much more in cases where the Name of Christ is sounded though by unauthorized or heretical preachers! God was with Balaam amid the altars of enchantment [Num 22-24]. If He was with the covetous prophet, can He not much more act through earnest, though mistaken, men? (v. 8; To Miss Formby?, 6 April 1841)

How Should Protestants and Catholics Personally Interact?

I thank you for your Lordship's note just received and the kindness it expresses. It gives me very great sorrow to pain members of your Lordship's communion in what I write; but is not this the state of Christendom, that we are all paining each other? If the terms I have used pain Roman Catholics, must not I be pained, though I am not so unreasonable as to complain of it, at their holding us to be heretics and schismatics, as they do? – is it not painful to be told that our Sacraments have imparted no grace to us, that we are still in the flesh, that we worship Christ in His Sacrament but that He is not there? Yet to hold this, is part of their religious system – they cannot help it; it is one of the necessities of their position. And it is part of our religious system and we cannot help it to think that they admit doctrines and practices of an idolatrous character into their communion. Such a belief is an essential element in our religious profession; else why are we separate from so great a portion of the Catholic world? have we placed ourselves in this miserable isolation for nothing? I trust I never make accusations against Rome in the way of railing or insult . . . I feel as much as any one the lamentable state of Christendom, and heartily wish that the Communions of Rome and England could be one – but the best way of tending to this great end seems to me to be, in charity and meekness, to state our convictions, not to stifle them. (v. 8; To Bishop Nicholas Wiseman, 6 April 1841)

It gave me great pleasure to receive your letter and paper. I rejoice to have any evidence, such as they give me, of kind feelings on the part of members of your [Catholic] communion towards our Church. I should hope that numbers among ourselves, while they feel it a duty to be zealous for the faith once delivered to the Saints, desire also to be on a better footing with Roman Catholics. Yet so great a work as that of bringing the opinions and hearts of vast masses of men into one, is not likely, according to the ordinary course of Divine Providence, to be effected in one generation. (v. 8; To Henry Elwes, 28 April 1841)

I earnestly pray that the longer we all live, the more our hearts and souls, and not ours only but those of all the Clergy of our Church and of the laity with them, may be opened and enlarged towards each other. Of course I cannot be surprised that parts of what I have published should not approve themselves to the judgment of the kind persons who have written to me; but it will be a blessed day for the Church when her children in general imitate them in thinking and hoping the best of others, view what is done in the most favorable light, desire and pray to be all at peace together and to edify one another. (v. 8; To J. K. Miller, 2 June 1841)

I am sure we have gained on neither side by hostility, and do think that it is high time, without compromising what we feel to be the Truth, to act toward them and their Church in the spirit of Charity. As it is, our conduct is *not* Christian, *unless* indeed they are actually reprobate and diabolical. I suppose we may only revile the evil spirit, though Michael the Archangel did not even this: but we not only hate the Church of Rome, as if it were a Satanical Church, but revile it. This cannot be right, and bears its own condemnation on the face of it. (v. 8; To Louis Shadwell, 11 October 1841)

It is a grievous thing that religious opinions among us should be so various and so opposite to each other – or rather, it is most mysterious – but it is an alleviation of the great evil to be bound to others from whom we differ by ties of personal good will and esteem, . . . (v. 21; To John Edward Nassau Molesworth, 30 Aug. 1864)

I must not close my letter without thanking you, as I do most sincerely, for the very kind words you use about my writings. Whatever tends to create a unity of heart between men of separate communions, lays the ground for advances towards a restoration of that visible unity, the absence of which among Christians is so great a triumph, and so great an advantage to the enemies of the Cross. Those actual advances, and still less that restoration, cannot, alas, be reasonably expected to take place in our day, but the ground may be laid – and those who, in laying it, have 'done what they could,' however small may be their work, have deep cause to thank Almighty God for having been allowed to do it. (v. 24; To Rev. Henry Allon, 28 Jan. 1868)

Of course, it has been a real pleasure to me, then and now, to read the favourable criticisms upon me of one who is himself so brave and powerful a champion of revealed religion, and certainly not the less pleasure because in many things he differs from me so much. For it suggests the welcome reflection that, in this unhappy age of division, unity of faith and communion is best promoted by the cultivation, in the first place, of an ethical union among those who differ. This is a levelling-up which may some day make controversy comparatively easy, as laying the ground for strong foundations, . . . (v. 25; To the Duke of Argyll [Scottish Presbyterian], 30 March 1870)

I am quite persuaded that in this way alone religious men will ultimately arrive at unity of thought and worship. Not that it will be attained in our day, but the first step is to lay the foundation, or rather to prepare the soil. It would be a great thing if certain theses could be drawn up, such as the two to which I have referred, which all would be willing to subscribe, not to Speak here of the all-important question of dogma. (v. 25; To John Campbell Shairp, 18 Dec. 1870)

[C]ultivate that great virtue, faith, which I acknowledge may be possessed in the Anglican Church; which, knowing your earnestness and sincerity, I will believe you possess in it, if you tell me so. This is not inconsistent with my holding that in reality there is 'no medium between scepticism and Catholicism –' and on the contrary quite consistent with my saying that if you join us, it must be 'to save your soul' . . . (v. 25; To an Unknown Correspondent, beginning of 1871?)

I saw Rogers in London, who is Lord Blachford now; and Church who is Dean of St Paul's. I don't suppose either of them has a chance of being a Catholic, humanly speaking, but we are very good friends. (v. 26; To Miss Maria Rosina Giberne, 20 July 1872)

Pray do not suppose that my delay in answering your very kind letter has arisen from indifference to it. I feel extremely and thank you for the warmth of your language about me, and I wish to return it to you. What a mystery it is in this day that there should be so much which draws religious minds together, and so much which separates them from each other. Never did members of the various Christian communions feel such tenderness for each other, yet never were the obstacles greater or stronger which divide them. What a melancholy thought is this – and when will a better day come! (v. 26; To David Brown, 24 Oct. 1872)

I know how honestly you try to approve yourself to God – and this is a claim on the reverence of any one who knows or reads you. There are many things as to which I most seriously differ from you . . . what you write perplexes me often – but when a man is really and truly seeking the Pearl of great price, how can one help joining oneself in heart and spirit with him? (v. 26; To Richard Holt Hutton, 29 Dec. 1872)

Does Protestantism Have Within it Much Truth?

Protestantism, so widely spread and so long enduring, must have in it, and must be witness for, a great truth or much truth. That I am an advocate for Protestantism, you cannot suppose – but I am forced into a Via Media, short of Rome, as it is at present. Let both communions pray for an increase of grace and illumination, and then, though no steps be made in our day towards a reconciliation, yet it may be effected after we have left the world by the generations which follow us. (v. 8; To Charles W. Russell, 26 April 1841)

The mixture of good and bad, which makes up the Protestantism of England, is a great mystery; He alone, whose infinite Intelligence can understand the union of the two, can also dissolve it, and set the truth and the right free; but, if any human agency is to be much His instrument in any part of this work, surely it must begin by acknowledging, not denying, what Protestants have that is good and true, and honoring it in them as coming from the one source of all light and holiness. Certainly, to my own mind one of the most affecting and discouraging elements in the action of Catholicism just now on English Society, is the scorn with which some of us treat proceedings and works among Protestants which it is but Christian charity to ascribe to the influence of divine grace. (v. 21; To Ambrose Phillips de Lisle, 18 Sep. 1864)

The article on Keble is very able and very beautiful. It must do a great deal of good, in this respect, if in no other, in interesting Anglicans in the Month, and again in interesting Catholics in a very remarkable adherent to Anglicanism. It is a mode of bringing two sets of men together more powerful than any other, and one which involves no violation of principle. And it tends to show that a rigidly Catholic publication, such as the Month is, is able to recognise facts, as facts, and is not afraid for the Catholic religion, if moral goodness is to be found in bodies not Catholic. (v. 22; To Henry James Coleridge, 20 April 1866)

I knew you would not convert me, and I did not see a reasonable hope of my converting you. I believe what *you* do – but I believe more. I rejoice to think that you with all your heart and soul believe our Lord Jesus Christ to be the Saviour of the world, and of every soul who comes to Him for salvation; and the sole Saviour. I wish you believed the whole counsel of God. But in this bad time, when there are so many unbelievers, I rejoice to think you are not one of them. (v. 25; To J. F. Lloyd, 14 April 1870)

I will think all good of the Protestants I meet with, and rejoice in the fruits of grace I may discern in them . . . (v. 26; To Miss Rowe, 16 Sep. 1873)

[W]hereas no Catholic would think of having recourse to Gnostic or Manichee in the conflict with unbelief, members of sects who are nevertheless in certain grave errors, as we think, are, as we rejoice to believe, not external to divine grace and the gradual leadings of divine mercy, and can be welcomed as aids in the defence of divine truth. (v. 31; To Richard Acland Armstrong, 25 April 1886)

Are Catholics Too Often Ignorant About Protestantism?

Would that Catholics who have never been Protestants knew us better. A convert like myself has the advantage of both knowing Catholic doctrine and having Protestant experience – but he is too often looked at with suspicion by the Protestant because he has become a Catholic and by the Catholic because he has been a Protestant. I will candidly say that, from the circumstances of their position, numbers of Catholics are narrowminded, they have no notion what a good Protestant is, and they are suspicious of anyone who tells them. We cannot help all this intolerance and bigotry; it does not belong to the Church herself, but, if the Church is intended, as she is, to gather in all men, good and bad, it is not wonderful that she has inclusively numbers who are weak or illogical, or at least simply ignorant, just as Protestants are of Catholics. (v. 20; To William Robert Brownlow, 25 Oct. 1863)

Does the Holy Spirit Act Beyond the Catholic Church?

Though your friend is not a Catholic, I do not know why he should not be able to bear witness to the same [divinity and incarnation of Christ] in his own case – for tho' ordinarily the Holy Spirit acts through the Visible Church, yet it is quite certain that He vouchsafes to act beyond its boundaries – and where He implants this faith and love, and where it is improved and assimilated by due correspondence with it and . . . devotion, this assurance is at last received. (v. 24; To G. A. Cox, 17 Jan. 1868)

How Should we Approach Religious Differences of Opinion?

You need not be afraid of hurting me by what you may say in contrariety to my own religious belief. I may think, as of course I do, that I am right and those who differ from me wrong – but it does not mend matters for us to conceal our mutual differences – and nothing is more unmeaning, as well as more untrue, than compromises and comprehensions. Of course unreal, and but verbal, differences do exist between religious men – but such are not the differences which exist between Catholics and their opponents. It would be best, if they did not exist – it is next best to confess them, plainly though in charity[.] (v. 26; To David Brown, 18 Jan. 1873)

What is the Ultimate Aim of Ecumenism?

Sad as it is to witness the ineffectual yearnings after unity on all hands, of which you speak, still it is helpful also. We may hope that our good God has not put-it into the hearts of religious men to wish and pray for unity, without intending in his own time to fulfil the prayer. And since the bar against unity is a conscientious feeling, and a reverence for what each party holds itself to be the truth, and a desire to maintain the Faith, we may humbly hope that in our day, and till He discloses to the hearts of men what the true faith is, He will, where hearts are honest, take the will for the deed. (v. 26; To David Brown, 3 Nov. 1873)

Chapter Twenty-Seven

Science

Is Process Antithetical to Creation?

Some Geologists (Lyell) tell us creation is still going on – Why should not the first introduction of the principle of vegetation be a *creation*, though unorganized matter existed before? – Many persons, I believe (and I, as far as I can judge on the subject) would call equivocal generations creations. Qu. whether we are not introducing an arbitrary distinction unknown to Scripture, when we distinguish between the first making de nihilo and the subsequent preparing? – whatever is added in the preparing, is a fresh de nihilo. (v. 8; To Edward B. Pusey, 20 March? 1841)

Is Theistic Evolution Antithetical to Catholicism or Theism?

It is a careful and severe examination of the theory of Darwin – and it shows, as is most certain he would be able to do, the various points which are to be made good before it can cohere. I do not fear the theory so much as he seems to do – and it seems to me that he is hard upon Darwin sometimes, . . . he might have interpreted him kindly. It does not seem to me to follow that creation is denied because the Creator, millions of years ago, gave laws to matter. He first created matter and then he created laws for it – laws which should *construct* it into its present wonderful beauty, and accurate adjustment and harmony of parts *gradually*. We do not deny or circumscribe the Creator, because we hold he has created the self acting originating human mind, which has almost a creative gift; much less then do we deny or circumscribe His power, if we hold that He gave matter such laws as by their blind instrumentality moulded and constructed through innumerable ages the world as we see it. If Mr Darwin in this or that point of his theory comes into collision with revealed truth, that is another matter – but I do not see that the *principle* of development, or what I have called construction, does. As to the Divine *Design*, is it not an instance Of incomprehensibly and infinitely marvellous Wisdom and Design to have given certain laws to matter millions of ages ago, which have surely and precisely worked out, in the long course of those ages, those effects which He from the first proposed. Mr Darwin's theory *need* not then be atheistical, be it true or not; it may simply be suggesting a larger idea of Divine Prescience and Skill. Perhaps your friend has got a surer clue to guide him than I have, who have never studied the question, and I do not like to put my opinion against his; but at first sight I do not [see] that 'the *accidental* evolution of organic beings' is inconsistent with divine design – It is accidental to *us*, not to *God*[.] (v. 24; To J. Walker of Scarborough, 22 May 1868; referring to the book, *The Darwinian Theory of the Transmutation of Species Examined by a Graduate of the University of Cambridge*, second edition, London 1868, by Robert Mackenzie Beverley)

I have not fallen in with Darwin's book. [*The Origin of Species*, 1859) I conceive it to be an advocacy of the theory that that principle of propagation, which we are accustomed to believe began with Adam, and with the patriarchs of the brute species, began in some one common ancestor millions of years before. 1. Is this against the distinct teaching of the inspired text? if it is, then he advocates an antichristian theory. For myself, speaking under correction, I don't see that it does – contradict it. 2 Is it against Theism (putting Revelation aside) – I don't see how it can be. Else, the fact of a propagation from Adam is against Theism. If second causes are conceivable at all, an Almighty Agent being supposed, I don't see why the series should not last for millions of years as well as for thousands. The former question is the more critical. Does Scripture contradict the theory? – was Adam *not* immediately taken from the dust of the earth? 'All are of dust' – Eccles iii, 20 – yet *we* never *were* dust – we are from fathers, Why may not the same be the case with Adam? I don't say that it *is* so – but, if the sun does not go round the earth and the earth stand still, as Scripture seems to say, I don't know why Adam needs be immediately out of dust – Formavit Deus hominem de limo terrae – i.e. out of what really was dust and mud in its nature, before He made it what it was, living. But I speak under correction. Darwin does not *profess* to oppose Religion. (v. 25; To Edward B. Pusey, 5 June 1870)

I shall be abundantly satisfied and pleased if my Essays do a quarter of the good which I hear your volume [*Genesis of Species*] is doing. Those who have a right to judge speak of it as a first rate book – and it is pleasant to find that the first real exposition of the logical insufficiency of Mr. Darwin's theory comes from a Catholic. In saying this, you must not suppose I have personally any great dislike or dread of his theory, but many good people are much troubled at it – and at all events, without any disrespect to him, it is well to show that Catholics may be better reasoners than philosophers. (v. 25; To St. George Jackson Mivart, 9 Dec. 1871)

Is Darwin's Theory of Evolution Indicated by Anatomy?

[T]he key to the whole inquiry which it contains lies in your statement towards the end that the phenomena which Comparative Anatomy presents to us is a net and not a ladder – and that Darwin's hypothesis with its supplements is not warranted by them, when you come close to them and catalogue them, . . . I am not so well satisfied with your own hypothesis, but I hardly think you mean it for one, but only as an indication for the direction in which to look for one – I mean the hypothesis, that chance variations are the ultimate resolution of the phenomenon, which meets our eyes, of distinct species. Of course chance is not a cause. (v. 26; To St. George Jackson Mivart, 10 Nov. 1873)

Do Science and Revelation Clash?

[C]ultivation of mind is at once a protection to religion, and a momentous social and political benefit; . . . the widest pursuit of scientific and historical truth never can interfere with even the most zealous acceptance of Revelation . . . (v. 18; To Benjamin Disraeli, 19 July 1858)

Do Scientists Unduly Interfere in the Domain of Religion?

[I]n the whole scientific world men seem going ahead most recklessly with their usurpations on the domain of religion. . . . I seem to wish that divine and human science might each be suffered in peace to take its own line, the one not interfering with the other. (v. 18; To Edward B. Pusey, 13 April 1858)

The two main instruments of infidelity just now are physical science and history; physical science is used against Scripture, and history against dogma; the Vatican Council by its decrees about the inspiration of Scripture and the Infallibility of the Pope has simply thrown down the gauntlet to the science and the historical research of the day. (v. 26; To J. Spencer Northcote, 7 April 1872)

Is There But One Interpretation of Genesis Chapter One?

The Fathers are not unanimous in their interpretation of the 1st chapter of Genesis. A commentator then does not impute untruth or error to Scripture, though he denies the fact of the creation or formation of the world in six days, or in six periods. He has a right to say that the chapter is a symbolical representation, for so St Augustine seems to consider. (v. 21; To William Wordsworth, 22 Oct. 1864)

Must Catholics Believe that Noah's Flood was Universal?

[T]he Church has not determined whether or not the sacred writer meant to say that the Deluge was universal. In such cases we may modestly exercise our own judgment, provided we are ever ready to submit, when the Church speaks[.] (v. 21; To an Unknown Correspondent, 19 March 1865)

Chapter Twenty-Eight

Miscellaneous

How Should Christians Regard Great Riches?

He seems to be withdrawing from us all those 'things of the earth' on which we might be tempted to 'set our affections', in order that we may look upwards, and, 'lay up treasure in Heaven', and sit loose to all earthly objects, and seek all our joys and pleasures from holiness and the love of God. I am convinced that nothing can be a greater snare and evil to a person than unalloyed prosperity. . . . in my present state of mind there is nothing I would rather deprecate than wealth, or fame, or great influence. (v. 1; To [Aunt] Elizabeth Newman, 7 Nov. 1821)

Is Exorcism a Legitimate Christian Practice?

Where has Pusey advocated Exorcism except on the ground of *expedience*? certainly, unless my memory fails me, his chief ground is that we have by giving it up lost a practical witness concerning the reality of the devil's power? (v. 5; To Hugh James Rose, 23 May 1836)

How Serious of a Matter are Vows?

I think it is well to be cautious and jealous with oneself as to any strong acts, such as vows. . . . If there be any matter, about which our Lord's caution holds, about 'counting the cost', it is the subject of vows. (v. 7; To Miss Mary Holmes, 10 June 1840)

Do Anti-Catholics Misrepresent Catholicism?

What I was thinking of, I believe, when I spoke . . . about the Reformers being disingenuous was this, that I thought, e.g. in the Homilies, when they would attack some tenet or practice of Rome, they attacked something which R C's could and do condemn as much as their opponents do – so that now we . . . *can agree to what our Reformers say* and *yet* agree with Rome too. E.g. 'The Invocation of Saints is a miserable and wicked thing, FOR is it not wrong to *offer sacrifice* to creatures?' – And I think that without perversions and misrepresentations of this kind the Reformers would not have succeeded. (v. 8; To Edward B. Pusey, 13 Aug. 1841)

[W]hat claims the respect of bystanders is the terms in which you speak of the good Fathers of Mount St Bernard, so different from the tone of insult or contempt in which Protestants commonly indulge towards them. Is it not possible, Dear Sir, that many other stories, whether of this day or of history, told of Catholics, would be found equally baseless, if they could be as fairly examined into? There was the tale of Maria Monk in America which, I believe, was equally proved to be a slander. The nuns of Yorkshire gained not so many years back a verdict against a (now beneficed) clergyman for defamation. You have had the advantage of *seeing* the monks and the Monastery of St Bernard's, – sight dissipates a multitude of suspicions: I in like manner have talked or lived both with the chief ecclesiastical authorities at Rome, and with Jesuits and Monks, and except when I grieve at the falsehood, I can but laugh out at the absurdity, of the ideas entertained of them in England. A Catholic, a Monk, a Jesuit, or a Pope is a monster, till he is seen and known to be a man with human feelings, a human heart, a conscience, and a love of mankind. Depend on it, the better you knew Catholics, whether you agreed with them or not, the more you would discard the views ordinarily taken of them. (v. 13; To Thomas Ragg, 2 July 1849)

I thank you for the kind feeling which has suggested your letter; and my confidence in that kind feeling is my warrant for believing that you will allow me without offence to tell you in reply, that you know nothing at all of our doctrines, though you think you do, that you have to learn what it is you are assailing before you can legitimately assail it, and that you cannot reasonably expect to convince me that I am wrong, till, putting aside assumption and Misconception, you address me with the weapons of Fact and Argument. To propose to convince a Catholic by such arguments as 'The Church of Rome does not appear to be aware of this certain fact, that God Almighty is neither a liar nor a quibbler' is like catching a bird by putting salt upon its tail. You assume what you have to prove. (v. 21; To J. F. Lloyd, 3 Oct. 1864)

Is There But One Interpretation of the Book of Revelation?

The remarks of the Presbyterian Review only confirm my persuasion that it is unfair to ourselves, and unkind to Protestants not to put out our own view of the drift of the Apocalypse. Their argument consists not so much in the evident correctness of their own interpretation, as in there being no other producible. 'If it does not mean this,' they seem to say, 'what else does it mean?' (v. 16; To A. Lisle Phillipps, 7 May 1855)

How Does Catholicism (and the Bible) View Slavery?

I think slavery is in the same order of things as despotism. . . . But I should hesitate to say that despotism is per se evil, for . . . a father is despotic over his young children. But . . . despotism is practically and certainly a great evil. So is slavery. Christianity destroys both the one and the other; but by *influence*, not by declaring their illegality. . . . That which is intrinsically and per se evil, we cannot give way to for an hour. That which is only accidentally evil, we can meet according to what is expedient, giving different rules, according to the particular case. St Paul would have got rid of despotism if he could. He could not, he left the desirable object to the slow working of Christian principles. So he would have got rid of slavery, if he could. He did not, because he could not, but had it been intrinsically evil, had it been *in se* a sin, he must have said to Philemon, liberate all your slaves at once. . . . . It is difficult to get an exact parallel – but take the profession of arms. This profession arises out of the corruption of nature, and it is, and ever has been, and I suppose ever will be, a hot bed of corruption itself. It is not in itself sinful. It may be restrained in its bad tendencies. Under circumstances it may not only be allowable for an individual, but *for him* the least dangerous. As things are, we have obligations, we men of peace, to the army, which never can be under valued, but I am looking at itself. . . . . can such an institution be practically, to the vast majority, be other than a school of vice and crime and spiritual ruin? Surely slavery can be *tamed* more easily than the military profession. Which did most harm to the soul the Jewish slavedom or the Jewish army? An army is a greater instrument of sin than slavery. It is the instrument of a Timour or an Alexander in introducing both slavery and despotism. Yet it is not in itself a sinful institution. St Peter bids us submit to every human creature; I suppose he included all these three. Slavery may be worse in a particular state of society than the other two, but not in itself. I had rather have been a slave in the Holy Land, than a courtier of Xerxes or a soldier of Zingis Khan. The Military Profession is not sinful, yet its particular professors or deeds. may be atrociously wicked. The institution of slavery, as of despotism, is one of its bad deeds. If a wicked effect does not make the profession of arms evil, I do not see why a wicked origin should make slavery per se evil. . . . . True, to enslave is a horrible sin, yet comparative good may come out of sin in this sinful world. . . . . Slavery then is not evil in se, except in such sense as despotism is, or the military profession, and therefore cannot be treated more than one of the symptoms, effects, aggravations, instruments of Roman corruption. . . . . Holding as I should do, that slavery admits of being better and worse, and fully allowing that its condition was as bad as it could be among the Roman nobles and in great cities, I wished to question, or rather I claimed to be *allowed* to ask proof, for its being so bad elsewhere, to ask proof whether what (e.g.) Seneca says, applies to the whole Roman Empire, or even as applied to Rome, has not something of rhetoric in it; and I do this on the ground that, whereas slavedom was not a sinful institution in itself, (for this I have to take for granted) though it came of sin and tended to sin, St Paul on the other hand does not add slave holders to man stealers, does not tell Philemon to manumit his slaves, and actually tells the slaves at Corinth to remain slaves though they could be free [1 Cor 7:21]. (v. 20; To T. W. Allies, 8 Nov. 1863)

A soldier's slavery seems to me to be something extraordinary. *Practically* he is a slave – an accident, a trick may bring him into it. He can't get out of it. He must do just what he is told, and he is exposed to the most shocking moral evil, to the worst temptations with not so much power as the female Carolina slave to resist; (at least he would need tenfold more grace than the slave). . . . I cannot understand people being so shocked at slavery, *and not* shocked at the army. Take any religious or refined officer's account of war, and though there is not such savageness, there is more immorality. Of course it has its heroic side, but you show that a slave may be a hero and a martyr. War seems to me a necessary evil, as *we are*, so might slavery be in the pagan world. Slavery is a far *worse* evil than the military profession, hence Christianity kills *it*, but has never yet killed the army. But I am not speaking about degrees of evil, but kind of evil. If slavery were *in se* evil, I don't think St Paul would have used it as a figure of our relation to our Creator and Redeemer. Are not all such figures taken from such facts of the world as are not intrinsically evil? – We are e.g. fishers of men, hunters of souls, – we could not be called seducers of souls, because the idea of seduction is wrong; or said to murder all sins in us, but to kill all sin. Now St Paul surely, by calling himself the slave of Christ means more than that he gives his labour to Him. No, he is bought, soul and body. Somehow, I can't make out that slavery is wrong in se. Children are slaves to their parents. I do not see that it is more than wrong from man's necessary abuse of it, but even then it may be the best thing under circumstances, e.g. better, in a *certain* state of man, of the soul etc, than freedom. I don't say that I have got at the bottom of the question. I only mean I cannot say all that you say. . . . Now, please, take all these as my *raw*, my crude thoughts. (v. 20; To T. W. Allies, 10 Nov. 1863)

[D]oes not Terence [Roman playwright; d. c. 159 BC] give a view of Slavery, whether of Athenian, or of contemporary, very different from what you gather from Seneca and the times of the Empire? Slaves could not be principals, or witnesses in the law courts, and they were subject to the mill and the prison; but they could possess property, and that when in town households, and so much, that they were expected to make presents to their masters at certain times. They married, and their wives were nurses in the family – and, while their freedom with their masters is something wonderful, the latter for some reason or other could not at will be severe with them. (v. 20; To T. W. Allies, 25 Dec. 1863)

What is Newman's Advice for Aspiring Writers?

[E]veryone must form his style for himself, and under a few general rules, . . . First, a man should be in earnest, by which I mean, he should write, not for *the sake of writing*, but to bring out his *thoughts*. He should never aim at being eloquent. He should keep his idea in view, and write sentences over and over again till he has expressed his meaning accurately, forcibly and in few words. He should aim at being understood by his hearers or readers. He should use words which are most likely to be understood – ornament and amplification will come to him spontaneously in due time, but he should never seek them. He must creep before he can fly, by which I mean that humility, which is a great Christian virtue, has a place in literary composition – He who is ambitious will never write well. But he who tries to say simply and exactly what he feels or thinks, what religion demands, what Faith teaches, what the Gospel promises, will be eloquent without intending it, and will write better English than if he made a study of English literature. (v. 24; To a Student at Maynooth, 2 March 1868)

Is Spanking or Corporal Punishment Permissible?

[T]here is one principle which comes into your discussion on which I certainly have an opinion, and in accordance with your own; it is on the expedience of corporal punishment for certain offences[.] We have a boys' school attached to our House here; and we certainly find that the good old punishment of flogging, is, in due moderation as to severity and frequency, the most efficacious of all punishments, while it is the most prompt and summary, and the least irritating and annoying to the subjects of it. It is done and over – there is nothing to brood over, nothing to create a grudge, at least to English boys. (v. 24; To Henry Taylor, 15 Feb. 1869)

How Do we Know that Souls Exist?

I trust you will think it enough, if I say now in a few words all I have to say to you, as to what I mean by a soul, from which it will be clear why I think it exists. I think, and I have emotions, and reason: I am conscious of my thoughts, emotions and reasonings; I have a memory of myself and of them in time past. I invest all this with a unity, as being parts of one, and call it 'I', as you do. This 'I' is what I mean by my 'soul'; when I say that I have a soul, I do but mean that I recognize the idea conveyed in the word 'I'. Then reflection leads me to think that this 'I' is distinct from my physical frame as conveying the idea of individuality and may last, though my physical frame which is divisible dissolves; but I consider this a property of the soul; and though I ended my being with this life, still I should at present be

I; that is I should have a soul. As to the proof that I, that is, my soul, lives after this life, I don't think the belief would be so widely spread, and so difficult to get rid of, if it were not true. The millions of men who hold that T is something distinct from the body are so many separate instances of one and the same phenomenon; and my own witness goes along with theirs. This would be enough for my thinking had a soul, if there were no other reasons[.] (v. 25; To Charles S. Hervé, 11 April 1870)

Are the Last Days Near?

Either the end of the world is coming, or a great purifying and perfecting of religious belief and ethics, which it may take centuries to complete. Trial does good, though it involves many cruel defections. (v. 26; To H. A. Woodgate, 26 Dec. 1872)

I think either Antichrist is coming, or that a great and purifying trial, which may last centuries, is coming on the Church[.] The course of God's Providence is as glorious as it is awful. (v. 26; To Mother Mary Imelda Poole, 27 Dec. 1872)

Should Unbaptized Persons be Married by Christian Clergymen?

I felt I could not on my own responsibility bestow the especial privilege of Christian matrimony on parties who had not taken on themselves even the public profession of Christianity . . . It seemed as if an inconsistency in me to profess that unbaptized persons are 'children of wrath' and outcast from God's covenanted mercies in Christ, yet to treat them as Christians; moreover that to do so was throwing suspicion on the sincerity of my own professed belief; – and uncharitable towards those whom I had few opportunities of warning and who I believed were disobeying a solemn command of our Lord's, and making light of a condition of Christian salvation. . . . And further the direction that the newly married persons should receive the Holy Communion would seem to imply that they had been already admitted to the first sacrament. – And lastly I believed that the Primitive Church was decidedly opposed both in its rule and practice to such marriages as that I was called to solemnize; and would take no part in promoting them. (v. 4; To Richard Bagot, Bishop of Oxford, 9 July 1834)

[S]uch a union as you mention, under the ordinary discipline of the Church, would not *be* marriage. Not only could not a priest marry the parties, but, if he did, it would not be a marriage. It would be null and void, as the form of Absolution without contrition, or the words of consecration, if used over any thing but bread and wine. There is this difference only, that it is one of those obstacles which the Pope has the powers to remove, though I never heard of his removing it, because he could not do it, except it was a duty to do so. How can a person be made partaker of a Christian Sacrament, who does not believe in Christ? How can a Catholic take part in bringing him before a God whom he does not acknowledge? (v. 23; To an Unknown Correspondent, 19 Feb. 1867)

What Did the First Protestants Think of Polygamy?

By the bye Luther and Co are believed (I think) to have been on the point of publishing their approval of Polygamy – You know they actually did allow it in the case of a Rheingrave, Luther Melanchthon, and 5 or 6 others, and that under their handwriting. (v. 6; To H. A. Woodgate, 23 Feb. 1838)

25686596R00216

Printed in Great Britain
by Amazon